SurviveJS - Webpack

From apprentice to master

Juho Vepsäläinen, Tobias Koppers and Jesús Rodríguez Rodríguez

SurviveJS - Webpack

From apprentice to master

Juho Vepsäläinen, Tobias Koppers and Jesús Rodríguez Rodríguez

ISBN 978-952-68688-0-6

Contents

CONTENTS

Foreword

It's a funny story how I started with webpack. Before getting addicted to JavaScript, I also developed in Java. I tried GWT (Google Web Toolkit) in that time. GWT is a Java-to-JavaScript Compiler, which has a great feature: code splitting[1]. I liked this feature and missed it in existing JavaScript tooling. I made a pull request to an existing module bundler, but it did not go through. Webpack was born.

Somehow the Instagram frontend team discovered an early version of webpack and started to use it for instagram.com. Pete Hunt, Facebook employee managing the Instagram web team, gave the first significant talk about webpack[2] at OSCON 2014. The talk boosted the popularity of webpack. One of the reasons for adoption of webpack by Instagram was **code splitting**.

I have been following this book since its early stages. It was once a combined React and webpack book. It has grown since then and become a book of its own filled with content.

Juho is an important part of the webpack documentation team for the webpack 2 documentation, so he knows best what complements the official documentation. He has used this knowledge to create a book that supplies you with a deep understanding of webpack and teaches you to use the tool to its full potential.

Tobias Koppers

---

[1] http://www.gwtproject.org/doc/latest/DevGuideCodeSplitting.html
[2] https://www.youtube.com/watch?v=VkTCL6Nqm6Y

Preface

The book you are reading right now goes years back. It all started from a comment I made at Christian Alfoni's blog in 2014. I had recently discovered webpack and React, and I felt there was a need for a cookbook about the topics. The work begun in a GitHub wiki early 2015.

After a while, I realized this should become an *actual* book and tried pitching it to a known publisher. As they weren't interested yet and I felt the book needed to happen, I started the **SurviveJS** effort. The book warped into "SurviveJS - Webpack and React", my first self-published book. It combined the two topics into one single book.

Given a book focusing only on a single technology can stand taller, I ended up splitting the book into two separate ones in 2016. The current book represents the webpack portion of it, and it has grown significantly due to this greater focus. The journey has not been a short one, but it has been possible thanks to community support and continued interest in the topic.

During these years webpack has transformed as a project. Instead of relying on a single prolific author, a core team including myself has grown around the project, and it has attracted more people around it to support the effort.

There is an open collective campaign[3] to help the project to succeed financially. Also, I am donating 30% of the book earnings to Tobias as he has more than earned it. By supporting the book, you literally support webpack development as most of the profit goes to its core team.

Juho Vepsäläinen

---

[3]https://opencollective.com/webpack

Introduction

Webpack[4] simplifies web development by solving a fundamental problem: bundling. It takes in various assets, such as JavaScript, CSS, and HTML, and then transforms these assets into a format that's convenient to consume through a browser. Doing this well takes away a significant amount of pain from web development.

It's not the easiest tool to learn due to its configuration-driven approach, but it's incredibly powerful. The purpose of this guide is to help you get started with webpack and then to go beyond the basics.

What Is Webpack

Web browsers are designed to consume HTML, CSS, and JavaScript. As a project grows, tracking and configuring all of these files grows too complex to manage without help. As an application develops, handling it becomes more difficult. Webpack was designed to counter these problems. Managing complexity is one of the fundamental issues of web development, and solving the problem well can help you a lot.

Webpack isn't the only solution for this problem, and a collection of different tools have emerged. Task runners, such as Grunt and Gulp, are good examples of higher level tools. Often the problem is that need to write the workflows by hand. Pushing that issue to a bundler, such as webpack, is a step forward.

---

[4]https://webpack.js.org/

How Does Webpack Change The Situation

Webpack takes another route. It allows you to treat your project as a dependency graph. You could have an *index.js* in your project that pulls in the dependencies the project needs through standard `require` or `import` statements. You can refer to your style files and other assets the same way if you want.

Webpack does all the preprocessing for you and gives you the bundles you specify through configuration and your code. This declarative approach is powerful, but it's difficult to learn. Webpack becomes an indispensable tool after you begin to understand how it works. This book has been designed to get through that initial learning curve and even go further.

What Will You Learn

This book has been designed to complement the official documentation of webpack[5]. The official documentation goes deeper in many aspects, and this book can be considered a companion to it. This book is more like a quick walkthrough that eases the initial learning curve while giving food for thought to more advanced users.

The book teaches you to develop a composable webpack configuration for both development and production purposes. Advanced techniques covered by the book allow you to get the most out of webpack.

 The book is based on webpack 2. If you want to apply its techniques to webpack 1, you should see the official migration guide[6] as it covers the changes made between the major versions. There are also codemods at the webpack-cli repository[7] for migrating from webpack 1 to 2.

---

[5]https://webpack.js.org/

[6]https://webpack.js.org/guides/migrating/

[7]https://github.com/webpack/webpack-cli

How Is The Book Organized

The book starts by explaining what webpack is. After that, you find multiple parts, each of which discusses webpack from a different direction. While going through those chapters, you develop your webpack configuration. The chapters also double as reference material.

The book has been split into the following parts:

- **Developing** gets you up and running with webpack. This part goes through features such as automatic browser refresh and explains how to compose your configuration so that it remains maintainable.
- **Styling** puts heavy emphasis on styling related topics. You will learn how to load styles with webpack and how to introduce techniques such as autoprefixing to your setup.
- **Loading** explains webpack's loader definitions in detail and shows you how to load assets such as images, fonts, and JavaScript.
- **Building** introduces source maps and the ideas of bundle and code splitting. You will learn to tidy up your build.
- **Optimizing** pushes your build to production quality level and introduces many smaller tweaks to make it smaller. You will learn to tune webpack for performance.
- **Output** discusses webpack's output options. Despite its name, it's not only for the web. You see how to manage multiple page setups with webpack and pick up the basic idea of Server Side Rendering.
- **Techniques** discusses several specific ideas including dynamic loading, web workers, internationalization, and deploying your applications.
- **Packages** has a heavy focus on npm and webpack related techniques. You will learn both to consume and author npm packages in an efficient way.
- **Extending** shows how to extend webpack with your loaders and plugins.

There's a short conclusion chapter after the main content that recaps the main points of the book. It contains checklists that allow you to go through your projects against the book techniques.

The appendices the end of the book cover secondary topics and sometimes dig deeper into the main ones. You can approach them in any order you want depending on your interest.

Given eventually webpack will give you an error, the *Troubleshooting* appendix at the end covers what to do then. It covers a basic process on what to do and how to debug the problem. When in doubt, study the appendix. If you are unsure of a term and its meaning, see the *Glossary* at the end of the book.

Who Is The Book For

You should have basic knowledge of JavaScript, Node, and npm. If you know something about webpack, that's great. By reading this book, you deepen your understanding of these tools.

If you don't know much about the topic, consider going carefully through the early parts. You can scan the rest to pick the bits you find worthwhile. If you know webpack already, skim and choose the techniques you find valuable.

In case you know webpack well already, there is still something in the book for you. Skim through it and see if you can pick up new techniques. Read especially the summaries at the end of the chapters and the conclusion chapter.

Book Versioning

Given this book receives a fair amount of maintenance and improvements due to the pace of innovation, there's a versioning scheme in place. Release notes for each new version are maintained at the book blog[8]. You can also use GitHub *compare* tool for this purpose. Example:

```
https://github.com/survivejs/webpack-book/compare/v1.9.0...v2.0.18
```

The page shows you the individual commits that went to the project between the given version range. You can also see the lines that have changed in the book.

The current version of the book is **2.0.18**.

---

[8]http://survivejs.com/blog/

Getting Support

If you run into trouble or have questions related to the content, there are several options:

- Contact me through GitHub Issue Tracker[9].
- Join me at Gitter Chat[10].
- Send me email at info@survivejs.com[11].
- Ask me anything about webpack or React at SurviveJS AmA[12].

If you post questions to Stack Overflow, tag them using **survivejs**. You can use the hashtag **#survivejs** on Twitter for the same result.

Additional Material

You can find more related material from the following sources:

- Join the mailing list[13] for occasional updates.
- Follow @survivejs[14] on Twitter.
- Subscribe to the blog RSS[15] to get access interviews and more.
- Subscribe to the Youtube channel[16].
- Check out SurviveJS related presentation slides[17].

---

[9] https://github.com/survivejs/webpack-book/issues
[10] https://gitter.im/survivejs/webpack
[11] mailto:info@survivejs.com
[12] https://github.com/survivejs/ama/issues
[13] https://eepurl.com/bth1v5
[14] https://twitter.com/survivejs
[15] https://survivejs.com/atom.xml
[16] https://www.youtube.com/channel/UCvUR-BJcbrhmRQZEEr4_bnw
[17] https://presentations.survivejs.com/

Acknowledgments

Big thanks to Christian Alfoni[18] for helping me craft the first version of this book. That inspired the whole SurviveJS effort. The version you see now is a complete rewrite.

The book wouldn't be half as good as it's without patient editing and feedback by my editors Jesús Rodríguez[19], Artem Sapegin[20], and Pedr Browne[21]. Thank you.

This book wouldn't have been possible without the original "SurviveJS - Webpack and React" effort. Anyone who contributed to it deserves my thanks. You can check that book for more accurate attributions.

Thanks to Mike "Pomax" Kamermans, Cesar Andreu, Dan Palmer, Viktor Jančík, Tom Byrer, Christian Hettlage, David A. Lee, Alexandar Castaneda, Marcel Olszewski, Steve Schwartz, Chris Sanders, Charles Ju, Aditya Bhardwaj, Rasheed Bustamam, José Menor, Ben Gale, Jake Goulding, Andrew Ferk, gabo, Giang Nguyen, @Coaxial, @khronic, Henrik Raitasola, Gavin Orland, David Riccitelli, Stephen Wright, Majky Bašista, Gunnari Auvinen, Jón Levy, Alexander Zaytsev, Richard Muller, Ava Mallory (Fiverr), Sun Zheng'an, Nancy (Fiverr), Aluan Haddad, Steve Mao, Craig McKenna, Tobias Koppers, Stefan Frede, Vladimir Grenaderov, Scott Thompson, Rafael De Leon, Gil Forcada Codinachs, Jason Aller, @pikeshawn, Stephan Klinger, Daniel Carral, Nick Yianilos, Stephen Bolton, and many others who have contributed direct feedback for this book!

---

[18] http://www.christianalfoni.com/
[19] https://github.com/Foxandxss
[20] https://github.com/sapegin
[21] https://github.com/Undistraction

What is Webpack

Webpack is a module bundler. You can use a separate task runner while leaving it to take care of bundling, however this line has become blurred as the community has developed plugins for it. Sometimes these plugins are used to perform tasks that are usually done outside of webpack, for example cleaning the build directory or deploying the build.

Webpack became particularly popular with React due to **Hot Module Replacement** (HMR) which helped greatly to popularize webpack and lead to its usage in other environments, such as Ruby on Rails[22]. Despite its name, web pack is not limited to web alone. It can bundle for other targets as well as discussed in the *Build Targets* chapter.

 If you want to understand build tools and their history in a better detail, check out the *Comparison of Build Tools* appendix.

Webpack Relies on Modules

The smallest project you could bundle with webpack consists of **input** and **output**. The bundling process begins from user defined **entries**. Entries themselves are **modules** and can point to other modules through **imports**.

When you bundle a project through webpack, it traverses through imports, constructing a **dependency graph** of the project and then generating the **output** based on the configuration. It's possible to define **split points** generating separate bundles within the project code itself.

Webpack supports ES6, CommonJS, and AMD module formats out of the box. The loader mechanism works for CSS as well, and @import and url() are supported

---

[22]https://github.com/rails/webpacker

through *css-loader*. You can also find plugins for specific tasks, such as minification, internationalization, HMR, and so on.

 A dependency graph describes is a directed graph that describes how nodes relate to each other. In this case the graph definition is defined through references (`require`, `import`) between files. Webpack traverses this information in a static manner without executing the source to generate the graph it needs to create bundles.

Webpack's Execution Process

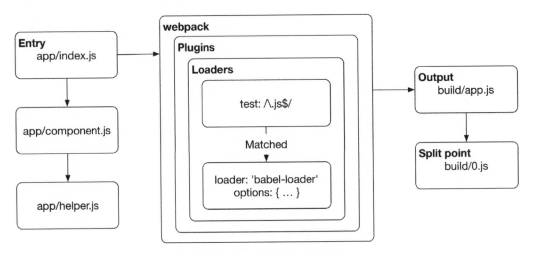

Webpack's execution process

Webpack begins its work from **entries**. Often these are JavaScript modules where webpack begins its traversal process. During this process webpack evaluates the matches against **loader** configuration that tells how to transform the files.

Resolution Process

An entry itself is a module and when webpack encounters one, it tries to match it against the file system using its `resolve` configuration. You can tell webpack to perform the lookup against specific directories in addition to *node_modules*. It's also possible to adjust the way it matches against file extensions and you can define specific aliases against directories. The *Package Consuming Techniques* chapter covers these ideas in greater detail.

If the resolution pass failed, webpack gives a runtime error. If webpack managed to resolve a file correctly, webpack performs processing over the matched file based on the loader definition. Each loader applies a specific transformation against the module contents.

The way a loader gets matched against a resolved file can be configured in multiple ways including file type and its location in the file system. Webpack provides even more flexible ways to achieve this as you can apply specific transformation against a file based on *where* it was imported to the project.

The same resolution process is performed against webpack's loaders. It allows you to apply similar logic there while it figures out which loader it should use. Loaders have resolve configuration of their own for this reason. If webpack fails to perform a loader lookup, you will get a runtime error.

Webpack Resolves Against Any File Type

Webpack will resolve against each module it encounters while constructing the dependency graph. If an entry contains dependencies, the process will be performed against each until the traversal has completed. Webpack performs this process against any file type unlike a specialized tool like Babel or Sass compiler.

Webpack gives you control over how to treat different assets it encounters. You can decide to **inline** assets to your JavaScript bundles to avoid requests for example. Webpack also allows you to use techniques, like CSS Modules, to couple styling with components and to avoid issues of standard CSS styling. It's this flexibility which makes webpack valuable.

Although webpack is used mainly to bundle JavaScript, it can capture assets like images or fonts and emit separate files for them. Entries are only a starting point of the bundling process. What webpack emits depends entirely on the way you configure it.

Evaluation Process

Assuming all loaders were found, webpack evaluates the matched loaders from bottom to top and right to left (`styleLoader(cssLoader('./main.css')))`, running the module through each loader in turn. As a result you get output which webpack will inject in the resulting **bundle**. The *Loader Definitions* chapter covers the topic in detail.

If all loader evaluation completed without a runtime error, webpack includes the source in the last bundle. **Plugins** allow you to intercept **runtime events** at different stages of the bundling process.

Although loaders can do a lot, they don't provide enough power for advanced tasks by themselves. Plugins intercept **runtime events** provided by webpack. A good example is bundle extraction performed by `ExtractTextPlugin` which, working in tandem with a loader, extracts CSS files out of the bundle and into a file of its own.

Without this step, CSS would end up in the resulting JavaScript as webpack treats all code as JavaScript by default. The extraction idea is discussed in the *Separating CSS* chapter.

Finishing

After every module has been evaluated, webpack writes **output**. The output includes a bootstrap script with a manifest that describes how to begin executing the result in the browser. The manifest can be extracted to a file of its own as discussed later in the book. The output differs based on the build target you are using and targeting web is not the only option.

That's not all there is to the bundling process. For example, you can define specific **split points** where webpack generates separate bundles that are loaded based on application logic. The idea is discussed in the *Code Splitting* chapter.

Webpack Is Configuration Driven

At its core webpack relies on configuration. Here is a sample adapted from the official webpack tutorial[23] that shows how the main ideas go together:

webpack.config.js

```javascript
const webpack = require('webpack');

module.exports = {
  // Where to start bundling
  entry: {
    app: './entry.js',
  },

  // Where to output
  output: {
    // Output to the same directory
    path: __dirname,

    // Capture name from the entry using a pattern
    filename: '[name].js',
  },

  // How to resolve encountered imports
  module: {
    rules: [
      {
        test: /\.css$/,
        use: ['style-loader', 'css-loader'],
      },
      {
        test: /\.js$/,
        use: 'babel-loader',
```

---

[23]https://webpack.js.org/get-started/

```
        exclude: /node_modules/,
      },
    ],
  },

  // What extra processing to perform
  plugins: [
    new webpack.optimize.UglifyJsPlugin(),
  ],

  // Adjust module resolution algorithm
  resolve: {
    alias: { ... },
  },
};
```

Webpack's configuration model can feel a bit opaque at times as the configuration file can appear monolithic. It can be difficult to understand what it's doing unless you understand the ideas behind it. Providing means to tame configuration is one of the main purposes why this book exists.

 To understand webpack on source code level, check out the artsy webpack tour[24].

Hot Module Replacement

You are likely familiar with tools, such as LiveReload[25] or BrowserSync[26], already. These tools refresh the browser automatically as you make changes. HMR takes things one step further. In the case of React, it allows the application to maintain

---

[24]https://github.com/TheLarkInn/artsy-webpack-tour

[25]http://livereload.com/

[26]http://www.browsersync.io/

its state without forcing a refresh. While this does not sound that special, it makes a big difference in practice.

HMR is available in Browserify via livereactload[27], so it's not a feature that's exclusive to webpack.

Code Splitting

Aside from the HMR feature, webpack's bundling capabilities are extensive. Webpack allows you to split code in various ways. You can even load code dynamically as your application gets executed. This sort of lazy loading comes in handy, especially for larger applications. You can load dependencies as you need them.

Even small applications can benefit from code splitting, as it allows the users to get something useable in their hands faster. Performance is a feature, after all. Knowing the basic techniques is worthwhile.

Asset Hashing

With webpack, you can inject a hash to each bundle name (e.g., *app.d587bbd6.js*) to invalidate bundles on the client side as changes are made. Bundle-splitting allows the client to reload only a small part of the data in the ideal case.

Conclusion

Webpack comes with a significant learning curve. However it's a tool worth learning, given it saves so much time and effort over the long term. To get a better idea how it compares to other tools, check out the official comparison[28].

Webpack won't solve everything, however, it does solve the problem of bundling. That's one less worry during development. Using *package.json* and webpack alone can take you far.

---

[27] https://github.com/milankinen/livereactload

[28] https://webpack.js.org/get-started/why-webpack/#comparison

To summarize:

- Webpack is a **module bundler**, but you can also use it for tasks as well.
- Webpack relies on a **dependency graph** underneath. Webpack traverses through the source to construct the graph and it uses this information and configuration to generate bundles.
- Webpack relies on **loaders** and **plugins**. Loaders operate on module level while plugins rely on hooks provided by webpack and have the best access to its execution process.
- Webpack's **configuration** describes how to transform assets of the graphs and what kind of output it should generate. A part of this information can be included in the source itself if features like **code splitting** are used.
- **Hot Module Replacement** (HMR) helped to popularize webpack. It's a feature that can enhance development experience by updating code in the browser without a full refresh.
- Webpack can generate **hashes** for filenames allowing you to invalidate bundles as their contents change.

In the next part of the book you'll learn to construct a development configuration using webpack while learning more about its basic concepts.

I Developing

In this part, you get up and running with webpack. You will learn to configure webpack-dev-server and linting. Finally, you compose the configuration so that it's possible to expand in the following parts of the book.

1. Getting Started

Before getting started, make sure you are using a recent version of Node[1]. You should use at least the most current LTS (long-term support) version. The configuration of the book has been written with Node 6 features in mind. You should have node and npm commands available at your terminal. Yarn[2] is a good alternative to npm and works for the tutorial as well.

It's possible to get a more controlled environment by using a solution such as Docker[3], Vagrant[4] or nvm[5]. Vagrant comes with a performance penalty as it relies on a virtual machine. Vagrant is valuable in a team: each developer can have the same environment that is usually close to production.

 The completed configuration is available at GitHub[6].

 If you are using an older version than Node 6, you have to adapt the code or process your webpack configuration through Babel as discussed in the *Loading JavaScript* chapter.

---

[1]http://nodejs.org/

[2]https://yarnpkg.com/

[3]https://www.docker.com/

[4]https://www.vagrantup.com/

[5]https://www.npmjs.com/package/nvm

[6]https://github.com/survivejs-demos/webpack-demo

1.1 Setting Up the Project

To get a starting point, you should create a directory for the project and set up a *package.json* there. npm uses that to manage project dependencies. Here are the basic commands:

```
mkdir webpack-demo
cd webpack-demo
npm init -y # -y generates *package.json*, skip for more control
```

You can tweak the generated *package.json* manually to make further changes to it even though a part of the operations modify the file automatically for you. The official documentation explains package.json options[7] in more detail.

You can set those npm init defaults at ∼/.*npmrc*.

This is a good place to set up version control using Git[8]. You can create a commit per step and tag per chapter, so it's easier to move back and forth if you want.

1.2 Installing Webpack

Even though webpack can be installed globally (npm install webpack -g), it's a good idea to maintain it as a dependency of your project to avoid issues, as then you have control over the exact version you are running. The approach works nicely in **Continuous Integration** (CI) setups as well. A CI system can install your local dependencies, compile your project using them, and then push the result to a server.

---

[7] https://docs.npmjs.com/files/package.json
[8] https://git-scm.com/

To add webpack to the project, execute:

```
npm install webpack --save-dev # -D if you want to save typing
```

You should see webpack at your *package.json* devDependencies section after this. In addition to installing the package locally below the *node_modules* directory, npm also generates an entry for the executable.

1.3 Executing Webpack

You can display the exact path of the executables using npm bin. Most likely it points at *./node_modules/.bin*. Try running webpack from there through the terminal using node_modules/.bin/webpack or a similar command.

After running, you should see a version, a link to the command line interface guide and an extensive list of options. Most aren't used in this project, but it's good to know that this tool is packed with functionality if nothing else.

```
webpack-demo $ node_modules/.bin/webpack
No configuration file found and no output filename configured via CL\
I option.
A configuration file could be named 'webpack.config.js' in the curre\
nt directory.
Use --help to display the CLI options.
```

To get a quick idea of webpack output, try this:

1. Set up *app/index.js* so that it contains console.log('Hello world');.
2. Execute node_modules/.bin/webpack app/index.js build/index.js.
3. Examine *build/index.js*. You should see webpack bootstrap code that begins executing the code. Below the bootstrap you should find something familiar.

 You can use --save and --save-dev to separate application and development dependencies. The former installs and writes to *package.json* dependencies field whereas the latter writes to devDependencies instead.

1.4 Directory Structure

To move further, you can implement a site that loads JavaScript, which you then build using webpack. After you progress a bit, you end up with a directory structure below:

- app/
  - index.js
  - component.js
- build/
- package.json
- webpack.config.js

The idea is that you transform *app/* to a bundle below *build/*. To make this possible, you should set up the assets needed and configure webpack through *webpack.config.js*.

1.5 Setting Up Assets

As you never get tired of Hello world, you will model a variant of that. Set up a component:

app/component.js

```
export default (text = 'Hello world') => {
  const element = document.createElement('div');

  element.innerHTML = text;

  return element;
};
```

Next, you are going to need an entry point for the application. It uses `import` against the component and renders it through the DOM:

app/index.js

```
import component from './component';

document.body.appendChild(component());
```

1.6 Setting Up Webpack Configuration

You need to tell webpack how to deal with the assets that were set up. For this purpose, you have to develop a *webpack.config.js* file. Webpack and its development server are able to discover this file through a convention.

To keep things convenient to maintain, you can use your first plugin: html-webpack-plugin[9]. `HtmlWebpackPlugin` generates an *index.html* for the application and adds a `script` tag to load the generated bundle. Install it:

```
npm install html-webpack-plugin --save-dev
```

At a minimum, it's nice to have at least `entry` and `output` fields in your configuration. Often you see a lot more as you specify how webpack deals with different file types and how it resolves them.

Entries tell webpack where to start parsing the application. In multi-page applications, you have an entry per page. Or you could have a configuration per entry as discussed later in this chapter.

All output related paths you see in the configuration are resolved against the `output.path` field. If you had an output relation option somewhere and wrote `styles/[name].css`, that would be expanded so that you get `<output.path>` + `<specific path>`. Example: ~/*webpack-demo/build/styles/main.css*.

---

[9] https://www.npmjs.com/package/html-webpack-plugin

To illustrate how to connect entry and output with HtmlWebpackPlugin, consider the code below:

webpack.config.js

```
const path = require('path');
const HtmlWebpackPlugin = require('html-webpack-plugin');

const PATHS = {
  app: path.join(__dirname, 'app'),
  build: path.join(__dirname, 'build'),
};

module.exports = {
  // Entries have to resolve to files! They rely on Node
  // convention by default so if a directory contains *index.js*,
  // it resolves to that.
  entry: {
    app: PATHS.app,
  },
  output: {
    path: PATHS.build,
    filename: '[name].js',
  },
  plugins: [
    new HtmlWebpackPlugin({
      title: 'Webpack demo',
    }),
  ],
};
```

The entry path could be given as a relative one using the context[10] field used to configure that lookup. However, given plenty of places expect absolute paths, preferring them over relative paths everywhere avoids confusion.

---

[10]https://webpack.js.org/configuration/entry-context/#context

Trailing commas are used in the book examples on purpose as it gives cleaner diffs for the code examples. You'll learn to enforce this rule in the *Linting JavaScript* chapter.

[name] is a placeholder. Placeholders are discussed in detail in the *Adding Hashes to Filenames* chapter, but they are effectively tokens that will be replaced when the string is evaluated. In this case [name] will be replaced by the name of the entry - 'app'.

If you execute node_modules/.bin/webpack, you should see output:

```
Hash: 3f76ae042ff0f2d98f35
Version: webpack 2.2.1
Time: 376ms
     Asset       Size   Chunks           Chunk Names
    app.js    3.13 kB        0  [emitted]  app
index.html   180 bytes          [emitted]
   [0] ./app/component.js 148 bytes {0} [built]
   [1] ./app/index.js 78 bytes {0} [built]
Child html-webpack-plugin for "index.html":
       [0] ./~/lodash/lodash.js 540 kB {0} [built]
       [1] (webpack)/buildin/global.js 509 bytes {0} [built]
       [2] (webpack)/buildin/module.js 517 bytes {0} [built]
       [3] ./~/html-webpack-plugin/lib/loader.js!./~/html-webpack-pl\
ugin/default_index.ejs 540 bytes {0} [built]
```

The output tells a lot:

- Hash: 3f76ae042ff0f2d98f35 - The hash of the build. You can use this to invalidate assets through [hash] placeholder. Hashing is discussed in detail in the *Adding Hashes to Filenames* chapter.
- Version: webpack 2.2.1 - Webpack version.
- Time: 377ms - Time it took to execute the build.

- `app.js 3.13 kB 0 [emitted]  app` - Name of the generated asset, size, the IDs of the **chunks** into which it's related, status information telling how it was generated, the name of the chunk.
- `index.html 180 bytes [emitted]` - Another generated asset that was emitted by the process.
- `[0] ./app/component.js 148 bytes {0} [built]` - The ID of the entry asset, name, size, entry chunk ID, the way it was generated.
- `Child html-webpack-plugin for "index.html":` - This is plugin-related output. In this case *html-webpack-plugin* is doing the output of its own.

Examine the output below `build/`. If you look closely, you can see the same IDs within the source. To see the application running, open the `build/index.html` file directly through a browser. On macOS `open ./build/index.html` works.

If you want webpack to stop execution on the first error, set `bail: true` option. Setting it kills the entire webpack process. The behavior is desirable if you are building in a CI environment.

In addition to a configuration object, webpack accepts an array of configurations. You can also return a `Promise` and eventually `resolve` to a configuration.

1.7 Adding a Build Shortcut

Given executing `node_modules/.bin/webpack` is verbose, you should do something about it. This is where npm and *package.json* can be used for running tasks.

Adjust the file as follows:

package.json

```
"scripts": {
  "build": "webpack"
},
```

Run `npm run build` to see the same output as before. This works because npm adds *node_modules/.bin* temporarily to the path. As a result, rather than having to write `"build": "node_modules/.bin/webpack"`, you can do `"build": "webpack"`.

You can execute this kind of scripts through *npm run* and you can use *npm run* anywhere within your project. If you run the command as is, it gives you the listing of available scripts.

 There are shortcuts like *npm start* and *npm test*. You can run these directly without *npm run* although that works too. For those in a hurry, you can use *npm t* to run your tests.

1.8 `HtmlWebpackPlugin` **Extensions**

Although you can replace `HtmlWebpackPlugin` template with your own, there are premade ones like html-webpack-template[11] or html-webpack-template-pug[12].

There are also specific plugins that extend `HtmlWebpackPlugin`'s functionality:

- favicons-webpack-plugin[13] is able to generate favicons.
- script-ext-html-webpack-plugin[14] gives you more control over script tags and allows you to tune script loading further.

---

[11] https://www.npmjs.com/package/html-webpack-template
[12] https://www.npmjs.com/package/html-webpack-template-pug
[13] https://www.npmjs.com/package/favicons-webpack-plugin
[14] https://www.npmjs.com/package/script-ext-html-webpack-plugin

- multipage-webpack-plugin[15] builds on top of *html-webpack-plugin* and makes it easier to manage multi-page configurations.
- resource-hints-webpack-plugin[16] adds resource hints[17] to your HTML files to speed up loading time.
- preload-webpack-plugin[18] enables `rel=preload` capabilities for scripts. This helps with lazy loading and it combines well with techniques discussed in the *Building* part of this book.

1.9 Conclusion

Even though you have managed to get webpack up and running, it does not do that much yet. Developing against it would be painful. Each time you wanted to check out the application, you would have to build it manually using `npm run build` and then refresh the browser. That's where webpack's more advanced features come in.

To recap:

- It's a good idea to use a locally installed version of webpack over a globally installed one. This way you can be sure of what version you are using. The local dependency works also in a Continuous Integration environment.
- Webpack provides a command line interface. You can use it even without configuration, but then you are limited by the options it provides.
- To write more complicated setups, you most likely have to write a separate *webpack.config.js* file.
- `HtmlWebpackPlugin` can be used to generate an HTML entry point to your application. Later in the book, you see how to generate multiple separate pages using. The *Multiple Pages* chapter covers that.
- It's handy to use npm *package.json* scripts to manage webpack. You can use it as a light task runner and use system features outside of webpack.

In the next chapter you will learn how to improve the developer experience by enabling automatic browser refresh.

---

[15] https://www.npmjs.com/package/multipage-webpack-plugin

[16] https://www.npmjs.com/package/resource-hints-webpack-plugin

[17] https://www.w3.org/TR/resource-hints/

[18] https://www.npmjs.com/package/preload-webpack-plugin

2. Automatic Browser Refresh

Tools, such as LiveReload[1] or Browsersync[2], allow to refresh the browser as you develop the application and avoid a refresh for CSS changes. It's possible to setup Browsersync to work with webpack through browser-sync-webpack-plugin[3], but webpack has more tricks in store.

2.1 Webpack watch Mode and webpack-dev-server

A good first step towards a better development environment is to use webpack in its **watch** mode. You can activate it through webpack --watch. Once enabled, it detects changes made to your files and recompiles automatically. *webpack-dev-server* (WDS) builds on top of the watch mode and goes even further.

WDS is a development server running **in-memory**, meaning the bundle contents aren't written out to files, but stored in memory. This is an important distinction when trying to debug code and styles.

By default WDS refreshes content automatically in the browser while you develop your application so you don't have to do it yourself. However it also supports an advanced webpack feature, **Hot Module Replacement** (HMR).

HMR allows patching the browser state without a full refresh making it particularly handy with libraries like React where a refresh blows away the application state. The *Hot Module Replacement* appendix covers the feature in detail.

WDS provides an interface that makes it possible to patch code on the fly, however for this to work effectively, you have to implement this interface for the client-side code. It's trivial for something like CSS because it's stateless, but the problem is harder with JavaScript frameworks and libraries.

---

[1]http://livereload.com/

[2]http://www.browsersync.io/

[3]https://www.npmjs.com/package/browser-sync-webpack-plugin

2.2 Emitting Files from WDS

Even though it's good that WDS operates in-memory by default for performance reasons, sometimes it can be good to emit files to the file system. This applies in particular, if you are integrating with another server that expects to find the files. webpack-disk-plugin[4], write-file-webpack-plugin[5], and more specifically html-webpack-harddisk-plugin[6] can achieve this.

 You should use WDS strictly for development. If you want to host your application, consider other standard solutions, such as Apache or Nginx.

2.3 Getting Started with WDS

To get started with WDS, install it first:

```
npm install webpack-dev-server --save-dev
```

As before, this command generates a command below the npm bin directory and you could run *webpack-dev-server* from there. After running the WDS, you have a development server running at http://localhost:8080. Automatic browser refresh is in place now, although at a basic level.

---

[4] https://www.npmjs.com/package/webpack-disk-plugin

[5] https://www.npmjs.com/package/write-file-webpack-plugin

[6] https://www.npmjs.com/package/html-webpack-harddisk-plugin

2.4 Attaching WDS to the Project

To integrate WDS to the project, define an npm script for launching it. To follow npm conventions, call it as *start*. To tell the targets apart, pass information about the environment to webpack configuration so you can specialize as needed:

package.json

```
"scripts": {
  "start": "webpack-dev-server --env development",
  "build": "webpack --env production"
  "build": "webpack"
},
```

 WDS picks up configuration like webpack itself. The same rules apply.

If you execute either *npm run start* or *npm start* now, you should see something in the terminal:

```
> webpack-dev-server --env development

Project is running at http://localhost:8080/
webpack output is served from /
Hash: c1b0a0508a91f4b1ac74
Version: webpack 2.2.1
Time: 757ms
      Asset       Size  Chunks                    Chunk Names
     app.js     314 kB       0  [emitted]  [big]  app
index.html  180 bytes          [emitted]
chunk    {0} app.js (app) 300 kB [entry] [rendered]
...
webpack: bundle is now VALID.
```

The server is running and if you open `http://localhost:8080/` at your browser, you should see something familiar:

Hello world

Hello world

If you try modifying the code, you should see output in your terminal. The browser should also perform a hard refresh on change.

WDS tries to run in another port in case the default one is being used. The terminal output tells you where it ends up running. You can debug the situation with a command like `netstat -na | grep 8080`. If something is running on the port 8080, it should display a message on Unix.

2.5 Verifying that `--env` Works

Webpack configuration is able to receive the value of `--env` if the configuration is defined within a function. To check that the correct environment is passed, adjust the configuration as follows:

webpack.config.js

```
module.exports = {
  // Entries have to resolve to files! It relies on Node.js
  // convention by default so if a directory contains *index.js*,
  // it resolves to that.
const commonConfig = {
  ...
};

module.exports = (env) => {
```

```
    console.log('env', env);

    return commonConfig;
};
```

If you run the npm commands now, you should see a different terminal output depending on which one you trigger:

```
> webpack-dev-server --env development
env development
...
```

 The result could be verified also by using the DefinePlugin to write it to the client code. The *Environment Variables* chapter discusses how to achieve this.

Understanding --env

Even though --env allows to pass strings to the configuration, it can do a bit more. Consider the following example:

package.json

```
"scripts": {
  "start": "webpack-dev-server --env development",
  "build": "webpack --env.target production"
},
```

Instead of a string, you should receive an object { target: 'production' } at configuration now. You could pass more key-value pairs, and they would go to the env object. If you set --env foo while setting --env.target, the string overrides the object.

Webpack relies on yargs underneath. To understand the dot notation in greater detail, see yargs documentation[7].

 Webpack 2 changed argument behavior compared to webpack 1. You are not allowed to pass custom parameters through the CLI anymore. Instead, it's better to go through the --env mechanism if you need to do this.

2.6 Configuring WDS Through Webpack Configuration

To customize WDS functionality it's possible to define a devServer field at webpack configuration. You can set most of these options through the CLI as well, but managing them through webpack is a good approach.

Enable additional functionality as below:

webpack.config.js

```
. . .

const productionConfig = () => commonConfig;

const developmentConfig = () => {
  const config = {
    devServer: {
      // Enable history API fallback so HTML5 History API based
      // routing works. Good for complex setups.
      historyApiFallback: true,

      // Display only errors to reduce the amount of output.
      stats: 'errors-only',
```

---

[7]http://yargs.js.org/docs/#parsing-tricks-dot-notation

```
      // Parse host and port from env to allow customization.
      //
      // If you use Docker, Vagrant or Cloud9, set
      // host: options.host || '0.0.0.0';
      //
      // 0.0.0.0 is available to all network devices
      // unlike default `localhost`.
      host: process.env.HOST, // Defaults to `localhost`
      port: process.env.PORT, // Defaults to 8080
    },
  };

  return Object.assign(
    {},
    commonConfig,
    config
  );
};

module.exports = (env) => {
  console.log('env', env);

  return commonConfig;
  if (env === 'production') {
    return productionConfig();
  }

  return developmentConfig();
};
```

After this change, you can configure the server host and port options through environment parameters. The merging portion of the code (Object.assign) is beginning to look knotty and it will be fixed in the *Splitting Configuration* chapter.

If you access through http://localhost:8080/webpack-dev-server/, WDS provides status information at the top. If your application relies on WebSockets and you use WDS proxying, you need to use this particular url as otherwise WDS logic interferes.

App ready.

Hello world

Status information

 dotenv[8] allows you to define environment variables through a *.env* file. *dotenv* allows you to control the host and port setting of the setup quickly.

2.7 Enabling Hot Module Replacement

Hot Module Replacement is one of those features that sets webpack apart. Implementing it requires additional effort on both server and client-side. The *Hot Module Replacement* appendix discusses the topic in greater detail. If you want to integrate HMR to your project, give it a look. It won't be needed to complete the tutorial, though.

2.8 Accessing the Development Server from Network

It's possible to customize host and port settings through the environment in the setup (i.e., `export PORT=3000` on Unix or `SET PORT=3000` on Windows). The default settings are enough on most platforms.

To access your server, you need to figure out the ip of your machine. On Unix, this can be achieved using `ifconfig | grep inet`. On Windows, `ipconfig` can be utilized.

---

[8]https://www.npmjs.com/package/dotenv

An npm package, such as node-ip[9] come in handy as well. Especially on Windows, you need to set your HOST to match your ip to make it accessible.

2.9 Making It Faster to Develop Configuration

WDS will handle restarting the server when you change a bundled file, but what about when you edit the webpack config? Restarting the development server each time you make a change tends to get boring after a while. This can be automated as discussed in GitHub[10] by using nodemon[11] monitoring tool.

To get it to work, you have to install it first through npm install nodemon --save-dev. After that, you can make it watch webpack config and restart WDS on change. Here's the script if you want to give it a go:

package.json

```
"scripts": {
  "start": "nodemon --watch webpack.config.js --exec \"webpack-dev-s\
erver --env development\"",
  "build": "webpack --env production"
},
```

It's possible WDS will support the functionality[12] itself in the future. If you want to make it reload itself on change, you should implement this workaround for now.

---

[9] https://www.npmjs.com/package/node-ip

[10] https://github.com/webpack/webpack-dev-server/issues/440#issuecomment-205757892

[11] https://www.npmjs.com/package/nodemon

[12] https://github.com/webpack/webpack/issues/3153

2.10 Polling Instead of Watching Files

Sometimes the file watching setup provided by WDS won't work on your system. It can be problematic on older versions of Windows, Ubuntu, Vagrant, and Docker. Enabling polling is a good option then:

webpack.config.js

```
const developmentConfig = merge([
  {
    devServer: {
      watchOptions: {
        // Delay the rebuild after the first change
        aggregateTimeout: 300,

        // Poll using interval (in ms, accepts boolean too)
        poll: 1000,
      },
    },
    plugins: [
      // Ignore node_modules so CPU usage with poll
      // watching drops significantly.
      new webpack.WatchIgnorePlugin([
        path.join(__dirname, 'node_modules')
      ]),
    ]
  },
  ...
]);
```

The setup is more resource intensive than the default but it's worth trying out.

 There are more details in *webpack-dev-server* issue #155[13].

---

[13]https://github.com/webpack/webpack-dev-server/issues/155

2.11 Alternate Ways to Use *webpack-dev-server*

You could have passed the WDS options through a terminal. It's clearer to manage the options within webpack configuration as that helps to keep *package.json* nice and tidy. It's also easier to understand what's going on as you don't need to dig out the answers from the webpack source.

Alternately, you could have set up an Express server and use a middleware. There are a couple of options:

- The official WDS middleware[14]
- webpack-hot-middleware[15]
- webpack-universal-middleware[16]

There's also a Node.js API[17] if you want more control and flexibility.

 There are slight differences[18] between the CLI and the Node API.

2.12 Other Features of *webpack-dev-server*

WDS provides functionality beyond what was covered above. There are a couple of relevant fields that you should be aware of:

- `devServer.contentBase` - Assuming you don't generate *index.html* dynamically and prefer to maintain it yourself in a specific directory, you need to point WDS to it. `contentBase` accepts either a path (e.g., `'build'`) or an array of paths (e.g., `['build', 'images']`). This defaults to the project root.

---

[14] https://webpack.js.org/guides/development/#webpack-dev-middleware

[15] https://www.npmjs.com/package/webpack-hot-middleware

[16] https://www.npmjs.com/package/webpack-universal-middleware

[17] https://webpack.js.org/configuration/dev-server/

[18] https://github.com/webpack/webpack-dev-server/issues/106

- `devServer.proxy` - If you are using multiple servers, you have to proxy WDS to them. The proxy setting accepts an object of proxy mappings (e.g., `{ '/api': 'http://localhost:3000/api' }`) that resolve matching queries to another server. Proxy settings are disabled by default.
- `devServer.headers` - Attach custom headers to your requests here.

 The official documentation[19] covers more options.

2.13 Development Plugins

The webpack plugin ecosystem is diverse and there are a lot of plugins that can help specifically with development:

- case-sensitive-paths-webpack-plugin[20] can be handy when you are developing on a case-insensitive environments like macOS or Windows but using case-sensitive environment like Linux for production.
- npm-install-webpack-plugin[21] allows webpack to install and wire the installed packages with your *package.json* as you import new packages to your project.
- system-bell-webpack-plugin[22] rings the system bell on failure instead of letting webpack fail silently.
- friendly-errors-webpack-plugin[23] improves on error reporting of webpack. It captures common errors and displays them in a friendlier manner.
- nyan-progress-webpack-plugin[24] can be used to get tidier output during the build process. Take care if you are using Continuous Integration (CI) systems like Travis as they can clobber the output. Webpack provides `ProgressPlugin` for the same purpose. No nyan there, though.

---

[19] https://webpack.js.org/configuration/dev-server/

[20] https://www.npmjs.com/package/case-sensitive-paths-webpack-plugin

[21] https://www.npmjs.com/package/npm-install-webpack-plugin

[22] https://www.npmjs.com/package/system-bell-webpack-plugin

[23] https://www.npmjs.com/package/friendly-errors-webpack-plugin

[24] https://www.npmjs.com/package/nyan-progress-webpack-plugin

- react-dev-utils[25] contains webpack utilities developed for Create React App[26]. Despite its name, they can find use beyond React.
- webpack-dashboard[27] gives an entire terminal based dashboard over the standard webpack output. If you prefer clear visual output, this one comes in handy.

In addition to plugins like these, it can be worth your while to set up linting to enforce coding standards. The *Linting JavaScript* chapter digs into that topic in detail.

2.14 Conclusion

WDS complements webpack and makes it more friendly by developers by providing development oriented functionality.

To recap:

- Webpack's watch mode is the first step towards a better development experience. You can have webpack compile bundles as you edit your source.
- Webpack's --env parameter allows you to control configuration target through terminal. You receive the passed env through a function interface.
- WDS can refresh the browser on change. It also implements **Hot Module Replacement**.
- The default WDS setup can be problematic on certain systems. For this reason, more resource intensive polling is an alternative.
- WDS can be integrated to an existing Node server using a middleware. This gives you more control than relying on the command line interface.
- WDS does far more than refreshing and HMR. For example proxying allows you to connect it with other servers.

In the next chapter, you make it harder to make mistakes by introducing JavaScript linting to the project.

---

[25] https://www.npmjs.com/package/react-dev-utils

[26] https://www.npmjs.com/package/create-react-app

[27] https://www.npmjs.com/package/webpack-dashboard

3. Linting JavaScript

Linting is one of those techniques that can help you make fewer mistakes while coding JavaScript. You can spot issues before they become actual problems. Modern editors and IDEs offer strong support for popular tools allowing you to detect possible issues as you are developing.

Despite this, it's a good idea to set them up with webpack or at least in a separate task that gets run regularly. That allows you to cancel a production build that is not up to your standards.

3.1 Brief Introduction to ESLint

The linter that started it all for JavaScript is Douglas Crockford's JSLint[1]. JSLint is known to be opinionated like Douglas himself. The next step in evolution was JSHint[2], which took the opinionated edge out of JSLint and allowed for more customization. ESLint[3] is the newest tool in vogue, and it goes even further.

ESLint Is Customizable

ESLint goes to the next level as it allows you to implement custom rules, parsers, and reporters. ESLint works with JSX syntax making it a good fit for React projects. You have to use a Babel specific parser with custom language features, although ESLint supports ES6 out of the box.

ESLint rules have been documented well, and you have full control over their severity. These features alone make it a powerful tool. Better yet, there is a significant number of rules and presets beyond the core as the community has built on top of it.

---

[1]http://www.jslint.com/

[2]http://jshint.com/

[3]http://eslint.org/

It's telling that a competing project, JSCS, decided to merge its efforts with ESLint[4]. JSCS reached the end of its life with its 3.0.0 release, and the core team joined with ESLint.

eslint-config-airbnb

eslint-config-airbnb[5] is a good example of a popular preset. Often it's enough to find a preset you like, tweak it to your liking with local rules or by deriving a preset of your own based on it, and then using that. This way you don't have to worry so much about all the available functionality.

 eslint-config-cleanjs[6] is a good example of how you can use ESLint to restrict JavaScript to a purely functional subset.

3.2 Linting Is About More than Catching Issues

Besides linting for issues, it can be valuable to manage the code style. Nothing is more annoying than having to work with source code that has mixed tabs and spaces. Stylistically consistent code reads better. When integrated with an Editor or IDE linting also points out your mistakes as you make them, making it easier to adjust your technique and avoid making more of the same errors.

Establishing strong linting can be beneficial, especially in a context where you need to collaborate with others. Even when working alone you benefit from linting as it can catch issues you could otherwise neglect. JavaScript as a language allows usage which, while valid, is not be the clearest to understand or may even be incorrect.

Linting does **not** replace proper testing, but it can complement testing approaches. It allows you to harden a codebase and make it more difficult to break. As the size of your project grows, and it becomes more challenging to manage, this becomes particularly important.

---

[4]http://eslint.org/blog/2016/04/welcoming-jscs-to-eslint
[5]https://www.npmjs.com/package/eslint-config-airbnb
[6]https://www.npmjs.com/package/eslint-config-cleanjs

3.3 Setting Up ESLint

ESLint

The pluggable linting utility for JavaScript and JSX

ESLint

ESLint[7] is the most versatile linting solution for JavaScript. It builds on top of ideas presented by JSLint and JSHint. More importantly, it allows you to develop custom rules.

 Since *v1.4.0* ESLint supports autofixing[8]. It allows you to perform certain rule fixes automatically. To activate it, pass the flag `--fix` to the tool. It's also possible to use this feature with webpack, although you should be careful with it. js-beautify[9] can perform a similar operation.

Connecting ESlint with *package.json*

To get started, install ESLint as a development dependency:

```
npm install eslint --save-dev
```

Next, you have to write configuration so you can run ESLint smoothly through npm. The `lint` namespace can be used to signify it's a linting related task. Caching should be enabled to improve performance on subsequent runs.

---

[7] http://eslint.org/

[8] http://eslint.org/blog/2015/09/eslint-v1.4.0-released/

[9] https://www.npmjs.com/package/js-beautify

Add the following to lint the application files and configuration:

package.json

```
"scripts": {
  "lint:js": "eslint app/ webpack.*.js --cache",
  ...
},
```

The potential problem with using an include based approach is that you forget to lint source code. Using excludes solves this but then you have to be careful to update the exclude list as your project grows to avoid linting too much.

The exclusion approach can be achieved by pointing ESLint to the project root through `eslint .` and setting up a *.eslintignore* file for the excludes like for *.gitignore*. You can point to your Git ignores using `--ignore-path .gitignore` for maximum reuse. Individual patterns are supported through `--ignore-pattern <pattern>`.

Defining Linting Rules

Given ESLint expects configuration to work, you need to define rules to describe what to lint and how to react if the rules aren't obeyed. The severity of an individual rule is defined by a number as follows:

- 0 - The rule has been disabled.
- 1 - The rule emits a warning.
- 2 - The rule emits an error.

Rules, such as `quotes`, accept an array instead allowing you to pass extra parameters to them. Refer to the ESLint rules documentation[10] for specifics.

---

[10]http://eslint.org/docs/rules/

Here's a starting point that works with the project:

.eslintrc.js

```js
module.exports = {
  env: {
    browser: true,
    commonjs: true,
    es6: true,
    node: true,
  },
  extends: 'eslint:recommended',
  parserOptions: {
    sourceType: 'module',
  },
  rules: {
    'comma-dangle': ['error', 'always-multiline'],
    indent: ['error', 2],
    'linebreak-style': ['error', 'unix'],
    quotes: ['error', 'single'],
    semi: ['error', 'always'],
    'no-unused-vars': ['warn'],
    'no-console': 0,
  },
};
```

If you invoke `npm run lint:js` now, it should execute without any warnings or errors. If you see either, this is a good time to try ESLint autofixing. You can run it through `npm run lint:js -- --fix`. Running an npm script this way allows you to pass extra parameters to it.

Another alternative would be to push it behind a *package.json* script. Autofix is not able to repair each error, but it can fix a lot. And as time goes by and ESLint improves, it can perform more work.

Beyond vanilla JSON, ESLint supports other formats, such as JavaScript or YAML. I.e., *.eslintrc.yaml* would expect YAML. See the documentation[11] for further details.

---

[11] http://eslint.org/docs/user-guide/configuring#configuration-file-formats

When ESLint gives errors, npm shows a long `ELIFECYCLE` error error block of its own. It's possible to disable that using the `silent` flag: `npm run lint:js --silent` or a shortcut `npm run lint:js -s`.

Connecting ESLint with Webpack

You can make webpack emit ESLint messages by using eslint-loader[12]. As the first step execute

```
npm install eslint-loader --save-dev
```

 eslint-loader uses a globally installed version of ESLint unless you have one included in the project itself. Make sure you have ESLint as a development dependency to avoid the strange behavior.

The loader needs wiring to work. Loaders are discussed in detail in the *Loading* part of this book, but the basic idea is fast to understand. A loader is connected to webpack through a rule that contains preconditions related to it and a reference to the loader itself.

In this case, you want to ensure that ESLint gets executed before anything else using the `enforce` field. It allows to guarantee that linting happens before any other processing. The idea is discussed in detail in the *Loader Definitions* chapter.

---

[12]https://www.npmjs.com/package/eslint-loader

To add linting to the project, adjust the configuration as follows:

webpack.config.js

```
const developmentConfig = () => {
  const config = {
    ...
    module: {
      rules: [
        {
          test: /\.js$/,
          enforce: 'pre',

          loader: 'eslint-loader',
          options: {
            emitWarning: true,
          },
        },
      ],
    },
  };


  ...
};
```

If you execute npm start now and break a linting rule while developing, you should
see that in the terminal output.

Webpack configuration lints only the application code you refer. If you
want to lint webpack configuration itself, execute npm run lint:js separately.

Attaching the linting process to Git through a prepush hook allows you to
catch problems earlier. husky[13] allows you to achieve this quickly. Doing
this allows you to rebase your commits and fix possible problems early.

---

[13] https://www.npmjs.com/package/husky

Enabling Error Overlay

WDS provides an overlay for capturing warnings and errors:

webpack.config.js

```
const developmentConfig = () => {
  const config = {
    devServer: {
      ...
      // overlay: true is equivalent
      overlay: {
        errors: true,
        warnings: true,
      },
    },
  };


  ...
};
```

Run the server now (npm start) and break the code to see an overlay in the browser:

```
Failed to compile.

./app/component.js

/Users/juhovepsalainen/Projects/tmp/webpack-demo/app/component.js
  4:1  error  Expected indentation of 2 spaces but found 0   indent
  4:1  error  'foo' is not defined                           no-undef
  4:4  error  Missing semicolon                              semi

✗ 3 problems (3 errors, 0 warnings)

  @ ./app/index.js 1:0-36
  @ multi (webpack)-dev-server/client?http://localhost:8080 ./app
```

Error overlay

3.4 ESLint Tips

The great thing about ESLint is that you can shape it to your purposes. The community around it's active, and you can find good integration in other tooling as well. Consider the tips below.

Usability Tips

- It can make sense to rely on an existing preset or set up custom configuration. That's where `--init` can come in handy. You can run it from `npm bin` and end up with a call like `node_modules/.bin/eslint --init`
- ESLint supports custom formatters through `--format` parameter. eslint-friendly-formatter[14] is an example of a formatter that provides terminal-friendly output. This way you can jump conveniently straight to the warnings and errors from there.

Performance Tips

- Especially on bigger projects it's beneficial to run ESLint outside of webpack. That keeps code compilation fast while still giving the advantage of linting. Solutions like lint-staged[15] and fastlint[16] can make this even more quickly.
- You can get more performance out of ESLint by running it through a daemon, such as eslint_d[17]. Using it brings down the overhead, and it can bring down linting times considerably.

Extension Tips

- ESLint supports ES6 features through configuration. You have to specify the features to use through the ecmaFeatures[18] property.

---

[14]https://www.npmjs.com/package/eslint-friendly-formatter

[15]https://www.npmjs.com/package/lint-staged

[16]https://www.npmjs.com/package/fastlint

[17]https://www.npmjs.com/package/eslint_d

[18]http://eslint.org/docs/user-guide/configuring.html#specifying-language-options

- Plugins, such as eslint-plugin-node[19], eslint-plugin-promise[20], eslint-plugin-compat[21], and eslint-plugin-import[22], are worth studying.
- Most IDEs and editors have good linter integration so you can spot issues as you develop.
- To learn about ESLint customizations options and how to write an ESLint plugin, check out the *Customizing ESLint* appendix.

Configuring ESLint Further

Since webpack 2, the configuration schema of webpack has become stricter, and it doesn't allow arbitrary fields at configuration root level anymore. To overcome this issue and to access all functionality of the *eslint-loader*, you have to use LoaderOptionsPlugin as below:

```
{
  plugins: [
    new webpack.LoaderOptionsPlugin({
      options: {
        eslint: {
          // Fail only on errors
          failOnWarning: false,
          failOnError: true,

          // Toggle autofix
          fix: false,

          // Output to Jenkins compatible XML
          outputReport: {
            filePath: 'checkstyle.xml',
            formatter: require('eslint/lib/formatters/checkstyle'),
          },
```

---

[19] https://www.npmjs.com/package/eslint-plugin-node
[20] https://www.npmjs.com/package/eslint-plugin-promise
[21] https://www.npmjs.com/package/eslint-plugin-compat
[22] https://www.npmjs.com/package/eslint-plugin-import

```
        },
      },
    }),
  ],
},
```

There are more options, and eslint-loader[23] documentation covers those in detail.

3.5 Webpack and JSHint

No JSLint particular loader exists for webpack yet. Fortunately, there's one for JSHint. You could set it up on a legacy project quickly. The key is in configuring jshint-loader[24].

JSHint looks into specific rules to apply from `.jshintrc`. You can also define custom settings within a `jshint` object at your webpack configuration. Exact configuration options have been covered by the JSHint documentation[25] in detail.

3.6 Prettier

Prettier[26] goes one step further and can format your code automatically according to your coding style. If you want to use Prettier with ESLint, you should use eslint-config-prettier[27] to disable ESLint rules that conflict with Prettier. Be warned that Prettier is highly opinionated in how it thinks code should look and offers few formatting options.

---

[23]https://www.npmjs.com/package/eslint-loader

[24]https://www.npmjs.com/package/jshint-loader

[25]http://jshint.com/docs/

[26]https://www.npmjs.com/package/prettier

[27]https://www.npmjs.com/package/eslint-config-prettier

3.7 Danger

Danger[28] operates on a higher level than other tools discussed. For example, it can check that the project change log was updated before a release is pushed to the public. You can also force pull requests of your project to comply specific standards.

3.8 EditorConfig

EditorConfig[29] allows you to maintain a consistent coding style across different IDEs and editors. Also, you need to set up a file:

.editorconfig

```
root = true

# General settings for whole project
[*]
indent_style = space
indent_size = 4
end_of_line = lf
charset = utf-8
trim_trailing_whitespace = true
insert_final_newline = true

# Format specific overrides
[*.js]
indent_style = space
indent_size = 2
```

---

[28] https://www.npmjs.com/package/danger
[29] http://editorconfig.org/

3.9 Conclusion

Linting is one of those techniques that yields benefits over the long term. You can fix possible problems before they become actual issues.

To recap:

- ESLint is the most versatile of the current options. You can expand it to fit your exact use case.
- ESLint can be run through webpack. It can terminate your build and even prevent it from getting deployed if your build does not pass the linting rules.
- To get a better development experience, consider enabling WDS `overlay` to capture errors and warnings emitted by webpack.
- EditorConfig complements ESLint by allowing you to define a project-level coding style. Editors integrate with EditorConfig making it easier to keep a project consistent regardless of the development platform.
- Prettier is a complimentary solution that can format your code automatically whilst Danger operates on repository level and can perform higher level tasks related to the development process.

Given the webpack configuration of the project is starting to get messy, it's a good time to discuss how to compose configuration and improve the situation.

4. Composing Configuration

Even though not a lot has been done with webpack yet, the amount of configuration is starting to feel substantial. Now you have to be careful about the way you compose it as you have separate production and development targets in the project. The situation can only get worse as you want to add more functionality to the project.

Using a single monolithic configuration file impacts comprehension and removes any potential for reusablity. As the needs of your project grow, you have to figure out the means to manage webpack configuration more effectively.

4.1 Possible Ways to Manage Configuration

You can manage webpack configuration in the following ways:

- Maintain configuration in multiple files for each environment and point web-pack to each through the `--config` parameter, sharing configuration through module imports. You can see this approach in action at webpack/react-starter[1].
- Push configuration to a library, which you then consume. Example: HenrikJoreteg/hjs-webpack[2].
- Maintain all configuration within a single file and branch there and by relying on the `--env` parameter.

These approaches can be combined to create a higher level configuration that is then composed of smaller parts. Those parts could then be added to a library which you then use through npm making it possible to consume the same configuration across multiple projects.

---

[1]https://github.com/webpack/react-starter
[2]https://www.npmjs.com/package/hjs-webpack

4.2 Composing Configuration by Merging

If the configuration file is broken into separate pieces, they have to be combined together again somehow. Normally this means merging objects and arrays. To eliminate the problem of dealing with `Object.assign` and `Array.concat`, webpack-merge[3] was developed.

webpack-merge does two things: it concatenates arrays and merges objects instead of overriding them. Even though a basic idea, this allows you to compose configuration and gives a degree of abstraction.

The example below shows the behavior in detail:

```
> merge = require('webpack-merge')
...
> merge(
... { a: [1], b: 5, c: 20 },
... { a: [2], b: 10, d: 421 }
... )
{ a: [ 1, 2 ], b: 10, c: 20, d: 421 }
```

webpack-merge provides even more control through strategies that enable you to control its behavior per field. Strategies allow you to force it to append, prepend, or replace content.

Even though *webpack-merge* was designed for this book, it has proven to be an invaluable tool beyond it. You can consider it as a learning tool and pick it up in your work if you find it handy.

 webpack-chain[4] provides a fluent API for configuring webpack allowing you to avoid configuration shape-related problems while enabling composition.

---

[3] https://www.npmjs.org/package/webpack-merge
[4] https://www.npmjs.com/package/webpack-chain

4.3 Setting Up *webpack-merge*

To get started, add *webpack-merge* to the project:

```
npm install webpack-merge --save-dev
```

To give a degree of abstraction, you can define *webpack.config.js* for higher level configuration and *webpack.parts.js* for configuration parts to consume. Here are the parts with small function-based interfaces extracted from the existing code:

webpack.parts.js

```
exports.devServer = ({ host, port } = {}) => ({
  devServer: {
    historyApiFallback: true,
    stats: 'errors-only',
    host, // Defaults to `localhost`
    port, // Defaults to 8080
    overlay: {
      errors: true,
      warnings: true,
    },
  },
});

exports.lintJavaScript = ({ include, exclude, options }) => ({
  module: {
    rules: [
      {
        test: /\.js$/,
        include,
        exclude,
        enforce: 'pre',

        loader: 'eslint-loader',
```

```
      options,
    },
  ],
 },
});
```

 The same stats idea works for production configuration as well. See the official documentation[5] for all the available options.

To connect these configuration parts, set up *webpack.config.js* as in the code example below:

webpack.config.js

```
const path = require('path');
const HtmlWebpackPlugin = require('html-webpack-plugin');
const merge = require('webpack-merge');

const parts = require('./webpack.parts');

const PATHS = {
  app: path.join(__dirname, 'app'),
  build: path.join(__dirname, 'build'),
};

const commonConfig = merge([
  {
    entry: {
      app: PATHS.app,
    },
    output: {
      path: PATHS.build,
      filename: '[name].js',
```

---

[5]https://webpack.js.org/configuration/stats/

```
    },
    plugins: [
      new HtmlWebpackPlugin({
        title: 'Webpack demo',
      }),
    ],
  },
  parts.lintJavaScript({ include: PATHS.app }),
]);

const productionConfig = merge([
]);

const developmentConfig = merge([
  parts.devServer({
    // Customize host/port here if needed
    host: process.env.HOST,
    port: process.env.PORT,
  }),
]);

module.exports = (env) => {
  if (env === 'production') {
    return merge(commonConfig, productionConfig);
  }

  return merge(commonConfig, developmentConfig);
};
```

After this change, the build should behave the same way as before. This time, however, you have room to expand, and you don't have to worry about how to combine different parts of the configuration.

You can add more targets by expanding the *package.json* definition and branching at *webpack.config.js* based on the need. *webpack.parts.js* grows to contain specific techniques you can then use to compose the configuration.

Webpack 2 validates the configuration by default. If you make a mistake like a typo, it lets you know.

4.4 Benefits of Composing Configuration

Splitting configuration allows you to keep on expanding the setup. The biggest win is the fact that you can extract commonalities between different targets. You can also identify smaller configuration parts to compose. These configuration parts can be pushed to packages of their own to consume across projects.

Instead of duplicating similar configuration across multiple projects, you can manage configuration as a dependency now. As you figure out better ways to perform tasks, all your projects receive the improvements.

Each approach comes with its pros and cons. Composition-based approach is a good starting point. In addition to composition, it gives you a limited amount of code to scan through, but it's a good idea to check out how other people do it too. You can find something that works the best based on your tastes.

Perhaps the biggest problem is that with composition you need to know what you are doing, and it's possible you aren't going to get the composition right the first time around. But that's a software engineering problem that goes beyond webpack.

You can always iterate on the interfaces and find better ones. By passing in a configuration object instead of multiple arguments, you can change the behavior of a part without effecting its API. You can expose API as you need it.

 If you have to support both webpack 1 and 2, you can perform branching based on version using `require('webpack/package.json').version` to detect it. After that, you have to set specific branches for each and merge.

4.5 Configuration Layouts

In the book project, you push all of the configuration into two files: *webpack.config.js* and *webpack.parts.js*. The former contains higher level configuration while the latter lower level and isolates you from webpack specifics. The chosen approach allows more layouts, and you can evolve it further.

Split per Configuration Target

If you split the configuration per target, you could end up with a file structure as below:

```
.
└── config
    ├── webpack.common.js
    ├── webpack.development.js
    ├── webpack.parts.js
    └── webpack.production.js
```

In this case, you would point to the targets through webpack `--config` parameter and `merge` common configuration through `module.exports = merge(common, config);`.

Split Parts per Purpose

To add hierarchy to the way configuration parts are managed, you could decompose *webpack.parts.js* per category:

```
.
└── config
    ├── parts
    │   ├── devserver.js
    ...
    │   ├── index.js
    │   └── javascript.js
    └── ...
```

This arrangement would make it faster to find configuration related to a category. A good option would be to arrange the parts within a single file and use comments to split it up.

Pushing Parts to Packages

Given all configuration is JavaScript, nothing prevents you from consuming it as a package or packages. It would be possible to package the shared configuration so that you can consume it across multiple projects. See the *Package Authoring Techniques* chapter for further information on how to achieve this.

4.6 Conclusion

Even though the configuration is technically the same as before, now you have room to grow it.

To recap:

- Given webpack configuration is JavaScript code underneath, there are many ways to manage it.
- You should choose a method to compose configuration that makes the most sense to you. webpack-merge[6] was developed to provide a light approach for composition, but you can find many other options in the wild.
- Composition can enable configuration sharing. Instead of having to maintain a custom configuration per repository, you can share it across repositories this way. Using npm packages enables this. Developing configuration is close to developing any other code. This time, however, you codify your practices as packages.

The next parts of this book cover different techniques, and *webpack.parts.js* sees a lot of action as a result. The changes to *webpack.config.js* fortunately remain minimal.

---

[6]https://www.npmjs.com/package/webpack-merge

II Styling

In this part, you will learn about styling-related concerns in detail including loading styles, refreshing styles during development, separating CSS, autoprefixing, eliminating unused CSS, and linting.

5. Loading Styles

Webpack doesn't handle styling out of the box and you will have to use loaders and plugins to allow loading style files. In this chapter, you will set up CSS with the project and see how it works out with automatic browser refreshing. When you make a change to the CSS webpack doesn't have to force a full refresh. Instead, it can patch the CSS without one.

5.1 Loading CSS

To load CSS, you need to use css-loader[1] and style-loader[2]. *css-loader* goes through possible `@import` and `url()` lookups within the matched files and treats them as a regular ES6 `import`. If an `@import` points to an external resource, *css-loader* skips it as only internal resources get processed further by webpack.

style-loader injects the styling through a `style` element. The way it does this can be customized. It also implements the *Hot Module Replacement* interface providing good development experience.

The matched files can be processed through loaders like file-loader[3] or url-loader[4] and these possibilities are discussed in the *Loading Assets* part of the book.

Since inlining CSS isn't a good idea for production usage, it makes sense to use `ExtractTextPlugin` to generate a separate CSS file. You will do this in the next chapter.

---

[1] https://www.npmjs.com/package/css-loader
[2] https://www.npmjs.com/package/style-loader
[3] https://www.npmjs.com/package/file-loader
[4] https://www.npmjs.com/package/url-loader

To get started, invoke

```
npm install css-loader style-loader --save-dev
```

Now let's make sure webpack is aware of them. Add a new function at the end of the part definition:

webpack.parts.js

```
exports.loadCSS = ({ include, exclude } = {}) => ({
  module: {
    rules: [
      {
        test: /\.css$/,
        include,
        exclude,

        use: ['style-loader', 'css-loader'],
      },
    ],
  },
});
```

You also need to connect the fragment with the main configuration:

webpack.config.js

```
const commonConfig = merge([
  ...
  parts.loadCSS(),
]);
```

The added configuration means that files ending with .css should invoke the given loaders. test matches against a JavaScript-style regular expression.

Loaders are transformations that are applied to source files, and return the new source and can be chained together like a pipe in Unix. They evaluated from right to left. This means that `loaders: ['style-loader', 'css-loader']` can be read as `styleLoader(cssLoader(input))`.

 If you want to disable *css-loader* `url` parsing, set `url: false`. The same idea applies to `@import` as to disable parsing imports you can set `import: false` through the loader options.

5.2 Setting Up the Initial CSS

You are missing the CSS still:

app/main.css

```
body {
  background: cornsilk;
}
```

Also, you need to make webpack aware of it. Without having an entry pointing to it somehow, webpack is not able to find the file:

app/index.js

```
import './main.css';
...
```

Execute `npm start` now. Browse to `http://localhost:8080` if you are using the default port and open up *main.css* and change the background color to something like `lime` (`background: lime`). Develop styles as needed to make it look a nicer.

You continue from here in the next chapter. Before that, though, you'll learn about styling-related techniques.

Hello world

Hello cornsilk world

5.3 Understanding CSS Scoping and CSS Modules

Perhaps the biggest challenge of CSS is that all rules exist within **global scope**, meaning that two classes with the same name will collide. The limitation is inherent to the CSS specification but projects have workarounds for the issue. CSS Modules[5] introduces **local scope** for every module by making every class declared within unique by including a hash in their name that is globally unique to the module.

Webpack's *css-loader* supports CSS Modules. You can enable it through a loader definition as above while enabling the support:

```
{
  loader: 'css-loader',
  options: {
    modules: true,
  },
},
```

After this change, your class definitions remain local to the files. In case you want global class definitions, you need to wrap them within :global(.redButton) { ... } kind of declarations.

---

[5]https://github.com/css-modules/css-modules

In this case, the `import` statement gives you the local classes you can then bind to elements. Assume you had CSS as below:

app/main.css

```css
body {
  background: cornsilk;
}

.redButton {
  background: red;
}
```

You could then bind the resulting class to a component:

app/component.js

```js
import styles from './main.css';

...

// Attach the generated class name
element.className = styles.redButton;
```

`body` remains as a global declaration still. It's that `redButton` that makes the difference. You can build component-specific styles that don't leak elsewhere this way.

CSS Modules provides additional features like composition to make it easier to work with your styles. You can also combine it with other loaders as long as you apply them before *css-loader*.

 CSS Modules behavior can be modified as discussed in the official documentation[6]. You have control over the names it generates for instance.

---

[6]https://www.npmjs.com/package/css-loader#local-scope

eslint-plugin-css-modules[7] is handy for tracking CSS Modules related problems.

Using CSS Modules with Third Party Libraries and CSS

If you are using CSS Modules in your project, you should process normal CSS through a separate loader definition without the modules option of *css-loader* enabled. Otherwise all classes will be scoped to their module. In the case of third party libraries this is almost certainly not what you want.

You can solve the problem by processing third party CSS differently through an include definition against *node_modules*. Alternately, you could use a file extension (.mcss) to tell files using CSS Modules apart from the rest and then manage this situation in a loader test.

5.4 Loading Less

Less

Less[8] is a CSS processor packed with functionality. Using Less doesn't take a lot of effort through webpack as less-loader[9] deals with the heavy lifting. You should install less[10] as well given it's a peer dependency of *less-loader*.

---

[7]https://www.npmjs.com/package/eslint-plugin-css-modules
[8]http://lesscss.org/
[9]https://www.npmjs.com/package/less-loader
[10]https://www.npmjs.com/package/less

Consider the following minimal setup:

```
{
  test: /\.less$/,
  use: ['style-loader', 'css-loader', 'less-loader'],
},
```

The loader supports Less plugins, source maps, and so on. To understand how those work you should check out the project itself.

5.5 Loading Sass

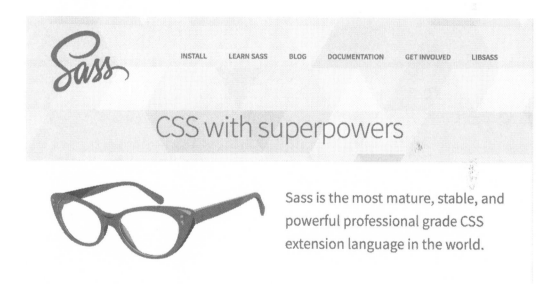

Sass

Sass[11] is a widely used CSS preprocessor. You should use sass-loader[12] with it. Remember to install node-sass[13] to your project as it's a peer dependency.

---

[11] http://sass-lang.com/

[12] https://www.npmjs.com/package/sass-loader

[13] https://www.npmjs.com/package/node-sass

Webpack doesn't take much configuration:

```
{
  test: /\.scss$/,
  use: ['style-loader', 'css-loader', 'sass-loader'],
},
```

 If you want more performance, especially during development, check out fast-sass-loader[14].

5.6 Loading Stylus and Yeticss

EXPRESSIVE, DYNAMIC, ROBUST CSS

Stylus

Stylus[15] is yet another example of a CSS processor. It works well through stylus-loader[16]. yeticss[17] is a pattern library that works well with it.

---

[14] https://www.npmjs.com/package/fast-sass-loader

[15] http://stylus-lang.com/

[16] https://www.npmjs.com/package/stylus-loader

[17] https://www.npmjs.com/package/yeticss

Consider the following configuration:

```
{
  ...
  module: {
    rules: [
      {
        test: /\.styl$/,
        use: ['style-loader', 'css-loader', 'stylus-loader'],
      },
    ],
  },
  plugins: [
    new webpack.LoaderOptionsPlugin({
      options: {
        // yeticss
        stylus: {
          use: [require('yeticss')],
        },
      },
    }),
  ],
},
```

To start using yeticss with Stylus, you must import it to one of your app's *.styl* files:

```
@import 'yeticss'

//or
@import 'yeticss/components/type'
```

5.7 PostCSS

PostCSS

PostCSS[18] allows you to perform transformations over CSS through JavaScript plugins. You can even find plugins that provide you Sass-like features. PostCSS is the equivalent of Babel for styling. postcss-loader[19] allows using it with webpack.

The example below illustrates how to set up autoprefixing using PostCSS. It also sets up precss[20], a PostCSS plugin that allows you to use Sass-like markup in your CSS. You can mix this technique with other loaders to allow autoprefixing there.

```
{
  test: /\.css$/,
  use: [
    'style-loader',
    'css-loader',
    {
      loader: 'postcss-loader',
      options: {
        plugins: () => ([
```

---

[18] http://postcss.org/

[19] https://www.npmjs.com/package/postcss-loader

[20] https://www.npmjs.com/package/precss

```
        require('autoprefixer'),
        require('precss'),
      ]),
    },
  },
],
},
```

You have to remember to include autoprefixer[21] and precss[22] to your project for this to work. The technique is discussed in detail in the *Autoprefixing* chapter.

 PostCSS supports *postcss.config.js* based configuration. It relies on cosmi-config[23] internally for other formats.

cssnext

cssnext[24] is a PostCSS plugin that allows to experience the future now with certain restrictions. You can use it through postcss-cssnext[25] and enable it as follows:

```
{
  loader: 'postcss-loader',
  options: {
    plugins: () => ([
      require('postcss-cssnext')(),
    ]),
  },
},
```

[21] https://www.npmjs.com/package/autoprefixer
[22] https://www.npmjs.com/package/precss
[23] https://www.npmjs.com/package/cosmiconfig
[24] http://cssnext.io/
[25] https://www.npmjs.com/package/postcss-cssnext

See the usage documentation[26] for available options.

 cssnext includes *autoprefixer*! You don't have to configure autoprefixing separately for it to work in this case.

5.8 Understanding Lookups

To get most out of *css-loader*, you should understand how it performs its lookups. Even though *css-loader* handles relative imports by default, it doesn't touch absolute imports (`url("/static/img/demo.png")`). If you rely on these kind of imports, you have to copy the files to your project.

copy-webpack-plugin[27] works for this purpose, but you can also copy the files outside of webpack. The benefit of the former approach is that webpack-dev-server can pick that up.

 resolve-url-loader[28] comes in handy if you use Sass or Less. It adds support for relative imports to the environments.

Processing *css-loader* Imports

If you want to process *css-loader* imports in a specific way, you should set up `importLoaders` option to a number that tells the loader how many loaders after the *css-loader* should be executed against the imports found. If you import other CSS files from your CSS through the `@import` statement and want to process the imports through specific loaders, this technique is essential.

---

[26] http://cssnext.io/usage/

[27] https://www.npmjs.com/package/copy-webpack-plugin

[28] https://www.npmjs.com/package/resolve-url-loader

Consider the following import from a CSS file:

```
@import "./variables.sass";
```

To process the Sass file, you would have to write configuration:

```
{
  test: /\.css$/,
  use: [
    'style-loader',
    {
      loader: 'css-loader',
      options: {
        importLoaders: 1,
      },
    },
    'sass-loader',
  ],
},
```

If you added more loaders, such as *postcss-loader*, to the chain, you would have to adjust the importLoaders option accordingly.

Loading from *node_modules* Directory

You can load files directly from your node_modules directory. Consider Bootstrap and its usage for example:

```
@import "~bootstrap/less/bootstrap";
```

The tilde character ($\sim$) tells webpack that it's not a relative import as by default. If tilde is included, it performs a lookup against node_modules (default setting) although this is configurable through the resolve.modules[29] field.

---

[29] https://webpack.js.org/configuration/resolve/#resolve-modules

If you are using *postcss-loader*, you can skip using $\sim$ as discussed in postcss-loader issue tracker[30]. *postcss-loader* can resolve the imports without a tilde.

5.9 Enabling Source Maps

If you want to enable source maps for CSS, you should enable `sourceMap` option for *css-loader* and set `output.publicPath` to an absolute url pointing to your development server. If you have multiple loaders in a chain, you have to enable source maps separately for each. *css-loader* issue 29[31] discusses this problem further.

5.10 Converting CSS to Strings

Especially with Angular 2, it can be convenient if you can get CSS in a string format that can be pushed to components. css-to-string-loader[32] achieves exactly this.

5.11 Using Bootstrap

There are a couple of ways to use Bootstrap[33] through webpack. One option is to point to the npm version[34] and perform loader configuration as above.

The Sass version[35] is another option. In this case, you should set `precision` option of *sass-loader* to at least 8. This is a known issue[36] explained at *bootstrap-sass*.

The third option is to go through bootstrap-loader[37]. It does a lot more but allows customization.

---

[30] https://github.com/postcss/postcss-loader/issues/166

[31] https://github.com/webpack/css-loader/issues/29

[32] https://www.npmjs.com/package/css-to-string-loader

[33] https://getbootstrap.com/

[34] https://www.npmjs.com/package/bootstrap

[35] https://www.npmjs.com/package/bootstrap-sass

[36] https://www.npmjs.com/package/bootstrap-sass#sass-number-precision

[37] https://www.npmjs.com/package/bootstrap-loader

5.12 Conclusion

Webpack can load a variety of style formats. It even supports advanced specifications like CSS Modules[38]. The approaches covered here inline the styling by default.

To recap:

- *css-loader* evaluates the `@import` and `url()` definitions of your styling. *style-loader* converts it to JavaScript and implements webpack's Hot Module Replacement interface.
- *css-loader* supports the CSS Modules specification. CSS Modules allow you maintain CSS in a local scope by default solving the biggest issue of CSS.
- Webpack supports a large variety of formats compiling to CSS through loaders. These include Sass, Less, and Stylus.
- PostCSS allows you to inject functionality to CSS in through its plugin system. cssnext is an example of a collection of plugins for PostCSS that implements future features of CSS.
- *css-loader* doesn't touch absolute imports by default. It allows customization of loading behavior through the `importLoaders` option. You can perform lookups against *node_modules* by prefixing your imports with a tilde ($\sim$) character.
- To use source maps, you have to enable `sourceMap` boolean through each style loader you are using except for *style-loader*. You should also set `output.publicPath` to an absolute url that points to your development server.
- Using Bootstrap with webpack requires special care. You can either go through generic loaders or a bootstrap specific loader for more customization options.

Although the loading approach covered here is enough for development purposes, it's not ideal for production as it inlines the styling to the JavaScript bundles. You'll learn to solve this problem in the next chapter by separating CSS from the source.

---

[38]https://github.com/css-modules/webpack-demo

6. Separating CSS

Even though there is a nice build set up now, where did all the CSS go? As per configuration, it has been inlined to JavaScript! Even though this can be convenient during development, it doesn't sound ideal.

The current solution doesn't allow to cache CSS. You can also get a **Flash of Unstyled Content** (FOUC). FOUC happens because the browser takes a while to load JavaScript and the styles would be applied only then. Separating CSS to a file of its own avoids the problem by letting the browser to manage it separately.

Webpack provides a means to generate a separate CSS bundles using ExtractTextPlugin[1]. It can aggregate multiple CSS files into one. For this reason, it comes with a loader that handles the extraction process. The plugin then picks up the result aggregated by the loader and emits a separate file.

Due to this process, `ExtractTextPlugin` comes with overhead during the compilation phase. It doesn't work with Hot Module Replacement by design. Given the plugin is used only for production, that is not a problem.

 This same technique can be employed with other assets, like templates, too.

 It can be potentially dangerous to use inline styles within JavaScript in production as it represents an attack vector. **Critical path rendering** embraces the idea and inlines the critical CSS to the initial HTML payload improving perceived performance of the site. In limited contexts inlining a small amount of CSS can be a viable option to speed up the initial load (fewer requests).

---

[1]https://www.npmjs.com/package/extract-text-webpack-plugin

6.1 Setting Up `ExtractTextPlugin`

Install the plugin first:

```
npm install extract-text-webpack-plugin --save-dev
```

`ExtractTextPlugin` includes a loader, `ExtractTextPlugin.extract` that marks the assets to be extracted. Then a plugin performs its work based on this annotation.

`ExtractTextPlugin.extract` accepts `use` and `fallback` definitions. `ExtractTextPlugin` processes content through `use` only from **initial chunks** by default and it uses `.fallback` for the rest. It doesn't touch any split bundles unless `allChunks: true` is set true. The *Bundle Splitting* chapter digs into greater detail.

If you wanted to extract CSS from a more involved format, like Sass, you would have to pass multiple loaders to the `use` option. Both `use` and `fallback` accept a loader (string), a loader definition, or an array of loader definitions.

The idea can be modeled as below:

webpack.parts.js

```
const ExtractTextPlugin = require('extract-text-webpack-plugin');

...

exports.extractCSS = ({ include, exclude, use }) => {
  // Output extracted CSS to a file
  const plugin = new ExtractTextPlugin({
    filename: '[name].css',
  });

  return {
    module: {
      rules: [
        {
          test: /\.css$/,
```

```
      include,
      exclude,

      use: plugin.extract({
        use,
        fallback: 'style-loader',
      }),
    },
  ],
},
plugins: [ plugin ],
};
};
```

That [name] placeholder uses the name of the entry where the CSS is referred. Placeholders and hashing are discussed in detail in the *Adding Hashes to Filenames* chapter.

It would be possible to have multiple plugin.extract calls against different file types. This would allow you to aggregate them to a single CSS file. Another option would be to extract multiple CSS files through separate plugin definitions and then concatenate them using merge-files-webpack-plugin[2].

 If you wanted to output the resulting file to a specific directory, you could do it by passing a path. Example: filename: 'styles/[name].css'.

[2]https://www.npmjs.com/package/merge-files-webpack-plugin

Connecting with Configuration

Connect the function with the configuration as below:

webpack.config.js

```
const commonConfig = merge([
  ...
  parts.loadCSS(),
]);

const productionConfig = merge([
  parts.extractCSS({ use: 'css-loader' }),
]);

const developmentConfig = merge([
  ...
  parts.loadCSS(),
]);
```

Using this setup, you can still benefit from the HMR during development. For a production build, it's possible to generate a separate CSS, though. `HtmlWebpackPlugin` picks it up automatically and injects it into `index.html`.

If you are using CSS Modules, remember to tweak `use` accordingly as discussed in the *Loading Styles* chapter. You can maintain separate setups for normal CSS and CSS Modules so that they get loaded through separate logic.

After running `npm run build`, you should see output similar to the following:

```
Hash: 57e54590377069688806
Version: webpack 2.2.1
Time: 952ms
      Asset       Size  Chunks                 Chunk Names
     app.js    3.79 kB       0  [emitted]  app
    app.css   32 bytes       0  [emitted]  app
 index.html  218 bytes          [emitted]
   [0] ./app/component.js 148 bytes {0} [built]
   [1] ./app/main.css 41 bytes {0} [built]
   [2] ./app/index.js 434 bytes {0} [built]
  ...
```

Now styling has been pushed to a separate CSS file. Thus, the JavaScript bundle has become slightly smaller. You also avoid the FOUC problem. The browser doesn't have to wait for JavaScript to load to get styling information. Instead, it can process the CSS separately, avoiding the flash.

If you are getting `Module build failed: CssSyntaxError:` or `Module build failed: Unknown word` error, make sure your `common` configuration doesn't have a CSS-related section set up.

extract-loader[3] is a light alternative to `ExtractTextPlugin`. It does less, but can be enough for basic extraction needs.

---

[3]https://www.npmjs.com/package/extract-loader

6.2 Managing Styles Outside of JavaScript

Even though referring to styling through JavaScript and then bundling is the
recommended option, it's possible to achieve the same result through an entry and
globbing[4]:

```
...
const glob = require('glob');

// Glob CSS files as an array of CSS files. This can be
// problematic due to CSS rule ordering so be careful!
const PATHS = {
  ...
  style: glob.sync('./app/**/*.css'),
};


...

const commonConfig = merge([
  {
    entry: {
      ...
      style: PATHS.style,
    },
    ...
  },
  ...
]);
```

After this type of change, you would not have to refer to styling from your
application code. It also means that CSS Modules stop working. As a result, you
should get both *style.css* and *style.js*. The latter file contains content like webpack-

---

[4]https://www.npmjs.com/package/glob

`Jsonp([1,3],[function(n,c){}]);` and it doesn't do anything as discussed in the webpack issue 1967[5].

If you want strict control over the ordering, you can set up a single CSS entry and then use `@import` to bring the rest to the project through it. Another option would be to set up a JavaScript entry and go through `import` to get the same effect.

 css-entry-webpack-plugin[6] has been designed to help with this usage pattern. The plugin is able to extract a CSS bundle from an entry without `ExtractTextPlugin`.

6.3 Conclusion

The current setup separates styling from JavaScript neatly. Even though the technique is most valuable with CSS, it can be used to extract HTML templates or any other files types you consume. The hard part about `ExtractTextPlugin` has to do with its setup, but the complexity can be hidden behind an abstraction.

To recap:

- Using `ExtractTextPlugin` with styling solves the problem of Flash of Unstyled Content (FOUC). Separating CSS from JavaScript also improves caching behavior and removes a potential attack vector.
- `ExtractTextPlugin` is not the only solution. *extract-loader* can give the same result in more limited contexts.
- If you don't prefer to maintain references to styling through JavaScript, an alternative is to handle them through an entry. You have to be careful with style ordering in this case, though.

In the next chapter, you'll learn to **autoprefix**. Enabling the feature makes it more convenient to develop complex CSS setups that work with older browsers as well.

---

[5]https://github.com/webpack/webpack/issues/1967

[6]https://www.npmjs.com/package/css-entry-webpack-plugin

7. Autoprefixing

It can be difficult to remember which vendor prefixes you have to use for specific CSS rules to support a large variety of users. **Autoprefixing** solves this problem. It can be enabled through PostCSS and the autoprefixer[1] plugin. *autoprefixer* uses Can I Use[2] service to figure out which rules should be prefixed and its behavior can be tuned further.

7.1 Setting Up Autoprefixing

Achieving autoprefixing takes a small addition to the current setup. Install *postcss-loader* and *autoprefixer* first:

```
npm install postcss-loader autoprefixer --save-dev
```

Add a fragment enabling autoprefixing:

webpack.parts.js

```
exports.autoprefix = () => ({
  loader: 'postcss-loader',
  options: {
    plugins: () => ([
      require('autoprefixer')(),
    ]),
  },
});
```

---

[1] https://www.npmjs.com/package/autoprefixer
[2] http://caniuse.com/

To connect the loader with `ExtractTextPlugin`, hook it up as follows:

webpack.config.js

```
const productionConfig = merge([
  parts.extractCSS({ use: 'css-loader' }),
  parts.extractCSS({
    use: ['css-loader', parts.autoprefix()],
  }),
]);
```

To confirm that the setup works, there should be something to autoprefix. Adjust the CSS:

app/main.css

```
body {
  background: cornsilk;
  display: flex;
}
```

If you build the application now (`npm run build`) and examine the built CSS, you should be able to find a declaration there:

```
body {
  background: cornsilk;
  display: -webkit-box;
  display: -ms-flexbox;
  display: flex;
}
```

As you can see, autoprefixing expands the rules. If you know what browsers you support, it's possible to set up a .browserslistrc[3] file. Different tools pick up this definition, *autoprefixer* included.

---

[3] https://www.npmjs.com/package/browserslist

Consider the example below where you select only specific browsers:

.browserslistrc

```
> 1% # Browser usage over 1%
Last 2 versions # Or last two versions
IE 8 # Or IE 8
```

7.2 Conclusion

Autoprefixing is a convenient technique as it decreases the amount of work needed while crafting CSS. You can maintain minimum browser requirements within a *.browserslistrc* file. The tooling can then use that information to generate optimal output.

To recap:

- Autoprefixing can be enabled through the *autoprefixer* PostCSS plugin.
- Autoprefixing writes missing CSS definitions based on your minimum browser definition.
- *.browserslistrc* is a standard file that works with tooling beyond *autoprefixer*

In the next chapter, you'll learn to eliminate unused CSS from the project.

8. Eliminating Unused CSS

Frameworks like Bootstrap[1] tend to come with a lot of CSS. Often you use only a small part of it. Typically, you bundle even the unused CSS. It's possible, however, to eliminate the portions you aren't using.

PurifyCSS[2] is a tool that can achieve this by analyzing files. It walks through your code and figures out which CSS classes are being used. Often there is enough information for it to strip unused CSS from your project. It also works with single page applications to an extent.

uncss[3] is a good alternative to PurifyCSS. It operates through PhantomJS and performs its work in a different manner. You can use uncss itself as a PostCSS plugin.

 You have to be careful if you are using CSS Modules. You have to **whitelist** the related classes as discussed in purifycss-webpack readme[4].

8.1 Setting Up Pure.css

To make the demo more realistic, let's install Pure.css[5], a small CSS framework, as well and refer to it from the project so that you can see PurifyCSS in action. These two projects aren't related in any way despite the naming.

```
npm install purecss --save
```

---

[1] https://getbootstrap.com/

[2] https://www.npmjs.com/package/purifycss

[3] https://www.npmjs.com/package/uncss

[4] https://github.com/webpack-contrib/purifycss-webpack#usage-with-css-modules

[5] http://purecss.io/

To make the project aware of Pure.css, `import` it:

app/index.js

```
import 'purecss';
...
```

You should also make the demo component use a Pure.css class, so there is something to work with:

app/component.js

```
module.exports = () => {
  const element = document.createElement('div');

  element.className = 'pure-button';
  element.innerHTML = 'Hello world';

  return element;
};
```

If you run the application (`npm start`), the "Hello world" should look like a button.

Styled hello

Building the application (npm run build) should yield output:

```
Hash: e8601af01b5c5a5e722c
Version: webpack 2.2.1
Time: 1255ms
     Asset        Size  Chunks              Chunk Names
    app.js     4.15 kB       0  [emitted]  app
   app.css     16.5 kB       0  [emitted]  app
index.html  218 bytes          [emitted]
   [0] ./app/component.js 185 bytes {0} [built]
   [1] ./app/main.css 41 bytes {0} [built]
   [2] ./~/purecss/build/pure-min.css 41 bytes {0} [built]
...
```

As you can see, the size of the CSS file grew. This is something to fix with PurifyCSS.

8.2 Enabling PurifyCSS

Using PurifyCSS can lead to significant savings. In the official example of the project, they purify and minify Bootstrap (140 kB) in an application using ~40% of its selectors to mere ~35 kB. That's a big difference.

purifycss-webpack[6] allows to achieve similar results. You should use the Extract-TextPlugin with it for the best results. Install it and a glob[7] helper first:

```
npm install glob purifycss-webpack purify-css --save-dev
```

---

[6]https://www.npmjs.com/package/purifycss-webpack
[7]https://www.npmjs.org/package/glob

You also need PurifyCSS configuration as below:

webpack.parts.js

```
. . .
const PurifyCSSPlugin = require('purifycss-webpack');

. . .

exports.purifyCSS = ({ paths }) => ({
  plugins: [
    new PurifyCSSPlugin({ paths }),
  ],
});
```

Next, the part has to be connected with the configuration. It's important the plugin is used *after* the ExtractTextPlugin; otherwise it doesn't work:

webpack.config.js

```
. . .
const glob = require('glob');

const parts = require('./webpack.parts');

. . .

const productionConfig = merge([
  . . .
  parts.purifyCSS({
    paths: glob.sync(`${PATHS.app}/**/*.js`, { nodir: true }),
  }),
]);
```

 The order matters. CSS extraction has to happen before purifying.

If you execute `npm run build` now, you should see something:

```
Hash: e8601af01b5c5a5e722c
Version: webpack 2.2.1
Time: 1363ms
       Asset       Size  Chunks              Chunk Names
      app.js    4.15 kB       0  [emitted]  app
     app.css    2.19 kB       0  [emitted]  app
  index.html  218 bytes          [emitted]
   [0] ./app/component.js 185 bytes {0} [built]
   [1] ./app/main.css 41 bytes {0} [built]
   [2] ./~/purecss/build/pure-min.css 41 bytes {0} [built]
...
```

The size of the style has decreased noticeably. Instead of 16k, you have roughly 2k now. The difference would be even bigger for heavier CSS frameworks.

PurifyCSS supports additional options[8] including `minify`. You can enable these through the `purifyOptions` field when instantiating the plugin. Given PurifyCSS cannot pick all of the classes you are using always, you should use `purifyOptions.whitelist` array to define selectors which it should leave in the result no matter what.

 Using PurifyCSS loses CSS source maps even if you have enabled them through loader specific configuration due to the way it works underneath.

---

[8]https://github.com/purifycss/purifycss#the-optional-options-argument

Critical Path Rendering

The idea of critical path rendering[9] takes a look at CSS performance from a different angle. Instead of optimizing for size, it optimizes for render order and puts emphasis on **above-the-fold** CSS.

isomorphic-style-loader[10] achieves this using webpack and React. critical-path-css-tools[11] listing by Addy Osmani lists other related tools.

8.3 Conclusion

Using PurifyCSS can lead to a significant decrease in file size. It's particularly valuable for static sites that rely on a heavy CSS framework. The more dynamic a site or an application becomes, the harder it becomes to analyze reliably.

To recap:

- Eliminating unused CSS is possible using PurifyCSS. It performs static analysis against the source.
- The functionality can be enabled through *purifycss-webpack* and the plugin should be applied *after* `ExtractTextPlugin`.
- At best, PurifyCSS can eliminate most, if not all, unused CSS rules.
- Critical path rendering is another CSS technique that puts emphasis on rendering the above-the-fold CSS first. The idea is to render something as fast as possible instead of waiting for all CSS to load.

The styling portion of the demo is in good shape. It can be made easier to develop by including CSS linting to the project.

---

[9] https://developers.google.com/web/fundamentals/performance/critical-rendering-path/

[10] https://www.npmjs.com/package/isomorphic-style-loader

[11] https://github.com/addyosmani/critical-path-css-tools

9. Linting CSS

As discussed earlier in the *Linting JavaScript* chapter, linting is a technique that allows to avoid certain categories of mistakes. Automation is good, as it can save effort. In addition to JavaScript, it's possible to lint CSS.

Stylelint[1] is a tool that allows linting. It can be used with webpack through postcss-loader[2].

9.1 Connecting Stylelint with *package.json*

To get started, install Stylelint as a development dependency:

```
npm install stylelint --save-dev
```

To connect Stylelint with npm and make it find the CSS files, adjust as follows:

package.json

```
"scripts": {
  "lint:style": "stylelint app/**/*.css",
  ...
},
```

---

[1] http://stylelint.io/
[2] https://www.npmjs.com/package/postcss-loader

To have something to test with, there should be a dummy rule:

.stylelintrc

```
{
  "rules": {
    "color-hex-case": "lower"
  }
}
```

If you break the rule at *app/main.css* and run `npm run lint:style`, you should see a message:

```
...
app/main.css
 2:15  Expected "#FFF" to be "#fff"   color-hex-case
...
```

To get less verbose output on error, use either `npm run lint:style --silent` or `npm run lint:style -s`.

The same rules can be connected with webpack.

9.2 Connecting Stylelint with Webpack

To get started, install *postcss-loader* unless you have it set up already:

```
npm install postcss-loader --save-dev
```

Next, to integrate with configuration, set up a part first:

webpack.parts.js

```
exports.lintCSS = ({ include, exclude }) => ({
  module: {
    rules: [
      {
        test: /\.css$/,
        include,
        exclude,
        enforce: 'pre',

        loader: 'postcss-loader',
        options: {
          plugins: () => ([
            require('stylelint')(),
          ]),
        },
      },
    ],
  },
});
```

Then add it to the common configuration:

webpack.config.js

```
const commonConfig = merge([
  ...
  parts.lintCSS({ include: PATHS.app }),
]);
```

If you define a CSS rule, such as background-color: #EFEFEF; at *main.css* now, you should see a warning at your terminal when you run the build (npm start or npm run build):

```
WARNING in ./~/css-loader!./~/postcss-loader!./app/main.css
stylelint: /webpack-demo/app/main.css:2:21: Expected "#EFEFEF" to be\
 "#efefef" (color-hex-case)
 @ ./app/main.css 4:14-117
 @ ./app/index.js
```

See the Stylelint documentation for a full list of rules. npm lists possible rulesets[3] you can enable through configuration.

  stylelint-scss[4] provides a collection of SCSS specific linting rules.

  The enforce idea is discussed in detail in the *Loader Definitions* chapter.

  If you get Module build failed: Error: No configuration provided for ... kind of error, check your *.stylelintrc*.

---

[3]https://www.npmjs.com/search?q=stylelint-config
[4]https://www.npmjs.com/package/stylelint-scss

9.3 *stylelint-webpack-plugin*

stylelint-webpack-plugin[5] allows you to reach the same result. Its greatest advantage over the setup above is that it follows possible @import statements you have in your styling.

 stylelint-bare-webpack-plugin[6] is a variant of *stylelint-webpack-plugin* that allows you to control the version of Stylelint you are using.

9.4 CSSLint

CSSLint[7] is another option to Stylelint. It can be used through csslint-loader[8] and follows a normal loader setup.

9.5 Conclusion

After these changes, there is style linting in place. Now you can catch CSS-related problems.

To recap:

- It's possible to lint CSS through **Stylelint**.
- Linting CSS allows you to capture common CSS-related problems and disallow problematic patterns.
- Stylelint can be treated as a PostCSS plugin, but it can also be used through *stylelint-webpack-plugin.*
- **CSSLint** is an option to Stylelint. It's possible the projects merge[9], though.

---

[5] https://www.npmjs.com/package/stylelint-webpack-plugin

[6] https://www.npmjs.com/package/stylelint-bare-webpack-plugin

[7] http://csslint.net/

[8] https://www.npmjs.com/package/csslint-loader

[9] https://github.com/CSSLint/csslint/issues/668

III Loading Assets

In this part, you will learn how to load different types of assets using webpack's loaders. Especially images, fonts, and JavaScript receive particular attention. You also learn how webpack's loader definitions work.

10. Loader Definitions

Webpack provides multiple ways to set up module loaders. Webpack 2 simplified the situation by introducing the use field. The legacy options (loader and loaders) still work, though. You see all the options for completeness, as they exist in older configurations online.

It can be a good idea to prefer absolute paths here as they allow you to move configuration without breaking assumptions. The other option is to set context field as this gives a similar effect and affects the way entry points and loaders are resolved. It doesn't have an impact on the output, though, and you still need to use an absolute path or / there.

Assuming you set an include or exclude rule, packages loaded from *node_modules* still work as the assumption is that they have been compiled in such way that they work out of the box. If they don't, then you have to apply techniques covered in the *Package Consuming Techniques* chapter.

 include/exclude is handy with *node_modules* as webpack processes and traverses the installed packages by default when you import JavaScript files to your project. Therefore you need to configure it to avoid that behavior. Other file types don't suffer from this issue.

10.1 Anatomy of a Loader

Webpack supports a large variety of formats through *loaders*. Also, it supports a couple of JavaScript module formats out of the box. The idea is the same. You always set up a loader, or loaders, and connect those with your directory structure.

Consider the example below where webpack is set to process JavaScript through Babel:

webpack.config.js

```
module.exports = {
  ...
  module: {
    rules: [
      {
        // **Conditions**
        // Match files against RegExp or a function.
        test: /\.js$/,

        // **Restrictions**
        // Restrict matching to a directory. This
        // also accepts an array of paths or a function.
        // The same applies to `exclude`.
        include: path.join(__dirname, 'app'),
        exclude(path) {
          // You can perform more complicated checks
          // through functions if you want.
          return path.match(/node_modules/);
        },

        // **Actions**
        // Apply loaders the matched files.
        use: 'babel-loader',
      },
    ],
  },
};
```

If you are not sure how a particular RegExp matches, consider using an online tool, such as regex101[1], RegExr[2], or Regexper[3].

10.2 Loader Evaluation Order

It's good to keep in mind that webpack's loaders are always evaluated from right to left and from bottom to top (separate definitions). The right-to-left rule is easier to remember when you think about as functions. You can read definition `use: ['style-loader', 'css-loader']` as `style(css(input))` based on this rule.

To see the rule in action, consider the example below:

```
{
  test: /\.css$/,
  use: ['style-loader', 'css-loader'],
},
```

Based on the right to left rule, the example can be split up while keeping it equivalent:

```
{
  test: /\.css$/,
  use: ['style-loader'],
},
{
  test: /\.css$/,
  use: ['css-loader'],
},
```

---

[1]https://regex101.com/
[2]http://regexr.com/
[3]https://regexper.com

Enforcing Order

Even though it would be possible to develop an arbitrary configuration using the rule above, it can be convenient to be able to force certain rules to be applied before or after regular ones. The enforce field can come in handy here. It can be set to either pre or post to push processing either before or after other loaders.

You used the idea earlier in the *Linting JavaScript* chapter. Linting is a good example as the build should fail before it does anything else. Using enforce: 'post' is rarer and it would imply you want to perform a check against the built source. Performing analysis against the built source is one potential example.

The basic syntax goes as below:

```
{
  // Conditions
  test: /\.js$/,
  enforce: 'pre', // 'post' too

  // Actions
  loader: 'eslint-loader',
},
```

It would be possible to write the same configuration without enforce if you chained the declaration with other loaders related to the test carefully. Using enforce removes the necessity for that allows you to split loader execution into separate stages that are easier to compose.

10.3 Passing Parameters to a Loader

There's a query format that allows passing parameters to loaders:

```
{
  // Conditions
  test: /\.js$/,
  include: PATHS.app,

  // Actions
  use: 'babel-loader?cacheDirectory,presets[]=es2015',
},
```

This style of configuration works in entries and source imports too as webpack picks it up. The format comes in handy in certain individual cases, but often you are better off using more readable alternatives.

It's preferable to use the combination of loader and options fields:

```
{
  // Conditions
  test: /\.js$/,
  include: PATHS.app,

  // Actions
  loader: 'babel-loader',
  options: {
    cacheDirectory: true,
    presets: ['react', 'es2015'],
  },
},
```

Or you can also go through use:

```
{
  // Conditions
  test: /\.js$/,
  include: PATHS.app,

  // Actions
  use: {
    loader: 'babel-loader',
    options: {
      cacheDirectory: true,
      presets: ['react', 'es2015'],
    },
  },
},
```

If you wanted to use more than one loader, you could pass an array to use and expand from there:

```
{
  test: /\.js$/,
  include: PATHS.app,

  use: [
    {
      loader: 'babel-loader',
      options: {
        cacheDirectory: true,
        presets: ['react', 'es2015'],
      },
    },
    // Add more loaders here
  ],
},
```

10.4 Branching at use Using a Function

In the book setup, you compose configuration on a higher level. Another option to achieve similar results would be to branch at use as webpack's loader definitions accept functions that allow you to branch depending on the environment. Consider the example below:

```
{
  test: /\.css$/,

  // resource refers to the resource path matched.
  // resourceQuery contains possible query passed to it (?sourceMap)
  // issuer tells about match context path
  use: ({ resource, resourceQuery, issuer }) => {
    // You have to return either something falsy,
    // string (i.e., 'style-loader'), or an object from here.
    //
    // Returning an array fails! To get around that,
    // it's possible to nest rules.
    if (env === 'development') {
      return {
        // Trigger css-loader first
        loader: 'css-loader',
        rules: [
          // And style-loader after it
          'style-loader',
        ],
      };
    }

    ...
  },
},
```

Carefully applied, this technique allows different means of composition.

10.5 Inline Definitions

Even though configuration level loader definitions are preferable, it's possible to write loader definitions inline:

```
// Process foo.png through url-loader and other
// possible matches.
import 'url-loader!./foo.png';

// Override possible higher level match completely
import '!!url-loader!./bar.png';
```

The problem with this approach is that it couples your source with webpack. But it's a good form to know still. Since configuration entries go through the same mechanism, the same forms work there as well:

```
{
  entry: {
    app: 'babel-loader!./app',
  },
},
```

10.6 Alternate Ways to Match Files

test combined with include or exclude to constrain the match is the most common approach to match files. These accept the data types as listed below:

- test - Match against a RegExp, string, function, an object, or an array of conditions like these.
- include - The same.
- exclude - The same, except the output is the inverse of include.
- resource: /inline/ - Match against a resource path including the query. Examples: /path/foo.inline.js, /path/bar.png?inline.

- issuer: /bar.js/ - Match against a resource requested from the match. Example: /path/foo.png would match if it was requested from /path/bar.js.
- resourcePath: /inline/ - Match against a resource path without its query. Example: /path/foo.inline.png.
- resourceQuery: /inline/ - Match against a resource based on its query. Example: /path/foo.png?inline.

Boolean based fields can be used to constrain these matchers further:

- not - Do **not** match against a condition (see test for accepted values).
- and - Match against an array of conditions. All must match.
- or - Match against an array while any must match.

10.7 Loading Based on resourceQuery

oneOf field makes it possible to route webpack to a specific loader based on a resource related match:

```
{
  test: /\.css$/,

  oneOf: [
    {
      resourceQuery: /inline/,
      use: 'url-loader',
    },
    {
      resourceQuery: /external/,
      use: 'file-loader',
    },
  ],
},
```

If you wanted to embed the context information to the filename, the rule could use resourcePath over resourceQuery.

10.8 Loading Based on `issuer`

`issuer` can be used to control behavior based on where a resource was imported. In the example below adapted from css-loader issue 287[4], *style-loader* is applied only when webpack captures a CSS file from a JavaScript import:

```
{
  test: /\.css$/,

  rules: [
    {
      issuer: /\.js$/,
      use: 'style-loader',
    },
    {
      use: 'css-loader',
    },
  ],
},
```

10.9 Understanding Loader Behavior

Loader behavior can be understood in greater detail by inspecting them. loader-runner[5] allows you to run them in isolation without webpack. Webpack uses this package internally and *Extending with Loaders* chapter covers it in detail.

inspect-loader[6] allows you to inspect what's being passed between loaders. Instead of having to insert `console.log`s within *node_modules*, you can attach this loader to your configuration and inspect the flow there.

---

[4]https://github.com/webpack-contrib/css-loader/pull/287#issuecomment-261269199

[5]https://www.npmjs.com/package/loader-runner

[6]https://www.npmjs.com/package/inspect-loader

10.10 LoaderOptionsPlugin

Given webpack 2 forbids arbitrary root level configuration, you have to use LoaderOptionsPlugin. The plugin exists for legacy compatibility and disappears in a future release. Consider the example below:

```
plugins: [
  new webpack.LoaderOptionsPlugin({
    sassLoader: {
      includePaths: [
        path.join(__dirname, 'style'),
      ],
    },
  }),
],
```

10.11 Conclusion

Webpack provides multiple ways to set up loaders but sticking with use is enough in webpack 2. Be careful with loader ordering, as it's a common source of problems.

To recap:

- **Loaders** allow you determine what should happen when webpack's module resolution mechanism encounters a file.
- A loader definition consists of **conditions** based on which to match and **actions** that should be performed when a match happens.
- Webpack 2 introduced the use field. It combines the ideas of old loader and loaders fields into a single construct.
- Webpack 2 provides multiple ways to match and alter loader behavior. You can, for example, match based on a **resource query** after a loader has been matched and route the loader to specific actions.
- LoaderOptionsPlugin exists for legacy purposes and allows you to get around the strict configuration schema of webpack 2.

In the next chapter, you'll learn to load images using webpack.

11. Loading Images

HTTP/1 application can be made slow by loading a lot of small assets. Each request comes with an overhead. HTTP/2 helps in this regard and changes the situation somewhat drastically. Till then you are stuck with different approaches. Webpack allows a couple of these. They are particularly relevant for loading images.

Webpack allows you to inline assets by using url-loader[1]. It emits your images as base64 strings within your JavaScript bundles. The process decreases the number of requests needed while growing the bundle size. It's enough to use *url-loader* during development. You want to consider other alternatives for the production build, though.

Webpack gives control over the inlining process and can defer loading to file-loader[2]. *file-loader* outputs image files and returns paths to them instead of inlining. This technique works with other assets types, such as fonts, as you see in the later chapters.

11.1 Setting Up *url-loader*

url-loader is a good starting point and it's the perfect option for development purposes, as you don't have to care about the size of the resulting bundle. It comes with a *limit* option that can be used to defer image generation to *file-loader* after a certain limit's reached. This way you can inline small files to your JavaScript bundles while generating separate files for the bigger ones.

If you use the limit option, you need to install both *url-loader* and *file-loader* to your project. Assuming you have configured your styles correctly, webpack resolves any url() statements your styling contains. You can point to the image assets through your JavaScript code as well.

In case the limit option is used, *url-loader* passes possible additional options to *file-loader* making it possible to configure its behavior further.

---

[1]https://www.npmjs.com/package/url-loader
[2]https://www.npmjs.com/package/file-loader

To load *.jpg*, *.png*, and *.svg* files while inlining files below 25kB, you would have to set up a loader:

```
{
  test: /\.(jpg|png|svg)$/,
  loader: 'url-loader',
  options: {
    limit: 25000,
  },
},
```

11.2 Setting Up *file-loader*

If you want to skip inlining altogether, you can use *file-loader* directly. The following setup customizes the resulting filename. By default, *file-loader* returns the MD5 hash of the file's contents with the original extension:

```
{
  test: /\.(jpg|png|svg)$/,
  loader: 'file-loader',
  options: {
    name: '[path][name].[hash].[ext]',
  },
},
```

 If you want to output your images below a particular directory, set it up with name: './images/[hash].[ext]'.

 Be careful not to apply both loaders on images at the same time! Use the include field for further control if *url-loader* limit isn't enough.

11.3 Integrating Images to the Project

The ideas above can be wrapped in a small helper that can be incorporated into the book project. To get started, install the dependencies:

```
npm install file-loader url-loader --save-dev
```

Set up a function as below:

webpack.parts.js

```
exports.loadImages = ({ include, exclude, options } = {}) => ({
  module: {
    rules: [
      {
        test: /\.(png|jpg|svg)$/,
        include,
        exclude,

        use: {
          loader: 'url-loader',
          options,
        },
      },
    ],
  },
});
```

To attach it to the configuration, adjust as follows. The configuration defaults to *url-loader* during development and uses both *url-loader* and *file-loader* in production to maintain smaller bundle sizes. *url-loader* uses *file-loader* implicitly when limit is set and both have to be installed for the setup to work.

webpack.config.js

```
const productionConfig = merge([
  ...
  parts.loadImages({
    options: {
      limit: 15000,
      name: '[name].[ext]',
    },
  }),
]);

const developmentConfig = merge([
  ...
  parts.loadImages(),
]);
```

To test that the setup works, download an image or generate it (`convert -size 100x100 gradient:blue logo.png`) and refer to it from the project:

app/main.css

```
body {
  background: cornsilk;
  background-image: url('./logo.png');
  background-repeat: no-repeat;
  background-position: center;
  display: flex;
}
```

The behavior changes depending on the `limit` you set. Below the limit, it should inline the image while above it should emit a separate asset and a path to it. The CSS lookup works because of *css-loader*. You can also try importing the image from JavaScript code and see what happens.

11.4 Loading SVGs

Webpack allows a couple ways[3] to load SVGs. However, the easiest way is through *file-loader* as follows:

```
{
  test: /\.svg$/,
  use: 'file-loader',
},
```

Assuming you have set up your styling correctly, you can refer to your SVG files as below. The example SVG path below is relative to the CSS file:

```
.icon {
    background-image: url('../assets/icon.svg');
}
```

If you want the raw SVG content, you can use the raw-loader[4] for this purpose. svg-inline-loader[5] goes a step further and eliminates unnecessary markup from your SVGs. These loaders can be valuable if you want to inject the SVG content to directly to JavaScript or HTML markup.

svg-sprite-loader[6] can merge separate SVG files into a single sprite, making it potentially more efficient to load as you avoid request overhead. It supports raster images (*.jpg, .png*) as well.

react-svg-loader[7] emits SVGs as React components meaning you could end up with code like `<Image width={50} height={50}/>` to render a SVG in your code after importing it.

 You can still use *url-loader* and the tips above with SVGs too.

---

[3]https://github.com/webpack/webpack/issues/595

[4]https://www.npmjs.com/package/raw-loader

[5]https://www.npmjs.com/package/svg-inline-loader

[6]https://www.npmjs.com/package/svg-sprite-loader

[7]https://www.npmjs.com/package/react-svg-loader

11.5 Optimizing Images

In case you want to compress your images, use image-webpack-loader[8], svgo-loader[9] (SVG specific), or imagemin-webpack-plugin[10]. This type of loader should be applied first to the data, so remember to place it as the last within use listing.

Compression is particularly valuable for production builds as it decreases the amount of bandwidth required to download your image assets and speed up your site or application as a result.

11.6 Utilizing `srcset`

resize-image-loader[11] and responsive-loader[12] allow you to generate `srcset` compatible collections of images for modern browsers. `srcset` gives more control to the browsers over what images to load and when resulting in higher performance.

11.7 Loading Images Dynamically

Webpack allows you to load images dynamically based on a condition. The techniques covered in the *Code Splitting* chapter are enough for this purpose. Doing this can save bandwidth and load images only when you need them or preload them while you have time.

11.8 Getting Image Dimensions

Sometimes getting the only reference to an image isn't enough. image-size-loader[13] emits image dimensions, type, and size in addition to the reference to the image itself.

---

[8]https://www.npmjs.com/package/image-webpack-loader

[9]https://www.npmjs.com/package/svgo-loader

[10]https://www.npmjs.com/package/imagemin-webpack-plugin

[11]https://www.npmjs.com/package/resize-image-loader

[12]https://www.npmjs.com/package/responsive-loader

[13]https://www.npmjs.com/package/image-size-loader

11.9 Referencing to Images

Webpack can pick up images from style sheets through `@import` and `url()` assuming *css-loader* has been configured. You can also refer to your images within code. In this case, you have to import the files explicitly:

```
const src = require('./avatar.png');

// Use the image in your code somehow now
const Profile = () => (
  <img src={src} />
);
```

If you are using React, then you use babel-plugin-transform-react-jsx-img-import[14] to generate the `require` automatically. In that case, you would end up with code:

```
const Profile = () => (
  <img src="avatar.png" />
);
```

It's also possible to set up dynamic imports as discussed in the *Code Splitting* chapter. Here's a small example:

```
// The name of the avatar is received from somewhere
const src = require(`./avatars/${avatar}`);
```

...

---

[14]https://www.npmjs.com/package/babel-plugin-transform-react-jsx-img-import

11.10 Loading Sprites

Spriting technique allows you to combine multiple smaller images into a single image. It has been used for games to describe animations and it's valuable for web development as well as you avoid request overhead.

webpack-spritesmith[15] converts provided images into a sprite sheet and Sass/-Less/Stylus mixins. You have to set up a SpritesmithPlugin, point it to target images, and set the name of the generated mixin. After that, your styling can pick it up:

```
@import '~sprite.sass';

.close-button {
  sprite($close);
}

.open-button {
  sprite($open);
}
```

11.11 Images and *css-loader* Source Map Gotcha

If you are using images and *css-loader* with the sourceMap option enabled, it's important that you set output.publicPath to an absolute value pointing to your development server. Otherwise, images aren't going to work. See the relevant webpack issue[16] for further explanation.

---

[15] https://www.npmjs.com/package/webpack-spritesmith
[16] https://github.com/webpack/style-loader/issues/55

11.12 Conclusion

Webpack allows you to inline images within your bundles when needed. Figuring out proper inlining limits for your images requires experimentation. You have to balance between bundle sizes and the number of requests.

To recap:

- *url-loader* inlines the assets within JavaScript. It comes with a `limit` option that allows you to defer assets above it to *file-loader*.
- *file-loader* emits image assets and returns paths to them to the code. It allows hashing the asset names.
- You can find image optimization related loaders and plugins that allow you to tune their size further.
- It's possible to generate **sprite sheets** out of smaller images to combine them into a single request.
- Webpack allows you to load images dynamically based on a given condition.
- If you are using source maps, you should remember to set `output.publicPath` to an absolute value for the images to show up.

You'll learn to load fonts using webpack in the next chapter.

12. Loading Fonts

Loading fonts is similar to loading images. It does come with special challenges, though. How to know what font formats to support? There can be up to four font formats to worry about if you want to provide first class support to each browser.

The problem can be solved by deciding a set of browsers and platforms that should receive first class service. The rest can use system fonts.

You can approach the problem in several ways through webpack. You can still use *url-loader* and *file-loader* as with images. Font test patterns tend to be more complicated, though, and you have to worry about font file related lookups.

 canifont[1] helps you to figure out which font formats you should support. It accepts a **.browserslistrc** definition and then checks font support of each browser based on the definition.

12.1 Choosing One Format

If you exclude Opera Mini, all browsers support the *.woff* format. Its newer version, *.woff2*, is widely supported by modern browsers and can be a good alternative.

---

[1]https://www.npmjs.com/package/canifont

Going with one format you can use a similar setup as for images and rely on both
file-loader and *url-loader* while using the limit option:

```
{
  test: /\.woff$/,
  loader: 'url-loader',
  options: {
    limit: 50000,
  },
},
```

A more elaborate approach to achieve a similar result that includes *.woff2* and others,
would be to end up with code as below:

```
{
  // Match woff2 in addition to patterns like .woff?v=1.1.1.
  test: /\.(woff|woff2)(\?v=\d+\.\d+\.\d+)?$/,
  loader: 'url-loader',
  options: {
    // Limit at 50k. Above that it emits separate files
    limit: 50000,

    // url-loader sets mimetype if it's passed.
    // Without this it derives it from the file extension
    mimetype: 'application/font-woff',

    // Output below fonts directory
    name: './fonts/[name].[ext]',
  },
},
```

12.2 Supporting Multiple Formats

In case you want to make sure the site looks good on a maximum amount of browsers, you can use *file-loader* and forget about inlining. Again, it's a trade-off as you get extra requests, but perhaps it's the right move. Here you could end up with a loader configuration:

```
{
  test: /\.(ttf|eot|woff|woff2)$/,
  loader: 'file-loader',
  options: {
    name: 'fonts/[name].[ext]',
  },
},
```

The way you write your CSS definition matters. To make sure you are getting the benefit from the newer formats, they should become first in the definition. This way the browser picks them up.

```
@font-face {
  font-family: 'myfontfamily';
  src: url('./fonts/myfontfile.woff2') format('woff2'),
    url('./fonts/myfontfile.woff') format('woff'),
    url('./fonts/myfontfile.eot') format('embedded-opentype'),
    url('./fonts/myfontfile.ttf') format('truetype');
    /* Add other formats as you see fit */
}
```

 MDN discusses the font-family rule[2] in detail.

---

[2]https://developer.mozilla.org/en/docs/Web/CSS/@font-face

12.3 Manipulating *file-loader* Output Path and
`publicPath`

As discussed above and in webpack issue tracker[3], *file-loader* allows shaping the output. This way you can output your fonts below fonts/, images below images/, and so on over using the root.

Furthermore, it's possible to manipulate `publicPath` and override the default per loader definition. The following example illustrates these techniques together:

```
{
  // Match woff2 in addition to patterns like .woff?v=1.1.1.
  test: /\.woff2?(\?v=\d+\.\d+\.\d+)?$/,
  loader: 'url-loader',
  options: {
    limit: 50000,
    mimetype: 'application/font-woff',

    // Output below the fonts directory
    name: './fonts/[name].[ext]',

    // Tweak publicPath to fix CSS lookups to take
    // the directory into account.
    publicPath: '../',
  },
},
```

12.4 Generating Font Files Based on SVGs

If you prefer to use SVG based fonts, they can be bundled as a single font file by using webfonts-loader[4].

---

[3]https://github.com/webpack/file-loader/issues/32#issuecomment-250622904
[4]https://www.npmjs.com/package/webfonts-loader

Take care with SVGs if you have SVG specific image setup in place already. If you want to process font SVGs differently, set their definitions carefully. The *Loader Definitions* chapter covers alternatives.

12.5 Using Font Awesome

The ideas above can be applied with Font Awesome[5]. It's a collection of high-quality font icons you can refer to using CSS classes.

Integrating Font Awesome to the Project

To integrate Font Awesome to the book project, install it first:

```
npm install font-awesome --save
```

Given Font Awesome doesn't define a `main` field in its *package.json* file, you need to point to it through a direct path instead of package name alone.

Refer to Font Awesome as follows:

app/index.js

```
import 'font-awesome/css/font-awesome.css';
...
```

Font Awesome includes Sass and Less versions as well, but given you have not set up either, this definition is enough.

 The `import` could be cleaned up as `import 'font-awesome'` by setting up a `resolve.alias`. The *Package Consuming Techniques* chapter discusses this idea in detail.

---

[5]https://www.npmjs.com/package/font-awesome

If you run the project now (`npm start`), webpack should give a long list of errors:

```
ERROR in ./~/font-awesome/fonts/fontawesome-webfont.woff2?v=4.7.0
Module parse failed: .../node_modules/font-awesome/fonts/fontawesome\
-webfont.woff2?v=4.7.0 Unexpected character '' (1:4)
You may need an appropriate loader to handle this file type.
(Source code omitted for this binary file)
 @ ./~/css-loader!./~/font-awesome/css/font-awesome.css 6:479-532
 @ ./~/font-awesome/css/font-awesome.css
 @ ./app/index.js
 @ multi (webpack)-dev-server/client?http://localhost:8080 webpack/h\
ot/only-dev-server react-hot-loader/patch ./app
```

Implementing Webpack Configuration

The result is expected as you haven't configured loaders for any of Font Awesome fonts yet and webpack doesn't know what to do with the files in question. To match the files and map them through *file-loader*, attach the following snippet to the project:

webpack.parts.js

```
exports.loadFonts = ({ include, exclude, options } = {}) => ({
  module: {
    rules: [
      {
        // Capture eot, ttf, woff, and woff2
        test: /\.(eot|ttf|woff|woff2)(\?v=\d+\.\d+\.\d+)?$/,
        include,
        exclude,

        use: {
          loader: 'file-loader',
          options,
        },
      },
```

```
    ],
  },
});
```

The idea is the same as for loading images. This time around you match font files. If you wanted, you could refactor the commonality to a function to share between the two.

You still need to connect the above with the main configuration:

webpack.config.js

```
const commonConfig = merge([
  ...
  parts.loadFonts({
    options: {
      name: '[name].[ext]',
    },
  }),
]);
```

The project should run (npm start) without any errors now.

To see Font Awesome in action, adjust the application as follows:

app/component.js

```
export default (text = 'Hello world') => {
  const element = document.createElement('div');

  element.className = 'pure-button';
  element.className = 'fa fa-hand-spock-o fa-1g';
  element.innerHTML = text;

  return element;
}
```

If you build the application (`npm run build`), you should see that it processed and Font Awesome assets were included.

```
Hash: e379b2c5a9f46663f367
Version: webpack 2.2.1
Time: 2547ms
          Asset      Size  Chunks                      Chunk Names
    ...font.eot    166 kB          [emitted]
    ...font.ttf    166 kB          [emitted]
  ...font.woff2   77.2 kB          [emitted]
   ...font.woff     98 kB          [emitted]
    ...font.svg    444 kB          [emitted]  [big]
       logo.png     77 kB          [emitted]
         app.js   4.22 kB       0  [emitted]             app
        app.css   7.72 kB       0  [emitted]             app
     index.html  227 bytes          [emitted]
   [0] ./app/component.js 185 bytes {0} [built]
   [1] ./~/font-awesome/css/font-awesome.css 41 bytes {0} [built]
   [2] ./app/main.css 41 bytes {0} [built]
   ...
```

The SVG file included in Font Awesome has been marked as [`big`]. It's beyond the performance budget defaults set by webpack and the topic is discussed in detail in the *Minifying* chapter.

 font-awesome-loader[6] allows more customization. Font Awesome 5 improves the situation further and make it easier to decide what fonts to consume. Font Awesome wiki[7] points to available online services that allow you to select specific fonts from Font Awesome collection.

---

[6]https://www.npmjs.com/package/font-awesome-loader
[7]https://github.com/FortAwesome/Font-Awesome/wiki/Customize-Font-Awesome

12.6 Conclusion

Loading fonts is similar to loading other assets. You have to consider the browsers you want to support and choose the loading strategy based on that.

To recap:

- When loading fonts, the same techniques as for images apply. You can choose to inline small fonts while bigger ones are served as separate assets.
- If you decide to provide first class support to only modern browsers, you can select only a font format or two and let the older browsers to use system level fonts.
- Using larger font collections, such as Font Awesome, can be problematic especially if you want to avoid loading additional rules. The problem is dependent on the packages in question and can be solved with webpack to an extent.

In the next chapter, you'll learn to load JavaScript using Babel and webpack. Webpack loads JavaScript by default but there's more to the topic as you have to consider what browsers you want to support.

13. Loading JavaScript

Webpack processes ES6 module definitions by default and transforms them into code. It does **not** transform ES6 specific syntax apart, such as const. The resulting code can be problematic especially in the older browsers.

To get a better idea of the default transform, consider the example output below:

build/app.js

```
webpackJsonp([1],{

/* 0 */
/***/ (function(module, __webpack_exports__, __webpack_require__) {

"use strict";
/* harmony default export */ __webpack_exports__["a"] = function (te\
xt = 'Hello world') {
  const element = document.createElement('div');

  element.className = 'fa fa-hand-spock-o fa-1g';
  element.innerHTML = text;

  return element;
};


...
```

The problem can be worked around by processing the code through Babel[1], a popular JavaScript compiler that supports ES6 features and more. It resembles ESLint in that it's built on top of presets and plugins. Presets are collections of plugins, and you can define your own as well.

---

[1]https://babeljs.io/

Given sometimes extending existing presets is not be enough, modify-babel-preset[2] allows you to go a step further and configure the base preset in a more flexible way.

13.1 Using Babel with Webpack Configuration

Even though Babel can be used standalone, as you can see in the *Package Authoring Techniques* chapter, you can hook it up with webpack as well. During development, it can make sense to skip processing if you are using language features supported by your browser.

Skipping processing is a good option especially if you don't rely on any custom language features and work using a modern browser. Processing through Babel becomes almost a necessity when you compile your code for production, though.

You can use Babel with webpack through babel-loader[3]. It can pick up project level Babel configuration or you can configure it at the webpack loader itself. babel-webpack-plugin[4] is another lesser known option.

Connecting Babel with a project allows you to process webpack configuration through it. To achieve this, name your webpack configuration using the *web-pack.config.babel.js* convention. interpret[5] package enables this and it supports other compilers as well.

 Given that Node supports the ES6 specification well[6] these days, you can use a lot of ES6 features without having to process configuration through Babel.

---

[2]https://www.npmjs.com/package/modify-babel-preset

[3]https://www.npmjs.com/package/babel-loader

[4]https://www.npmjs.com/package/babel-webpack-plugin

[5]https://www.npmjs.com/package/interpret

[6]http://node.green/

Babel isn't the only option although it's the most popular one. Buble[7] by Rich Harris is another compiler worth checking out. There's experimental buble-loader[8] that allows you to use it with webpack. Buble doesn't support ES6 modules, but that's not a problem as webpack provides that functionality.

 If you use *webpack.config.babel.js*, take care with the `"modules": false,` setting. If you want to use ES6 modules, you could skip the setting in your global Babel configuration and then configure it per environment as discussed below.

Setting Up *babel-loader*

The first step towards configuring Babel to work with webpack is to set up babel-loader[9]. It takes the code and turns it into a format older browsers can understand. Install *babel-loader* and include its peer dependency *babel-core*:

```
npm install babel-loader babel-core --save-dev
```

[7] https://buble.surge.sh
[8] https://www.npmjs.com/package/buble-loader
[9] https://www.npmjs.com/package/babel-loader

As usual, let's define a part for Babel:

webpack.parts.js

```
exports.loadJavaScript = ({ include, exclude }) => ({
  module: {
    rules: [
      {
        test: /\.js$/,
        include,
        exclude,

        loader: 'babel-loader',
        options: {
          // Enable caching for improved performance during
          // development.
          // It uses default OS directory by default. If you need
          // something more custom, pass a path to it.
          // I.e., { cacheDirectory: '<path>' }
          cacheDirectory: true,
        },
      },
    ],
  },
});
```

Next, you need to connect this with the main configuration. If you are using a modern browser for development, you can consider processing only the production code through Babel. To play it safe, it's used for both production and development environments in this case. In addition, only application code is processed through Babel.

Adjust as below:

webpack.config.js

```
const commonConfig = merge([
  ...
  parts.loadJavaScript({ include: PATHS.app }),
]);
```

Even though you have Babel installed and set up, you are still missing one bit: Babel configuration. This can be achieved using a *.babelrc* dotfile as other tooling can pick it up as well.

 There are times when caching Babel compilation can surprise you if your dependencies change in a way that *babel-loader* default caching mechanism doesn't notice. Override `cacheIdentifier` with a string that has been derived based on data that should invalidate the cache for better control. Node crypto API[10] and especially its MD5 related functions can come in handy.

 If you try to import files **outside** of your configuration root directory and then process them through *babel-loader*, this fails. It's a known issue[11], and there are workarounds including maintaining *.babelrc* at a higher level in the project and resolving against Babel presets through `require.resolve` at webpack configuration.

Setting Up *.babelrc*

At a minimum, you need babel-preset-env[12]. It's a Babel preset that enables the needed plugins based on the environment definition you pass to it. It follows the **browserslist** definition discussed in the *Autoprefixing* chapter.

---

[10]https://nodejs.org/api/crypto.html

[11]https://github.com/babel/babel-loader/issues/313

[12]https://www.npmjs.com/package/babel-preset-env

Install the preset first:

```
npm install babel-preset-env --save-dev
```

To make Babel aware of the preset, you need to write a *.babelrc*. Given webpack supports ES6 modules out of the box, you can tell Babel to skip processing them. Skipping this step would break webpack's HMR mechanism although the production build would still work. You can also constrain the build output to work only in recent versions of Chrome.

Adjust the target definition as you like. As long as you follow browserslist[13], it should work. Here's a sample configuration:

.babelrc

```
{
  "presets": [
    [
      "env",
      {
        "modules": false,
        "targets": {
          "browsers": ["last 2 Chrome versions"]
        }
      }
    ]
  ]
}
```

 If you omit the `targets` definition, *babel-preset-env* compiles to ES5 compatible code. If you are using UglifyJS, see the *Minifying* chapter for more information on why this is required. You can also target Node through the `node` field. Example: `"node": "current"`.

---

[13] https://www.npmjs.com/package/browserslist

babel-preset-env does **not** support *.browserslistrc* file yet. See issue #26[14] for more information.

If you execute `npm run build` now and examine *build/app.js*, the result should be similar to the earlier since it supports the features you are using in the code.

To see that the target definition works, change it to work such as `"browsers": ["IE 8"]`. Since IE 8 doesn't support `const`s, the code should change. If you build (`npm run build`), now, you should see something different:

build/app.js

```
webpackJsonp([1],{

/* 0 */
/***/ (function(module, __webpack_exports__, __webpack_require__) {

"use strict";
/* harmony default export */ __webpack_exports__["a"] = function () {
  var text = arguments.length > 0 && arguments[0] !== undefined ? ar\
guments[0] : 'Hello world';

  var element = document.createElement('div');

  element.className = 'fa fa-hand-spock-o fa-1g';
  element.innerHTML = text;

  return element;
};


...
```

Note especially how the function was transformed. You can try out different browser definitions and language features to see how the output changes based on the selection.

---

[14]https://github.com/babel/babel-preset-env/issues/26

13.2 Polyfilling Features

babel-preset-env allows you to polyfill certain language features for older browsers. For this to work, you should enable its `useBuiltIns` option (`"useBuiltIns": true`) and install babel-polyfill[15]. You have include it to your project either through an import or an entry (`app: ['babel-polyfill', PATHS.app]`). *babel-preset-env* rewrites the import based on your browser definition and loads only the polyfills that are needed.

babel-polyfill pollutes the global scope with objects like `Promise`. Given this can be problematic for library authors, there's transform-runtime[16] option. It can be enabled as a Babel plugin, and it avoids the problem of globals by rewriting the code in such way that they aren't be needed.

 Certain webpack features, such as *Code Splitting*, write `Promise` based code to webpack's bootstrap after webpack has processed loaders. The problem can be solved by applying a shim before your application code is executed. Example: `entry: { app: ['core-js/es6/promise', PATHS.app] }`.

13.3 Babel Tips

There are other possible *.babelrc* options[17] beyond the ones covered here. Like ESLint, *.babelrc* supports JSON5[18] as its configuration format meaning you can include comments in your source, use single quoted strings, and so on.

Sometimes you want to use experimental features that fit your project. Although you can find a lot of them within so-called stage presets, it's a good idea to enable them one by one and even organize them to a preset of their own unless you are working on a throwaway project. If you expect your project to live a long time, it's better to document the features you are using well.

---

[15] https://babeljs.io/docs/usage/polyfill/

[16] https://babeljs.io/docs/plugins/transform-runtime/

[17] https://babeljs.io/docs/usage/options/

[18] https://www.npmjs.com/package/json5

13.4 Babel Presets and Plugins

Perhaps the greatest thing about Babel is that it's possible to extend with presets and plugins:

- babel-preset-es2015[19] includes ES2015 features.
- babel-preset-es2016[20] includes **only** ES2016 features. Remember to include the previous preset as well if you want both!
- babel-plugin-import[21] rewrites module imports so that you can use a form such as `import { Button } from 'antd';` instead of pointing to the module through an exact path.
- babel-plugin-import-asserts[22] asserts that your imports have been defined.
- babel-plugin-log-deprecated[23] adds `console.warn` to functions that have `@deprecate` annotation in their comment.
- babel-plugin-annotate-console-log[24] annotates `console.log` calls with information about invocation context so it's easier to see where they logged.
- babel-plugin-webpack-loaders[25] allows you to use certain webpack loaders through Babel.
- babel-plugin-syntax-trailing-function-commas[26] adds trailing comma support for functions.
- babel-react-optimize[27] implements a variety of React specific optimizations you can experiment with.
- babel-plugin-transform-react-remove-prop-types[28] allows you to remove `propType` related code from your production build. It also allows component authors to generate code that's wrapped so that setting environment at `DefinePlugin` can kick in as discussed in the book.

---

[19] https://www.npmjs.org/package/babel-preset-es2015

[20] https://www.npmjs.org/package/babel-preset-es2016

[21] https://www.npmjs.com/package/babel-plugin-import

[22] https://www.npmjs.com/package/babel-plugin-import-asserts

[23] https://www.npmjs.com/package/babel-plugin-log-deprecated

[24] https://www.npmjs.com/package/babel-plugin-annotate-console-log

[25] https://www.npmjs.com/package/babel-plugin-webpack-loaders

[26] https://www.npmjs.com/package/babel-plugin-syntax-trailing-function-commas

[27] https://github.com/thejameskyle/babel-react-optimize

[28] https://www.npmjs.com/package/babel-plugin-transform-react-remove-prop-types

It's possible to connect Babel with Node through babel-register[29] or babel-cli[30]. These packages can be handy if you want to execute your code through Babel without using webpack.

13.5 Enabling Presets and Plugins per Environment

Babel allows you to control which presets and plugins are used per environment through its env option[31]. You can manage Babel's behavior per build target this way.

env checks both NODE_ENV and BABEL_ENV and functionality to your build based on that. If BABEL_ENV is set, it overrides any possible NODE_ENV. Consider the example below:

.babelrc

```
{
  ...
  "env": {
    "development": {
      "plugins": [
        "react-hot-loader/babel"
      ]
    }
  }
}
```

Any shared presets and plugins are available to all targets still. env allows you to specialize your Babel configuration further.

---

[29] https://www.npmjs.com/package/babel-register

[30] https://www.npmjs.com/package/babel-cli

[31] https://babeljs.io/docs/usage/babelrc/#env-option

It's possible to pass the webpack environment to Babel with a tweak:

webpack.config.js

```
module.exports = (env) => {
  process.env.BABEL_ENV = env;


  ...

};
```

 The way env works is subtle. Consider logging env and make sure it matches your Babel configuration or otherwise the functionality you expect is not applied to your build.

 The technique is used in the *Server Side Rendering* chapter to enable the Babel portion of *react-hot-loader* for development target only.

13.6 Setting Up TypeScript

Microsoft's TypeScript[32] is a compiled language that follows a similar setup as Babel. The neat thing is that in addition to JavaScript, it can emit type definitions. A good editor can pick those up and provide enhanced editing experience. Stronger typing is valuable for development as it becomes easier to state your type contracts.

Compared to Facebook's type checker Flow, TypeScript is a more established option. As a result, you find more premade type definitions for it, and overall, the quality of support should be better.

---

[32]http://www.typescriptlang.org/

You can use TypeScript with webpack using the following loaders:

- ts-loader[33]
- awesome-typescript-loader[34]
- light-ts-loader[35]

 There's a TypeScript parser for ESLint[36]. It's also possible to lint it through tslint[37].

13.7 Setting Up Flow

Flow[38] performs static analysis based on your code and its type annotations. You have to install it as a separate tool and then run it against your code. There's flow-status-webpack-plugin[39] that allows you to run it through webpack during development.

If you use React, the React specific Babel preset does most of the work through babel-plugin-syntax-flow[40]. It can strip Flow annotations and convert your code into a format that is possible to transpile further.

There's also babel-plugin-typecheck[41] that allows you to perform runtime checks based on your Flow annotations. flow-runtime[42] goes a notch further and provides more functionality. These approaches complement Flow static checker and allow you to catch even more issues.

---

[33] https://www.npmjs.com/package/ts-loader

[34] https://www.npmjs.com/package/awesome-typescript-loader

[35] https://www.npmjs.com/package/light-ts-loader

[36] https://www.npmjs.com/package/typescript-eslint-parser

[37] https://www.npmjs.com/package/tslint

[38] https://flow.org/

[39] https://www.npmjs.com/package/flow-status-webpack-plugin

[40] https://www.npmjs.com/package/babel-plugin-syntax-flow

[41] https://www.npmjs.com/package/babel-plugin-typecheck

[42] https://codemix.github.io/flow-runtime/

flow-coverage-report[43] shows how much of your code is covered by Flow type annotations.

13.8 Conclusion

Babel has become an indispensable tool for developers given it bridges the standard with older browsers. Even if you targeted modern browsers, transforming through Babel is an option.

To recap:

- Babel gives you control over what browsers to support. It can compile ES6 features to a form the older browser understand. *babel-preset-env* is valuable as it can choose which features to compile and which polyfills to enable based on your browser definition.
- Babel allows you to use experimental language features. You can find numerous plugins that improve development experience and the production build through optimizations.
- Babel functionality can be enabled per development target. This way you can be sure you are using the correct plugins at the right place.
- Besides Babel, webpack supports other solutions like TypeScript of Flow. Flow can complement Babel while TypeScript represents an entire language compiling to JavaScript.

---

[43]https://www.npmjs.com/package/flow-coverage-report

IV Building

In this part, you enable source maps on the build, discuss how to split it into separate bundles in various ways, and learn to tidy up the result.

14. Source Maps

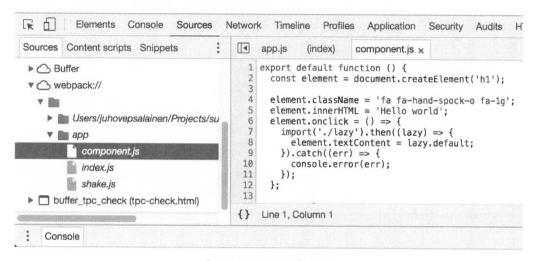

Source maps in Chrome

When your source code has gone through any transformations, debugging becomes a problem. When debugging in a browser, how to tell where the original code is? **Source maps** solve this problem by providing a mapping between the original and the transformed source code. In addition to source compiling to JavaScript, this works for styling as well.

One approach is to simply skip source maps during development and rely on browser support of language features. If you use ES6 without any extensions and develop using a modern browser, this can work. The advantage of doing this is that you avoid all the problems related to source maps while gaining better performance.

 If you want to understand the ideas behind source maps in greater detail, read Ryan Seddon's introduction to the topic[1].

---

[1]https://www.html5rocks.com/en/tutorials/developertools/sourcemaps/

14.1 Inline Source Maps and Separate Source Maps

Webpack can generate both inline source maps included within bundles or separate source map files. The former are valuable during development due to better performance while the latter are handy for production usage as it keeps the bundle size small. In this case, loading source maps is optional.

It's possible you **don't** want to generate a source map for your production bundle as this makes it effortless to inspect your application. By disabling them you are performing a sort of obfuscation. Whether or not you want to enable source maps for production, they are handy for staging. Skipping source maps entirely speeds up your build as generating source maps at the best quality can be a complex operation.

Hidden source maps give stack trace information only. You can connect them with a monitoring service to get traces as the application crashes allowing you to fix the problematic situations. While this isn't ideal, it's better to know about possible problems than not.

 It's a good idea to study the documentation of the loaders you are using to see loader specific tips. For example, with TypeScript, you have to set a particular flag to make it work as you expect.

14.2 Enabling Source Maps

Webpack provides two ways to enable source maps. There's a `devtool` shortcut field. You can also find two plugins that give more options to tweak. The plugins are be discussed briefly at the end of this chapter. Beyond webpack, you also have to enable support for source maps at the browsers you are using for development.

Enabling Source Maps in Webpack

To get started, you can wrap the core idea within a configuration part. You can convert this to use the plugins later if you want:

webpack.parts.js

```
exports.generateSourceMaps = ({ type }) => ({
  devtool: type,
});
```

Webpack supports a wide variety of source map types. These vary based on quality and build speed. For now, you can enable eval-source-map for development and source-map for production. This way you get good quality while trading off performance, especially during development.

Set these up as follows:

webpack.config.js

```
const productionConfig = merge([
  parts.generateSourceMaps({ type: 'source-map' }),
  ...
]);

const developmentConfig = merge([
  {
    output: {
      devtoolModuleFilenameTemplate: 'webpack:///[absolute-resource-\
path]',
    },
  },
  parts.generateSourceMaps({ type: 'cheap-module-eval-source-map' }),
  ...
]);
```

`eval-source-map` builds slowly initially, but it provides fast rebuild speed. More rapid development specific options, such as `cheap-module-eval-source-map` and `eval`, produce lower quality source maps. All `eval` options emit source maps as a part of your JavaScript code.

`source-map` is the slowest and highest quality option of them all, but that's fine for a production build.

If you build the project now (`npm run build`), you should see source maps in the output:

```
Hash: 79905cd66e14d3455b7d
Version: webpack 2.2.1
Time: 2817ms
             Asset       Size  Chunks                     Chunk Names
          logo.png      77 kB          [emitted]
       ...font.eot     166 kB          [emitted]
     ...font.woff2    77.2 kB          [emitted]
      ...font.woff      98 kB          [emitted]
       ...font.svg     444 kB          [emitted]  [big]
       ...font.ttf     166 kB          [emitted]
            app.js    4.46 kB       0  [emitted]             app
           app.css    3.89 kB       0  [emitted]             app
        app.js.map    4.15 kB       0  [emitted]             app
       app.css.map    84 bytes       0  [emitted]             app
        index.html   218 bytes          [emitted]
   [0] ./app/component.js 272 bytes {0} [built]
   [1] ./~/font-awesome/css/font-awesome.css 41 bytes {0} [built]
   [2] ./app/main.css 41 bytes {0} [built]
...
```

Take a good look at those *.map* files. That's where the mapping between the generated and the original source happens. During development, it writes the mapping information in the bundle itself.

Enabling Source Maps in Browsers

To use source maps within a browser, you have to enable source maps explicitly as per browser-specific instructions:

- Chrome[2]. Sometimes source maps will not update in Chrome inspector[3]. For now, the temporary fix is to force the inspector to reload itself by using *alt-r*.
- Firefox[4]
- IE Edge[5]
- Safari[6]

 If you want to use breakpoints (i.e., a `debugger;` statement or ones set through the browser), the `eval`-based options won't work in Chrome!

14.3 Source Map Types Supported by Webpack

Source map types supported by webpack can be split into two categories:

- **Inline** source maps add the mapping data directly to the generated files.
- **Separate** source maps emit the mapping data to separate source map files and link the original source to them using a comment. Hidden source maps omit the comment on purpose.

Thanks to their speed, inline source maps are ideal for development. Given they make the bundles big, separate source maps are the preferable solution for production. Separate source maps work during development as well if the performance overhead is acceptable.

---

[2]https://developer.chrome.com/devtools/docs/javascript-debugging

[3]https://github.com/webpack/webpack/issues/2478

[4]https://developer.mozilla.org/en-US/docs/Tools/Debugger/How_to/Use_a_source_map

[5]https://developer.microsoft.com/en-us/microsoft-edge/platform/documentation/f12-devtools-guide/debugger/#source-maps

[6]https://developer.apple.com/library/safari/documentation/AppleApplications/Conceptual/Safari_Developer_Guide/ResourcesandtheDOM/ResourcesandtheDOM.html#//apple_ref/doc/uid/TP40007874-CH3-SW2

14.4 Inline Source Map Types

Webpack provides multiple inline source map variants. Often eval is the starting point and webpack issue #2145[7] recommends cheap-module-eval-source-map as it's a good compromise between speed and quality while working reliably in Chrome and Firefox browsers.

To get a better idea of the available options, they are listed below while providing a small example for each. The source code contains only a single console.log('Hello world') and webpack.NamedModulesPlugin is used to keep the output easier to understand. In practice, you would see a lot more code to handle the mapping.

 webpack.NamedModulesPlugin replaces number based module IDs with paths. It's discussed in the *Hot Module Replacement* appendix.

devtool: 'eval'

eval generates code in which each module is wrapped within an eval function:

```
webpackJsonp([1, 2], {
  "./app/index.js": function(module, exports) {
    eval("console.log('Hello world');\n\n//////////////////\n// WEBP\
ACK FOOTER\n// ./app/index.js\n// module id = ./app/index.js\n// mod\
ule chunks = 1\n\n//# sourceURL=webpack:///./app/index.js?")
  }
}, ["./app/index.js"]);
```

---

[7]https://github.com/webpack/webpack/issues/2145#issuecomment-294361203

devtool: 'cheap-eval-source-map'

cheap-eval-source-map goes a step further and it includes base64 encoded version of the code as a data url. The result includes only line data while losing column mappings.

```
webpackJsonp([1, 2], {
  "./app/index.js": function(module, exports) {
    eval("console.log('Hello world');//# sourceMappingURL=data:appli\
cation/json;charset=utf-8;base64,eyJ2ZXJzaW9uIjozLCJmaWxlIjoiLi9hcHA\
vaW5kZXguanMuanMiLCJzb3VyY2VzIjpbIndlYnBhY2s6Ly8vLi9hcHAvaW5kZXguanM\
/MGUwNCJdLCJzb3VyY2VzQ29udGVudCI6WyJjb25zb2xlLmxvZygnSGVsbG8gd29ybGQ\
nKTtcblxuXG4vLy8vLy8vLy8vLy8vLy8vLy9cbi8vIFdFQlBBQ0sgRk9PVEVSXG4vLyA\
uL2FwcC9pbmRleC5qc1xuLy8gbW9kdWxlIGlkID0gLi9hcHAvaW5kZXguanNcbi8vIG1\
vZHVsZSBjaHVua3MgPSAxIl0sIm1hcHBpbmdzIjoiQUFBQSIsInNvdXJjZVJvb3QiOiI\
ifQ==")
  }
}, ["./app/index.js"]);
```

If you decode that base64 string, you get output containing the mapping:

```
{
  "file": "./app/index.js.js",
  "mappings": "AAAA",
  "sourceRoot": "",
  "sources": [
    "webpack:///./app/index.js?0e04"
  ],
  "sourcesContent": [
    "console.log('Hello world');\n\n\n//////////////////////\n// WEBPACK\
FOOTER\n// ./app/index.js\n// module id = ./app/index.js\n// module\
chunks = 1"
  ],
  "version": 3
}
```

devtool: 'cheap-module-eval-source-map'

`cheap-module-eval-source-map` is the same idea, except with higher quality and lower performance:

```
webpackJsonp([1, 2], {
  "./app/index.js": function(module, exports) {
    eval("console.log('Hello world');//# sourceMappingURL=data:appli\
cation/json;charset=utf-8;base64,eyJ2ZXJzaW9uIjozLCJmaWxlIjoiLi9hcHA\
vaW5kZXguananMuanMiLCJzb3VyY2VzIjpbIndlYnBhY2s6Ly8vYXBwL2luZGV4LmpzPzI\
wMTgiXSwic291cmNlc0NvbnRlbnQiOlsiY29uc29sZS5sb2coJ0hlbGxvIHdvcmxkJyk\
7XG5cblxuLy8gV0VCUEFDSyBGT09URVIgLy9cbi8vIGFwcC9pbmRleC5qcyJdLCJtYXB\
waW5ncyI6IkFBQUEiLCJzb3VyY2VSb290IjoiIn0=")
  }
}, ["./app/index.js"]);
```

Again, decoding the data reveals more:

```
{
  "file": "./app/index.js.js",
  "mappings": "AAAA",
  "sourceRoot": "",
  "sources": [
    "webpack:///app/index.js?2018"
  ],
  "sourcesContent": [
    "console.log('Hello world');\n\n\n// WEBPACK FOOTER //\n// app/i\
ndex.js"
  ],
  "version": 3
}
```

In this particular case, the difference between the options is minimal.

devtool: 'eval-source-map'

eval-source-map is the highest quality option of the inline options. It's also the slowest one as it emits the most data:

```
webpackJsonp([1, 2], {
  "./app/index.js": function(module, exports) {
    eval("console.log('Hello world');//# sourceMappingURL=data:appli\
cation/json;charset=utf-8;base64,eyJ2ZXJzaW9uIjozLCJzb3VyY2VzIjpbInd\
lYnBhY2s6Ly8vLi9hcHAvaW5kZXguanM/ZGFkYyJdLCJuYW1lcyI6WyJjb25zb2xlIiw\
ibG9nIl0sIm1hcHBpbmdzIjoiQUFBQUEsUUFBUUMsR0FBUixDQUFZLGFBQVoiLCJmaWx\
lIjoiLi9hcHAvaW5kZXguanMuanMiLCJzb3VyY2VzQ29udGVudCI6WyJjb25zb2xlLmx\
vZygnSGVsbG8gd29ybGQnKTtcbiXuXG4vLyBXRUJQQUNLIEZPT1RFUiAvLlxuLy8gLi9\
hcHAvaW5kZXguanMiXSwic291cmNlUm9vdCI6IiJ9")
  }
}, ["./app/index.js"]);
```

This time around there's more mapping data available for the browser:

```
{
  "file": "./app/index.js.js",
  "mappings": "AAAAA,QAAQC,GAAR,CAAY,aAAZ",
  "names": [
    "console",
    "log"
  ],
  "sourceRoot": "",
  "sources": [
    "webpack:///./app/index.js?dadc"
  ],
  "sourcesContent": [
    "console.log('Hello world');\n\n\n// WEBPACK FOOTER //\n// ./app\
/index.js"
  ],
  "version": 3
}
```

14.5 Separate Source Map Types

Webpack can also generate production usage friendly source maps. These end up in separate files ending with .map extension and are loaded by the browser only when required. This way your users get good performance while it's easier for you to debug the application.

source-map is a good default here. Even though it takes longer to generate the source maps this way, you get the best quality. If you don't care about production source maps, you can simply skip the setting there and get better performance in return.

devtool: 'cheap-source-map'

cheap-source-map is similar to the cheap options above. The result is going to miss column mappings. Also, source maps from loaders, such as *css-loader*, are not going to be used.

Examining the .map file reveals the following output in this case:

```
{
  "file": "app.9aff3b1eced1f089ef18.js",
  "mappings": "AAAA",
  "sourceRoot": "",
  "sources": [
    "webpack:///app.9aff3b1eced1f089ef18.js"
  ],
  "sourcesContent": [
    "webpackJsonp([1,2],{\"./app/index.js\":function(o,n){console.lo\
g(\"Hello world\")}},[\"./app/index.js\"]);\n\n\n// WEBPACK FOOTER /\
/\n// app.9aff3b1eced1f089ef18.js"
  ],
  "version": 3
}
```

The original source contains //# sourceMappingURL=app.9a...18.js.map kind of comment at its end to map to this file.

devtool: 'cheap-module-source-map'

cheap-module-source-map is the same as previous except source maps from loaders
are simplified to a single mapping per line. It yields the following output in this case:

```
{
  "file": "app.9aff3b1eced1f089ef18.js",
  "mappings": "AAAA",
  "sourceRoot": "",
  "sources": [
    "webpack:///app.9aff3b1eced1f089ef18.js"
  ],
  "version": 3
}
```

 cheap-module-source-map is currently broken if minification is used[8] and
this is a good reason to avoid the option for now.

---

[8]https://github.com/webpack/webpack/issues/4176

devtool: 'source-map'

source-map provides the best quality with the complete result, but it's also the slowest option. The output reflects this:

```json
{
  "file": "app.9aff3b1eced1f089ef18.js",
  "mappings": "AAAAA,cAAc,EAAE,IAEVC,iBACA,SAAUC,EAAQC,GCHxBC,QAAQC,\
IAAI,kBDST",
  "names": [
    "webpackJsonp",
    "./app/index.js",
    "module",
    "exports",
    "console",
    "log"
  ],
  "sourceRoot": "",
  "sources": [
    "webpack:///app.9aff3b1eced1f089ef18.js",
    "webpack:///./app/index.js"
  ],
  "sourcesContent": [
    "webpackJsonp([1,2],{\n\n/***/ \"./app/index.js\":\n/***/ (funct\
ion(module, exports) {\n\nconsole.log('Hello world');\n\n/***/ })\n\\
n},[\"./app/index.js\"]);\n\n\n// WEBPACK FOOTER //\n// app.9aff3b1e\
ced1f089ef18.js",
    "console.log('Hello world');\n\n\n// WEBPACK FOOTER //\n// ./app\
/index.js"
  ],
  "version": 3
}
```

devtool: 'hidden-source-map'

hidden-source-map is the same as source-map except it doesn't write references to the source maps to the source files. If you don't want to expose source maps to development tools directly while you want proper stack traces, this is handy.

 The official documentation[9] contains more information about devtool options.

14.6 Other Source Map Options

There are a couple of other options that affect source map generation:

```
{
  output: {
    // Modify the name of the generated source map file.
    // You can use [file], [id], and [hash] replacements here.
    // The default option is enough for most use cases.
    sourceMapFilename: '[file].map', // Default

    // This is the source map filename template. It's default
    // format depends on the devtool option used. You don't
    // need to modify this often.
    devtoolModuleFilenameTemplate: 'webpack:///[resource-path]?[load\
ers]'
  },
}
```

 The official documentation[10] digs into output specifics.

[9] https://webpack.js.org/configuration/devtool/#devtool
[10] https://webpack.js.org/configuration/output/#output-sourcemapfilename

If you are using any UglifyJsPlugin and still want source maps, you need to enable sourceMap: true for the plugin. Otherwise, the result isn't be what you expect because UglifyJS will perform a further transformation on the code, breaking the mapping. The same has to be done with other plugins and loaders performing transformations. *css-loader* and related loaders are a good example.

14.7 SourceMapDevToolPlugin **and** EvalSourceMapDevToolPlugin

If you want more control over source map generation, it's possible to use the SourceMapDevToolPlugin or EvalSourceMapDevToolPlugin instead. The latter is a more limited alternative, and as stated by its name, it's handy for generating eval based source maps.

Both plugins can allow more granular control over which portions of the code you want to generate source maps for, while also having strict control over the result with SourceMapDevToolPlugin. Using either plugin allows you to skip the devtool option altogether.

You could model a configuration part using SourceMapDevToolPlugin (adapted from the official documentation[11]):

```
exports.generateSourceMaps = ({
  test, include, separateSourceMaps, columnMappings
}) => ({
  // Enable functionality as you want to expose it
  plugins: [
    new webpack.SourceMapDevToolPlugin({
      // Match assets like for loaders. This is
      // convenient if you want to match against multiple
      // file types.
      test: test, // string | RegExp | Array,
```

---

[11] https://webpack.js.org/plugins/source-map-dev-tool-plugin/

```
      include: include, // string | RegExp | Array,

      // `exclude` matches file names, not package names!
      // exclude: string | RegExp | Array,

      // If filename is set, output to this file.
      // See `sourceMapFileName`.
      // filename: string,

      // This line is appended to the original asset processed.
      // For instance '[url]' would get replaced with an url
      // to the source map.
      // append: false | string,

      // See `devtoolModuleFilenameTemplate` for specifics.
      // moduleFilenameTemplate: string,
      // fallbackModuleFilenameTemplate: string,

      // If false, separate source maps aren't generated.
      module: separateSourceMaps,

      // If false, column mappings are ignored.
      columns: columnMappings,

      // Use plain line to line mappings for the matched modules.
      // lineToLine: bool | {test, include, exclude},

      // Remove source content from source maps. This is handy
      // especially if your source maps are big (over 10 MB)
      // as browsers can struggle with those.
      // See https://github.com/webpack/webpack/issues/2669.
      // noSources: bool,
    }),
  ],
});
```

Given webpack matches only `.js` and `.css` files by default for source maps, you can use `SourceMapDevToolPlugin` to overcome this issue. This can be achieved by passing a `test` pattern like `/\.(js|jsx|css)($|\?)/i`.

`EvalSourceMapDevToolPlugin` accepts only `module` and `lineToLine` options as described above. Therefore it can be considered as an alias to `devtool: 'eval'` while allowing a notch more flexibility.

14.8 Changing Source Map Prefix

You can prefix a source map option with a **pragma** character that gets injected to the source map reference. Webpack uses `#` by default that is supported by modern browsers so you don't have to set it.

To override this, you have to prefix your source map option with it (e.g., `@source-map`). After the change, you should see `//@` kind of reference to the source map over `//#` in your JavaScript files assuming a separate source map type was used.

14.9 Using Dependency Source Maps

Assuming you are using a package that uses inline source maps in its distribution, you can use source-map-loader[12] to make webpack aware of them. Without setting it up against the package, you get minified debug output. Often you can skip this step as it's a special case.

14.10 Source Maps for Styling

If you want to enable source maps for styling files, you can achieve this by enabling the `sourceMap` option. The same idea works with style loaders such as *css-loader*, *sass-loader*, and *less-loader*.

The *css-loader* is known to have issues[13] when you are using relative paths in imports. To overcome this problem, you should set `output.publicPath` to resolve against the server url.

---

[12]https://www.npmjs.com/package/source-map-loader
[13]https://github.com/webpack-contrib/css-loader/issues/232

14.11 Conclusion

Source maps can be convenient during development. They provide better means to debug applications as you can still examine the original code over a generated one. They can be valuable even for production usage and allow you to debug issues while serving a client-friendly version of your application.

To recap:

- **Source maps** can be helpful both during development and production. They provide more accurate information about what's going on and make it faster to debug possible problems.
- Webpack supports a large variety of source map variants. They can be split into inline and separate source maps based on where they are generated. Inline source maps are handy during development due to their speed. Separate source maps work for production as then loading them becomes optional.
- `devtool: 'source-map'` is the highest quality option making it valuable for production.
- `cheap-module-eval-source-map` is a good starting point for development.
- If you want to get only stack traces during production, use `devtool: 'hidden-source-map'`. You can capture the output and send it to a third party service for you to examine. This way you can capture errors and fix them.
- `SourceMapDevToolPlugin` and `EvalSourceMapDevToolPlugin` provide more control over the result than the `devtool` shortcut.
- *source-map-loader* can come in handy if your dependencies provide source maps.
- Enabling source maps for styling requires additional effort. You have to enable `sourceMap` option per styling related loader you are using.

In the next chapter, you'll learn to split bundles and separate the current bundle into application and vendor bundles.

15. Bundle Splitting

Currently, the production version of the application is a single JavaScript file. If the application is changed, the client must download vendor dependencies as well.

It would be better to download only the changed portion. If the vendor dependencies change, then the client should fetch only the vendor dependencies. The same goes for actual application code. **Bundle splitting** can be achieved using `CommonsChunkPlugin`.

 To invalidate the bundles properly, you have to attach hashes to the generated bundles as discussed in the *Adding Hashes to Filenames* chapter.

15.1 The Idea of Bundle Splitting

With bundle splitting, you can push the vendor dependencies to a bundle of their own and benefit from client level caching. This can be done in such a way that the whole size of the application remains the same. Given there are more requests to perform, there's a slight overhead. But the benefit of caching makes up for this cost.

To give you a quick example, instead of having *app.js* (100 kB), you could end up with *app.js* (10 kB) and *vendor.js* (90 kB). Now changes made to the application are cheap for the clients that have already used the application earlier.

Caching comes with its problems. One of those is cache invalidation. A potential approach related to that is discussed in the *Adding Hashes to Filenames* chapter.

Bundle splitting isn't the only way out. The *Code Splitting* chapter discusses another, more granular way.

15.2 Adding Something to Split

Given there's not much to split into the vendor bundle yet, you should add something there. Add React to the project first:

```
npm install react --save
```

Then make the project depend on it:

app/index.js

```
import 'react';
...
```

Execute npm run build to get a baseline build. You should end up with something as below:

```
Hash: 2db5a05e02ac73897fd4
Version: webpack 2.2.1
Time: 2864ms
          Asset       Size  Chunks                    Chunk Names
       logo.png      77 kB          [emitted]
    ...font.eot     166 kB          [emitted]
  ...font.woff2    77.2 kB          [emitted]
   ...font.woff      98 kB          [emitted]
    ...font.svg     444 kB          [emitted]  [big]
    ...font.ttf     166 kB          [emitted]
         app.js     140 kB       0  [emitted]         app
        app.css    3.89 kB       0  [emitted]         app
     app.js.map     165 kB       0  [emitted]         app
    app.css.map    84 bytes       0  [emitted]         app
     index.html   218 bytes          [emitted]
   [0] ./~/process/browser.js 5.3 kB {0} [built]
   [3] ./~/react/lib/ReactElement.js 11.2 kB {0} [built]
  [18] ./app/component.js 272 bytes {0} [built]
...
```

As you can see, *app.js* is big. That is something to fix next.

15.3 Setting Up a vendor Bundle

So far, the project has only a single entry named as app. The configuration tells webpack to traverse dependencies starting from the app entry directory and then to output the resulting bundle below the build directory using the entry name and .js extension.

To improve the situation, you can define a vendor entry containing React by matching the dependency name. It's possible to generate this information automatically as discussed at the end of this chapter, but a static array is enough to illustrate the basic idea. Change the code:

webpack.config.js

```
const productionConfig = merge([
  {
    entry: {
      vendor: ['react'],
    },
  },
  ...
]);
```

You have two separate entries, or **entry chunks**, now. [name].js of the existing output.path the configuration kicks in based on the entry name. If you try to generate a build now (npm run build), you should see something along this:

```
Hash: ebf1b976090ff95e4fcd
Version: webpack 2.2.1
Time: 2814ms
           Asset       Size  Chunks                    Chunk Names
          app.js     140 kB       0  [emitted]         app
    ...font.eot      166 kB          [emitted]
    ...font.woff2   77.2 kB          [emitted]
    ...font.woff       98 kB          [emitted]
    ...font.svg      444 kB          [emitted]  [big]
        logo.png       77 kB          [emitted]
    ...font.ttf      166 kB          [emitted]
       vendor.js     138 kB       1  [emitted]         vendor
         app.css    3.89 kB       0  [emitted]         app
      app.js.map     165 kB       0  [emitted]         app
     app.css.map   84 bytes       0  [emitted]         app
   vendor.js.map     164 kB       1  [emitted]         vendor
      index.html  274 bytes          [emitted]
     [3] ./~/react/lib/ReactElement.js 11.2 kB {0} {1} [built]
    [18] ./~/react/react.js 56 bytes {0} {1} [built]
    [21] ./~/react/lib/React.js 2.69 kB {0} {1} [built]
   ...
```

app.js and *vendor.js* have separate chunk IDs right now given they are entry chunks of their own. The output size is off, though. Intuitively *app.js* should be smaller to attain the goal with this build.

If you examine the resulting bundle, you can see that it contains React given that's how the default definition works. Webpack pulls the related dependencies to a bundle by default as illustrated by the image below:

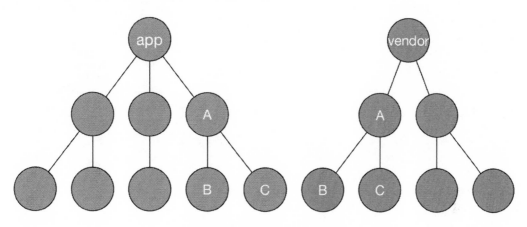

Separate app and vendor bundles

CommonsChunkPlugin is a webpack plugin that allows to alter this default behavior.

 This step can fail on Windows due to letter casing. Instead of c:\ you have to force your terminal to read C:\. There's more information in the related webpack issue[1].

 Webpack doesn't allow referring to entry files within entries. If you inadvertently do this, webpack complains loudly. Consider refactoring the module structure of your code to eliminate the situation.

---

[1]https://github.com/webpack/webpack/issues/2362

15.4 Setting Up `CommonsChunkPlugin`

CommonsChunkPlugin[2] is a powerful and complex plugin. In this case, the target is clear. You have to tell it to extract vendor related code to a bundle of its own. Before abstraction, implement it:

webpack.config.js

```
const webpack = require('webpack');

...

const productionConfig = merge([
  {
    entry: {
      vendor: ['react'],
    },
    plugins: [
      new webpack.optimize.CommonsChunkPlugin({
        name: 'vendor',
      }),
    ],
  },
  ...
]);
```

The configuration tells the plugin to extract React to a bundle named `vendor`.

---

[2]https://webpack.js.org/guides/code-splitting-libraries/#commonschunkplugin

If you execute the build now using npm run build, you should see something along this:

```
Hash: af634c8857c0ffb5c5e0
Version: webpack 2.2.1
Time: 2790ms
        Asset       Size  Chunks                    Chunk Names
       app.js    2.15 kB       0  [emitted]         app
  ...font.eot     166 kB          [emitted]
...font.woff2    77.2 kB          [emitted]
  ...font.woff      98 kB          [emitted]
   ...font.svg     444 kB          [emitted]  [big]
     logo.png      77 kB          [emitted]
   ...font.ttf     166 kB          [emitted]
    vendor.js     141 kB       1  [emitted]         vendor
      app.css    3.89 kB       0  [emitted]         app
   app.js.map    1.67 kB       0  [emitted]         app
  app.css.map    84 bytes       0  [emitted]         app
vendor.js.map     167 kB       1  [emitted]         vendor
   index.html   274 bytes          [emitted]
   [0] ./~/process/browser.js 5.3 kB {1} [built]
   [3] ./~/react/lib/ReactElement.js 11.2 kB {1} [built]
   [7] ./~/react/react.js 56 bytes {1} [built]
...
```

Now the bundles look the way they should. The image below illustrates the current situation.

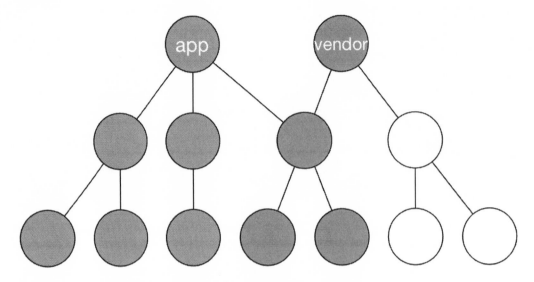

App and vendor bundles after applying `CommonsChunkPlugin`

If the vendor entry contained extra dependencies (white on the image), the setup would pull those into the project as well. Resolving this problem is possible by examining which packages are being used in the project using the `minChunks` parameter of the `CommonsChunksPlugin`. But before that, let's abstract the solution a bit.

 The technique could be implemented only for `productionConfig`. It's sensible to maintain it at `commonConfig` as it improved performance.

15.5 Abstracting Bundle Extraction

The following code combines the `entry` idea above with a basic `CommonsChunkPlugin` setup. It has been designed so that it's possible to access advanced features of `CommonsChunkPlugin` while allowing you to define multiple splits through it:

webpack.parts.js

```
...
const webpack = require('webpack');

...

exports.extractBundles = (bundles) => ({
  plugins: bundles.map((bundle) => (
    new webpack.optimize.CommonsChunkPlugin(bundle)
  )),
});
```

Given the function handles the entry, you can drop the `vendor`-related configuration and use the function instead:

webpack.config.js

```
const webpack = require('webpack');

...

const productionConfig = merge([
  {
    entry: {
      vendor: ['react'],
    },
    plugins: [
      new webpack.optimize.CommonsChunkPlugin({
        name: 'vendor',
```

```
          }),
        },
    },
    ...
    parts.extractBundles([
      {
        name: 'vendor',
      },
    ]),
]);
```

Everything should work the same way as earlier. This time around, however, it's more convenient to work with the plugin. You still have access to its functionality as before, but with a smaller amount of code.

To pick React to the vendor build automatically based on usage, you have to drop the entries option and adjust the setup so that it picks up JavaScript files from *node_-modules* to the vendor bundle.

15.6 Loading dependencies to a vendor Bundle Automatically

CommonsChunkPlugin gives control over its behavior through its minChunks options. In addition to a number and certain other values, minChunks accepts a function with a signature (module, count). The first parameter contains a lot of information about the matches module and allows to deduce which modules are used by the project. The second one tells how many times a particular module has been imported into the project.

The most important module properties have been listed below. These assume an import like import 'purecss'; and ExtractTextPlugin:

- resource represents the path of the full path of the resource being imported. Example: .../webpack-demo/node_modules/purecss/build/pure-min.css.

- context returns the path to the directory in which the resource is. Example: `.../webpack-demo/node_modules/purecss/build`.
- rawRequest contains the whole unresolved request. Example: `!!../../css-loader/index.js!.../pure-min.css`.
- userRequest is a version of the request that has been resolved to a query. Example: `.../node_modules/css-loader/index.js!.../pure-min.css`.
- chunks tells in which chunks the module is contained. Check `chunks.length` to tell how many times webpack has included it to control output on the chunk level.

Particularly resource and userRequest can return the same value if you are operating with imports that aren't being processed in any way. In the example above, ExtractTextPlugin caused a difference between the values.

To capture only JavaScript files from *node_modules*, you should perform a check against each request using the resource since it contains the needed information:

webpack.config.js

```
const productionConfig = merge([
  {
    entry: {
      vendor: ['react'],
    },
  },
  ...
  parts.extractBundles([
    {
      name: 'vendor',
      minChunks: ({ resource }) => (
        resource &&
        resource.indexOf('node_modules') >= 0 &&
        resource.match(/\.js$/)
      ),
    },
  ]),
]);
```

The build result should remain the same. This time, however, webpack pulls only dependencies that are used in the project, and you don't have to maintain the list anymore.

15.7 Performing a More Granular Split

Sometimes having only an app and a vendor bundle isn't enough. Especially when your application grows and gains more entry points, you could split the vendor bundle into multiples ones per each entry. CommonsChunkPlugin operates against all entry chunks by default. This behavior can be constrained through the chunks option for more granular control.

Consider the example adapted from a GitHub comment[3] below where chunks are extracted from login and app entries:

```
const config = {
  ...
  plugins: [
    new webpack.optimize.CommonsChunkPlugin({
      name: 'login',
      chunks: ['login'],
      minChunks: isVendor,
    }),
    new webpack.optimize.CommonsChunkPlugin({
      name: 'vendor',
      chunks: ['app'],
      minChunks: isVendor,
    }),
    // Extract chunks common to both app and login
    new webpack.optimize.CommonsChunkPlugin({
      name: 'common',
      chunks: ['login', 'app'],
      minChunks: (module, count) => count >= 2 && isVendor(module),
```

---

[3]https://github.com/webpack/webpack/issues/2855#issuecomment-239606760

```
    }),
  ],
  ...
};

function isVendor({ resource }) {
  return resource &&
    resource.indexOf('node_modules') >= 0 &&
    resource.match(/\.js$/);
}
```

The same code would look as below using the `parts.extractBundles` abstraction:

```
parts.extractBundles([
  {
    name: 'login',
    chunks: ['login'],
    minChunks: isVendor,
  },
  {
    name: 'vendor',
    chunks: ['app'],
    minChunks: isVendor,
  },
  {
    name: 'common',
    chunks: ['login', 'app'],
    minChunks: (module, count) => (
      count >= 2 && isVendor(module),
    ),
  },
]),
```

 The chunks option refers to the entry chunks of your configuration.

15.8 `CommonsChunkPlugin` `children` **and** `async` **Flags**

`CommonsChunkPlugin` provides more control through `children` and `async` flags:

- `children` - If `children` is set to `true`, webpack detects which modules are the same in the resulting bundles and push them to the parent bundle.
- `async` - The idea is the same if `async` is set to `true`. In this case, webpack generates a separate bundle with the commonalities and load it asynchronously from the parent. You can pass a string to `async` option to name the output bundle. The idea is the same as for *Code Splitting* as you will see in the next chapter.

The image below shows the difference compared to the default. The top circles represent the parent bundles. The way B is treated depends on the chosen option:

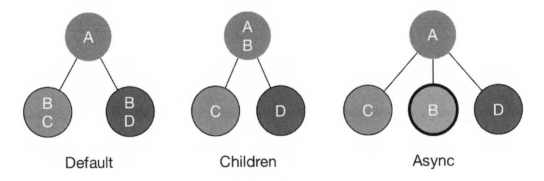

CommonsChunkPlugin **children and async**

 `children` and `async` can be used together if you are using *Code Splitting* and want to extract commonalities.

 The `children` behavior applies only to immediate children. The algorithm is not applied recursively. Webpack issue 3981[4] explains this in detail.

---

[4]https://github.com/webpack/webpack/issues/3981

15.9 Splitting and Merging Chunks

Webpack provides more control over the generated chunks by providing two plugins: AggressiveSplittingPlugin and AggressiveMergingPlugin. The former allows you to emit more and smaller bundles. The behavior is handy with HTTP/2 due to the way the new standard works.

Here's the basic idea of aggressive splitting:

```
{
  plugins: [
    new webpack.optimize.AggressiveSplittingPlugin({
        minSize: 10000,
        maxSize: 30000,
    }),
  ],
},
```

There's a trade-off as you lose out in caching if you split to multiple small bundles. You also get request overhead in HTTP/1 environment. For now, the approach doesn't work when HtmlWebpackPlugin is enabled due to a bug in the plugin[5].

The aggressive merging plugin works the opposite way and allows you to combine too small bundles into bigger ones:

```
{
  plugins: [
    new AggressiveMergingPlugin({
        minSizeReduce: 2,
        moveToParents: true,
    }),
  ],
},
```

---

[5]https://github.com/ampedandwired/html-webpack-plugin/issues/446

It's possible to get good caching behavior with these plugins if a webpack **records** are used. The idea is discussed in detail in the *Adding Hashes to Filenames* chapter.

 Tobias Koppers discusses aggressive merging in detail at the official blog of webpack[6].

 `webpack.optimize.LimitChunkCountPlugin`   and `webpack.optimize.MinChunkSizePlugin` give further control over chunk size.

15.10 Chunk Types in Webpack

In the example above, you used different types of webpack chunks. Webpack treats chunks in three types:

- **Entry chunks** - Entry chunks contain webpack runtime and modules it then loads.
- **Normal chunks** - Normal chunks **don't** contain webpack runtime. Instead, these can be loaded dynamically while the application is running. A suitable wrapper (JSONP for example) is generated for these. You generate a normal chunk in the next chapter as you set up code splitting.
- **Initial chunks** - Initial chunks are normal chunks that count towards initial loading time of the application and are generated by the `CommonsChunkPlugin`. As a user, you don't have to care about these. It's the split between entry chunks and normal chunks that is important.

---

[6]https://medium.com/webpack/webpack-http-2-7083ec3f3ce6

15.11 Conclusion

The situation is better now compared to the earlier. Note how small app bundle compared to the vendor bundle. To benefit from this split, you set up caching in the next part of this book in the *Adding Hashes to Filenames* chapter.

To recap:

- Webpack allows you to split bundles from configuration entries through the CommonsChunkPlugin.
- The most basic use case for CommonsChunkPlugin is to extract so-called **vendor bundle**.
- A vendor bundle contains the third party code of your project. The vendor dependencies can be detected by inspecting where the modules are imported. If they come from the *node_modules* directory, they can be split automatically through a minChunks rule.
- CommonsChunkPlugin provides control over the splitting process. You can control the position of shared modules through its async and children flags. async extracts shared modules to an asynchronously loaded bundle while children pushes the shared modules to the parent bundle.
- The chunks option of CommonsChunkPlugin allows you to control where the plugin is performing splitting. The option gives more granular control, especially in more complex setups.
- Webpack offers more control over chunking through specific plugins, such as AggressiveSplittingPlugin and AggressiveMergingPlugin. Particularly the splitting plugin can be handy in HTTP/2 oriented setups.
- Internally webpack relies on three chunk types: entry, normal, and initial chunks. CommonsChunkPlugin flags modules using these types.

In the next chapter, you'll learn about code splitting and loading code on demand.

16. Code Splitting

Web applications have the tendency to grow big as features are developed. The longer it takes for your application to load, the more frustrating it's to the user. This problem is amplified in a mobile environment where the connections can be slow.

Even though splitting bundles can help a notch, they are not the only solution, and you can still end up having to download a lot of data. Fortunately, it's possible to do better thanks to **code splitting**. It allows to load code lazily as you need it.

You can load more code as the user enters a new view of the application. You can also tie loading to a specific action like scrolling or clicking a button. You could also try to predict what the user is trying to do next and load code based on your guess. This way the functionality would be already there as the user tries to access it.

 Incidentally, it's possible to implement Google's PRPL pattern[1] using webpack's lazy loading. PRPL (Push, Render, Pre-cache, Lazy-load) has been designed with mobile web in mind.

16.1 Code Splitting Formats

Code splitting can be done in two primary ways in webpack: through a dynamic `import` or `require.ensure` syntax. The former is used in this project.

The goal is to end up with a split point that gets loaded on demand. There can be splits inside splits, and you can structure an entire application based on splits. The advantage of doing this is that then the initial payload of your application can be smaller than it would be otherwise.

---

[1] https://developers.google.com/web/fundamentals/performance/prpl-pattern/

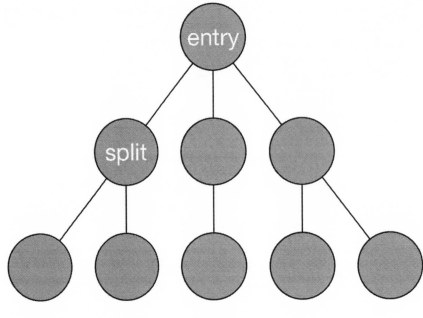

Code splitting

Dynamic `import`

The dynamic `import` syntax[2] isn't in the official language specification yet. To use it, minor tweaks are needed especially at ESLint and Babel.

Dynamic imports are defined as `Promises`:

```
import(/* webpackChunkName: "optional-name" */ './module').then(
  module => {...}
).catch(
  error => {...}
);
```

---

[2]https://github.com/tc39/proposal-dynamic-import

The optional name allows you to pull multiple split points into a single bundle. As long as they have the same name, they will be grouped together. Each split point generates a separate bundle by default.

The interface allows composition, and you could load multiple resources in parallel:

```
Promise.all([
  import('lunr'),
  import('../search_index.json'),
]).then(([lunr, search]) => {
  return {
    index: lunr.Index.load(search.index),
    lines: search.lines,
  };
});
```

This creates separate bundles to request. If you wanted only one, you would have to use naming or define an intermediate module to import.

 Webpack provided support for System.import in the early versions of webpack 2 and it still does. The functionality has been deprecated and gets removed in webpack 3. Until then, you can use the functionality interchangeably.

 The syntax works only with JavaScript after configured the right way. If you use another environment, you have to use alternatives covered in the following sections.

`require.ensure`

require.ensure[3] provides an alternate way:

```
require.ensure(
  // Modules to load, but not execute yet
  ['./load-earlier'],
  () => {
    const loadEarlier = require('./load-earlier');

    // Load later on demand and include to the same chunk
    const module1 = require('./module1');
    const module2 = require('./module2');

    ...
  },
  err => console.error(err),
  'optional-name'
);
```

Often you can achieve what you want through a dynamic `import`, but it's good to know this alternate form exists as well. `require.ensure` supports naming as well and the official example[4] shows the output in detail.

 `require.ensure` relies on `Promise`s internally. If you use `require.ensure` with older browsers, remember to shim `Promise` using a polyfill such as es6-promise[5].

---

[3] https://webpack.js.org/guides/code-splitting-require/#require-ensure-

[4] https://github.com/webpack/webpack/tree/master/examples/named-chunks

[5] https://www.npmjs.com/package/es6-promise

`require.include`

The example above could be rewritten using webpack particular `require.include`:

```
require.ensure(
  [],
  () => {
    require.include('./load-earlier');

    const loadEarlier = require('./load-earlier');

    // Load later on demand and include to the same chunk
    const module1 = require('./module1');
    const module2 = require('./module2');


    ...
  }
);
```

If you had nested `require.ensure` definitions, you could pull a module to the parent chunk using either syntax. It's a similar idea as you saw in the *Bundle Splitting* chapter.

 The formats respect `output.publicPath` option. You can also use `output.chunkFilename` to shape where they output. Example: `chunkFilename: '[name].js'`.

16.2 Setting Up Code Splitting

To demonstrate the idea of code splitting, you can use dynamic `import`. Both ESLint and Babel setup of the project needs additions to make the syntax work.

Configuring ESLint

Given ESLint supports only standard ES6 out of the box, it requires tweaking to work with dynamic `import`. Install *babel-eslint* parser first:

```
npm install babel-eslint --save-dev
```

Tweak ESLint configuration as follows:

.eslintrc.js

```
module.exports = {
  ...
  parser: 'babel-eslint',
  parserOptions: {
    sourceType: 'module',
    allowImportExportEverywhere: true,
  },
  ...
}
```

After these changes, ESLint doesn't complain if you write `import` in the middle of the code.

Configuring Babel

Given Babel doesn't support the dynamic `import` syntax out of the box, it needs babel-plugin-syntax-dynamic-import[6] to work. Install it first:

```
npm install babel-plugin-syntax-dynamic-import --save-dev
```

To connect it with the project, adjust the configuration as follows:

.babelrc

```
{
  "plugins": ["syntax-dynamic-import"],
  ...
}
```

Defining a Split Point Using a Dynamic `import`

The idea can be demonstrated by setting up a module that contains a string that replaces the text of the demo button:

app/lazy.js

```
export default 'Hello from lazy';
```

---

[6]https://www.npmjs.com/package/babel-plugin-syntax-dynamic-import

You also need to point the application to this file, so the application knows to load it. This can be done by binding the loading process to click. Whenever the user happens to click the button, you trigger the loading process and replace the content:

app/component.js

```
export default () => {
  const element = document.createElement('div');

  element.className = 'fa fa-hand-spock-o fa-1g';
  element.innerHTML = 'Hello world';
  element.onclick = () => {
    import('./lazy').then((lazy) => {
      element.textContent = lazy.default;
    }).catch((err) => {
      console.error(err);
    });
  };

  return element;
};
```

If you open up the application (npm start) and click the button, you should see the new text in the button.

🖖Hello from lazy

Lazy loaded content

If you run npm run build, you should see something:

```
Hash: e61343b53de634da8aac
Version: webpack 2.2.1
Time: 2890ms
          Asset       Size  Chunks                      Chunk Names
         app.js     2.4 kB       1  [emitted]           app
    ...font.eot      166 kB          [emitted]
  ...font.woff2    77.2 kB          [emitted]
   ...font.woff       98 kB          [emitted]
    ...font.svg      444 kB          [emitted]  [big]
       logo.png       77 kB          [emitted]
           0.js   313 bytes       0  [emitted]
    ...font.ttf      166 kB          [emitted]
      vendor.js      150 kB       2  [emitted]           vendor
        app.css    3.89 kB       1  [emitted]           app
       0.js.map   233 bytes       0  [emitted]
     app.js.map    2.13 kB       1  [emitted]           app
    app.css.map    84 bytes       1  [emitted]           app
  vendor.js.map      178 kB       2  [emitted]           vendor
     index.html   274 bytes          [emitted]
   [0] ./~/process/browser.js 5.3 kB {2} [built]
   [3] ./~/react/lib/ReactElement.js 11.2 kB {2} [built]
  [18] ./app/component.js 461 bytes {1} [built]
...
```

That *0.js* is your split point. Examining the file reveals that webpack has wrapped the code in a webpackJsonp block and processed the code bit.

Lazy Loading Styles

Lazy loading can be applied to styling as well. Expand the definition:

app/lazy.js

```
import './lazy.css';

export default 'Hello from lazy';
```

And to have a style definition to load, set up a rule:

app/lazy.css

```
body {
  color: blue;
}
```

The idea is that after *lazy.js* gets loaded, *lazy.css* is applied as well. You can confirm this by running the application (npm start). The same behavior is visible if you build the application (npm run build) and examine the output (0.js). This is due to the ExtractTextPlugin definition.

🖐Hello from lazy

Lazy styled content

Defining a Split Point Using `require.ensure`

It's possible to achieve the same with `require.ensure`. Consider the full example below:

```
export default () => {
  const element = document.createElement('div');

  element.className = 'pure-button';
  element.innerHTML = 'Hello world';
  element.onclick = () => {
    require.ensure([], (require) => {
      element.textContent = require('./lazy').default;
    });
  };

  return element;
};
```

You could name the split point as outlined above. If you add another split point and give it the same name, the splits should end up in the same bundle.

 bundle-loader[7] gives similar results, but through a loader interface. It supports bundle naming through its `name` option.

 The *Dynamic Loading* chapter covers other techniques that come in handy when you have to deal with more complicated splits.

---

[7] https://www.npmjs.com/package/bundle-loader

16.3 Code Splitting in React

The splitting pattern can be wrapped into a React component. Airbnb uses the following solution as described by Joe Lencioni[8]:

```
import React from 'react';

...

// Somewhere in code
<AsyncComponent loader={() => import('./SomeComponent')} />

...

// React wrapper for loading
class AsyncComponent extends React.Component {
  constructor(props) {
    super(props);

    this.state = {
      Component: null,
    };
  }

  componentDidMount() {
    // Load the component now
    this.props.loader().then(Component => {
      this.setState({ Component });
    });
  }

  render() {
    const { Component } = this.state;
```

---

[8]https://gist.github.com/lencioni/643a78712337d255f5c031bfc81ca4cf

```
    const { Placeholder } = this.props;

    if (Component) {
      return <Component {...this.props} />;
    }

    return <Placeholder>
  }
}


AsyncComponent.propTypes = {
  // A loader is a function that should return a Promise.
  loader: PropTypes.func.isRequired,

  // A placeholder to render while waiting completion.
  Placeholder: PropTypes.node.isRequired
};
```

 react-async-component[9] wraps the pattern in a createAsyncComponent call and provides server side rendering specific functionality. react-loadable[10] is another option.

---

[9]https://www.npmjs.com/package/react-async-component
[10]https://www.npmjs.com/package/react-loadable

16.4 Conclusion

Code splitting is one of those features that allows you to push your application a notch further. You can load code when you need it to gain faster initial load times and improved user experience especially in a mobile context where bandwidth is limited.

To recap:

- **Code splitting** comes with extra effort as you have to decide what to split and where. Often, you find good split points within a router. Or you notice that specific functionality is required only when a particular feature is used. Charting is a good example of this.
- To use dynamic `import` syntax, both Babel and ESLint require careful tweaks. Webpack supports the syntax ouf of the box.
- Use naming to pull separate split points into the same bundles.
- The techniques can be used within modern frameworks and libraries like React. You can wrap related logic to a specific component that handles the loading process in a user-friendly manner.

You'll learn to tidy up the build in the next chapter.

 The *Searching with React* appendix contains a complete example of code splitting. It shows how to set up a static site index that's loaded when the user searches information.

 webpack-pwa[11] illustrates the idea on a larger scale and discusses different shell based approaches. You get back to this topic in the *Multiple Pages* chapter.

---

[11] https://github.com/webpack/webpack-pwa

17. Tidying Up

The current setup doesn't clean the *build* directory between builds. As a result, it keeps on accumulating files as the project changes. Given this can get annoying, you should clean it up in between.

Another nice touch would be to include information about the build itself to the generated bundles as a small comment at the top of each file including version information at least.

17.1 Cleaning the Build Directory

This issue can be resolved either by using a webpack plugin or solving it outside of it. You could trigger `rm -rf ./build && webpack` or `rimraf ./build && webpack` in an npm script to keep it cross-platform. A task runner could work for this purpose as well.

Setting Up `CleanWebpackPlugin`

Install the clean-webpack-plugin[1] first:

```
npm install clean-webpack-plugin --save-dev
```

---

[1]https://www.npmjs.com/package/clean-webpack-plugin

Next, you need to define a function to wrap the basic idea. You could use the plugin directly, but this feels like something that could be used across projects, so it makes sense to push it to the library:

webpack.parts.js

```
. . .
const CleanWebpackPlugin = require('clean-webpack-plugin');

. . .

exports.clean = (path) => ({
  plugins: [
    new CleanWebpackPlugin([path]),
  ],
});
```

Connect it with the project:

webpack.config.js

```
const productionConfig = merge([
  parts.clean(PATHS.build),
  . . .
]);
```

After this change, the build directory should remain nice and tidy while building. You can verify this by building the project and making sure no old files remained in the output directory.

17.2 Attaching a Revision to the Build

Attaching information related to the current build revision to the build files themselves can be used for debugging. webpack.BannerPlugin[2] allows you to achieve this.
It can be used in combination with git-revision-webpack-plugin[3] to generate a small
comment at the beginning of the generated files.

Setting Up BannerPlugin and GitRevisionPlugin

To get started, install the revision plugin:

```
npm install git-revision-webpack-plugin --save-dev
```

Then define a part to wrap the idea:

webpack.parts.js

```
...
const GitRevisionPlugin = require('git-revision-webpack-plugin');

...

exports.attachRevision = () => ({
  plugins: [
    new webpack.BannerPlugin({
      banner: new GitRevisionPlugin().version(),
    }),
  ],
});
```

---

[2]https://webpack.js.org/plugins/banner-plugin/

[3]https://www.npmjs.com/package/git-revision-webpack-plugin

And connect it to the main configuration:

webpack.config.js

```
const productionConfig = merge([
  ...
  parts.attachRevision(),
]);
```

If you build the project (npm run build), you should notice the built files contain comments like /*! 0b5bb05 */ or /*! v1.7.0-9-g5f82fe8 */ in the beginning.

The output can be customized further by adjusting the banner. You can also pass revision information to the application using webpack.DefinePlugin. This technique is discussed in detail in the *Environment Variables* chapter.

 The code expects you run it within a Git repository! Otherwise, you get a fatal: Not a git repository (or any of the parent directories): .git error. If you are not using Git, you can replace the banner with other data.

17.3 Copying Files

Copying files is another common operation you can handle with webpack. copy-webpack-plugin[4] can be handy if you need to bring external files to your build without having webpack pointing at them directly.

cpy-cli[5] is a good option if you want to copy outside of webpack in a cross-platform way. Plugins should be cross-platforms by definition.

---

[4]https://www.npmjs.com/package/copy-webpack-plugin
[5]https://www.npmjs.com/package/cpy-cli

17.4 Conclusion

Often, you work with webpack by identifying a problem and then finding a plugin to tackle it. It's entirely acceptable to solve these types of issues outside of webpack, but webpack can often handle them as well.

To recap:

- You can find many small plugins that work as tasks and push webpack closer to a task runner.
- These tasks include cleaning the build and deployment. The *Deploying Applications* chapter discusses the latter topic in detail.
- It can be a good idea to include small comments to the production build to tell what version has been deployed. This way you can debug potential issues faster.
- Secondary tasks like these can be performed outside of webpack. If you are using a multi-page setup as discussed in the *Multiple Pages* chapter, this becomes a necessity.

V Optimizing

In this part, you will learn about aspects like code minification, setting environment variables, adding hashing to filenames, webpack manifest, and analyzing build statistics. Understanding these techniques allows you to reach production level output. You also learn about tuning webpack performance.

18. Minifying

The build output hasn't received attention yet and no doubt it's going to be chunky, especially as you included React in it. You can apply a variety of techniques to bring down the size of the vendor bundle. You can also leverage client level caching and load individual assets lazily as you saw earlier.

Minification is a process where the code is simplified without losing any meaning that matters to the interpreter. As a result, your code most likely looks jumbled, and it's hard to read. But that's the point.

 Even if you minify the build, you can still generate source maps through the devtool option that was discussed earlier to gain a better debugging experience, even production code if you want.

18.1 Generating a Baseline Build

To get started, you should generate a baseline build, so you have something to optimize. Execute npm run build to see output below:

```
Hash: 12aec469d54202150429
Version: webpack 2.2.1
Time: 2863ms
         Asset      Size  Chunks             Chunk Names
        app.js   2.42 kB       1  [emitted]  app
   ...font.eot    166 kB          [emitted]
 ...font.woff2   77.2 kB          [emitted]
  ...font.woff     98 kB          [emitted]
   ...font.svg    444 kB          [emitted]  [big]
      logo.png     77 kB          [emitted]
```

```
         0.js    1.89 kB      0    [emitted]
   ...font.ttf     166 kB           [emitted]
     vendor.js     150 kB      2    [emitted]            vendor
       app.css     3.9 kB      1    [emitted]            app
     0.js.map    2.22 kB      0    [emitted]
   app.js.map    2.13 kB      1    [emitted]            app
  app.css.map    84 bytes     1    [emitted]            app
vendor.js.map     178 kB      2    [emitted]            vendor
    index.html  274 bytes          [emitted]
   [3] ./~/react/lib/ReactElement.js 11.2 kB {2} [built]
  [18] ./app/component.js 461 bytes {1} [built]
  [19] ./~/font-awesome/css/font-awesome.css 41 bytes {1} [built]
...
```

150 kB for a vendor bundle is a lot! Minification should bring the size down.

18.2 Enabling a Performance Budget

Webpack allows you to define a **performance budget**. The idea is that it gives your build size constraint which it has to follow. The feature is disabled by default, but if enabled it defaults to 250 kB limit per entries and assets. The calculation includes extracted chunks to entry calculation.

Performance budget can be configured to provide warnings or errors. If a budget isn't met and it has been configured to emit an error, it would terminate the entire build.

To integrate the feature into the project, adjust the configuration:

webpack.config.js

```
const productionConfig = merge([
  {
    performance: {
      hints: 'warning', // 'error' or false are valid too
      maxEntrypointSize: 100000, // in bytes
      maxAssetSize: 450000, // in bytes
    },
  },
  ...
]);
```

In practice you want to maintain lower limits. The current ones are enough for this demonstration. If you build now (npm run build), you should see a warning within the output:

```
...
WARNING in entrypoint size limit: The following entrypoint(s) combin\
ed asset size exceeds the recommended limit (100 kB). This can impac\
t web performance.
Entrypoints:
  app (156 kB)
      vendor.js
,      app.js
,      app.css
...
```

If minification works, the warning should disappear. That's the next challenge.

18.3 Minifying JavaScript

The point of **minification** is to convert the code into a smaller form. Safe **transformations** do this without losing any meaning by rewriting code. Good examples of this include renaming variables or even removing entire blocks of code based on the fact that they are unreachable (`if (false)`).

Unsafe transformations can break code as they can lose something implicit the underlying code relies upon. For example, Angular 1 expects specific function parameter naming when using modules. Rewriting the parameters breaks code unless you take precautions against it in this case.

Minification in webpack can be enabled through `webpack -p` (same as `--optimize-minimize`). This uses webpack's `UglifyJsPlugin` underneath. The problem is that UglifyJS doesn't support ES6 syntax yet making it problematic if Babel and *babel-preset-env* are used while targeting specific browsers. You have to go another route in this case for this reason.

Setting Up JavaScript Minification

babili[1] is a JavaScript minifier maintained by the Babel team and it provides support for ES6 and newer features. babili-webpack-plugin[2] makes it possible to use it through webpack.

To get started, include the plugin to the project:

```
npm install babili-webpack-plugin --save-dev
```

---

[1]https://www.npmjs.com/package/babili
[2]https://www.npmjs.com/package/babili-webpack-plugin

To attach it to the configuration, define a part for it first:

webpack.parts.js

```
...
const BabiliPlugin = require('babili-webpack-plugin');

...

exports.minifyJavaScript = () => ({
  plugins: [
    new BabiliPlugin(),
  ],
});
```

The plugin exposes more functionality, but having the possibility of toggling source maps is enough. Hook it up with the configuration:

webpack.config.js

```
const productionConfig = merge([
  ...
  parts.clean(PATHS.build),
  parts.minifyJavaScript(),
  ...
]);
```

If you execute `npm run build` now, you should see smaller results:

```
Hash: 12aec469d54202150429
Version: webpack 2.2.1
Time: 5265ms
          Asset       Size  Chunks             Chunk Names
         app.js  669 bytes       1  [emitted]  app
    ...font.eot     166 kB          [emitted]
  ...font.woff2    77.2 kB          [emitted]
   ...font.woff      98 kB          [emitted]
    ...font.svg     444 kB          [emitted]
       logo.png      77 kB          [emitted]
           0.js  399 bytes       0  [emitted]
    ...font.ttf     166 kB          [emitted]
      vendor.js    45.2 kB       2  [emitted]  vendor
        app.css     3.9 kB       1  [emitted]  app
       0.js.map    2.07 kB       0  [emitted]
     app.js.map    1.64 kB       1  [emitted]  app
    app.css.map   84 bytes       1  [emitted]  app
  vendor.js.map     169 kB       2  [emitted]  vendor
     index.html  274 bytes          [emitted]
    [3] ./~/react/lib/ReactElement.js 11.2 kB {2} [built]
   [18] ./app/component.js 461 bytes {1} [built]
   [19] ./~/font-awesome/css/font-awesome.css 41 bytes {1} [built]
...
```

Given it needs to do more work, it took longer to execute the build. But on the plus side, the build is now smaller, the size limit warning disappeared, and the vendor build went from 150 kB to roughly 45 kB.

You should check *babili-webpack-plugin* and Babili documentation for more options. Babili gives you control over how to handle code comments for example.

18.4 Other Ways to Minify JavaScript

Although Babili works for this use case, there are more options you can consider:

- webpack-closure-compiler[3] runs parallel and gives even smaller result than Babili at times.
- optimize-js-plugin[4] complements the other solutions by wrapping eager functions and it enhances the way your JavaScript code gets parsed initially. The plugin relies on optimize-js[5] by Nolan Lawson.
- webpack.optimize.UglifyJsPlugin[6] is the official UglifyJS plugin for webpack. It doesn't support ES6 yet.
- uglifyjs-webpack-plugin[7] allows you to try out an experimental version of UglifyJS that provides better support for ES6 than the stable version.
- uglify-loader[8] gives more granular control than webpack's `UglifyJsPlugin` in case you prefer to use UglifyJS.
- webpack-parallel-uglify-plugin[9] allows you to parallelize the minifying step and can yield extra performance as webpack doesn't run in parallel by default.

18.5 Minifying CSS

css-loader allows minifying CSS through cssnano[10]. Minification needs to be enabled explicitly using the `minimize` option. You can also pass cssnano specific options[11] to the query to customize the behavior further.

clean-css-loader[12] allows you to use a popular CSS minifier clean-css[13].

---

[3]https://www.npmjs.com/package/webpack-closure-compiler

[4]https://www.npmjs.com/package/optimize-js-plugin

[5]https://github.com/nolanlawson/optimize-js

[6]https://webpack.js.org/plugins/uglifyjs-webpack-plugin/

[7]https://www.npmjs.com/package/uglifyjs-webpack-plugin

[8]https://www.npmjs.com/package/uglify-loader

[9]https://www.npmjs.com/package/webpack-parallel-uglify-plugin

[10]http://cssnano.co/

[11]http://cssnano.co/optimisations/

[12]https://www.npmjs.com/package/clean-css-loader

[13]https://www.npmjs.com/package/clean-css

optimize-css-assets-webpack-plugin[14] is a plugin based option that applies a chosen minifier on CSS assets. Using `ExtractTextPlugin` can lead to duplicated CSS given it only merges text chunks. `OptimizeCSSAssetsPlugin` avoids this problem by operating on the generated result and thus can lead to a better result.

 In webpack 1 `minimize` was set on by default if `UglifyJsPlugin` was used. This confusing behavior was fixed in webpack 2, and now you have explicit control over minification.

Setting Up CSS Minification

Out of the available solutions, `OptimizeCSSAssetsPlugin` composes the best. To attach it to the setup, install it and *cssnano* first:

```
npm install optimize-css-assets-webpack-plugin cssnano --save-dev
```

Like for JavaScript, you can wrap the idea in a configuration part:

webpack.parts.js

```
...
const OptimizeCSSAssetsPlugin = require('optimize-css-assets-webpack\
-plugin');
const cssnano = require('cssnano');

...

exports.minifyCSS = ({ options }) => ({
  plugins: [
    new OptimizeCSSAssetsPlugin({
      cssProcessor: cssnano,
      cssProcessorOptions: options,
```

---

[14]https://www.npmjs.com/package/optimize-css-assets-webpack-plugin

```
    canPrint: false,
  }),
 ],
});
```

 If you use `--json` output with webpack as discussed in the *Analyzing Build Statistics* chapter, you should set `canPrint: false` to avoid output. You can solve by exposing the flag as a parameter so you can control it based on the environment.

Then, connect with main configuration:

webpack.config.js

```
const productionConfig = merge([
  ...
  parts.minifyJavaScript(),
  parts.minifyCSS({
    options: {
      discardComments: {
        removeAll: true,
      },
      // Run cssnano in safe mode to avoid
      // potentially unsafe transformations.
      safe: true,
    },
  }),
  ...
]);
```

If you build the project now (`npm run build`), you should notice that CSS has become smaller as it's missing comments:

```
Hash: 12aec469d54202150429
Version: webpack 2.2.1
Time: 4764ms
          Asset      Size  Chunks           Chunk Names
         app.js  669 bytes      1  [emitted]  app
    ...font.eot    166 kB          [emitted]
  ...font.woff2   77.2 kB          [emitted]
   ...font.woff     98 kB          [emitted]
    ...font.svg    444 kB          [emitted]
       logo.png     77 kB          [emitted]
           0.js  399 bytes      0  [emitted]
    ...font.ttf    166 kB          [emitted]
      vendor.js   45.2 kB      2  [emitted]  vendor
        app.css   2.48 kB      1  [emitted]  app
       0.js.map   2.07 kB      0  [emitted]
     app.js.map   1.64 kB      1  [emitted]  app
    app.css.map   84 bytes      1  [emitted]  app
  vendor.js.map    169 kB      2  [emitted]  vendor
     index.html  274 bytes          [emitted]
    [3] ./~/react/lib/ReactElement.js 11.2 kB {2} [built]
   [18] ./app/component.js 461 bytes {1} [built]
   [19] ./~/font-awesome/css/font-awesome.css 41 bytes {1} [built]
...
```

cssnano[15] has a lot more options to try out.

---

[15] http://cssnano.co/

18.6 Minifying HTML

If you consume HTML templates through your code using html-loader[16], you can preprocess it through posthtml[17] with posthtml-loader[18]. You can use posthtml-minifier[19] to minify your HTML through it.

18.7 Conclusion

Minification is the easiest step you can take to make your build smaller. To recap:

- **Minification** process analyzes your source code and turns it into a smaller form with the same meaning if you use safe transformations. Certain unsafe transformations allow you to reach even smaller results while potentially breaking code that relies, for example, on exact parameter naming.
- **Performance budget** allows you to set limits to the build size. Maintaining a budget can keep developers more conscious of the size of the generated bundles.
- Webpack includes `UglifyJsPlugin` for minification. Other solutions, such as Babili, provide similar functionality with costs of their own. While Babili supports ES6, it can be less performant than UglifyJS.
- Besides JavaScript, it's possible to minify other assets, such as CSS and HTML, too. Minifying these requires specific technologies that have to be applied through loaders and plugins of their own.

You'll learn to apply tree shaking against code in the next chapter.

---

[16] https://www.npmjs.com/package/html-loader

[17] https://www.npmjs.com/package/posthtml

[18] https://www.npmjs.com/package/posthtml-loader

[19] https://www.npmjs.com/package/posthtml-minifier

19. Tree Shaking

Tree shaking is a feature enabled by the ES6 module definition. The idea is that given it's possible to analyze the module definition in a static way without running it, webpack can tell which parts of the code are being used and which are not. It's possible to verify this behavior by expanding the application and adding code there that should be eliminated.

19.1 Demonstrating Tree Shaking

To shake code, you have to define a module and use only a part of its code. Set one up:

app/shake.js

```
const shake = () => console.log('shake');
const bake = () => console.log('bake');

export { shake, bake };
```

To make sure you use a part of the code, alter the application entry point:

app/index.js

```
...
import { bake } from './shake';

bake();

...
```

If you build the project again (`npm run build`) and examine the build (*build/app.js*), it should contain `console.log('bake')`, but miss `console.log('shake')`. That's tree shaking in action.

To get a better idea of what webpack is using for tree shaking, run it through `npm run build -- --display-used-exports`. You should see additional output like `[no exports used]` or `[only some exports used: bake]` in the terminal.

 If you are using `UglifyJsPlugin`, enable warnings for a similar effect. In addition to other messages, you should see lines like `Dropping unused variable treeShakingDemo [./app/component.js:17,6]`.

 There is a CSS Modules related tree shaking proof of concept at dead-css-loader[1].

19.2 Tree Shaking on Package Level

The same idea works with dependencies that use the ES6 module definition. Given the related packaging standards are still emerging, you have to be careful when consuming such packages. Webpack tries to resolve *package.json* `module` field for this reason.

For tools like webpack to allow tree shake npm packages, you should generate a build that has transpiled everything else except the ES6 module definitions and then point to it through *package.json* `module` field. In Babel terms, you have to let webpack to manage ES6 modules by setting `"modules": false`.

---

[1]https://github.com/simlrh/dead-css-loader

To get most out of tree shaking with external packages, you have to use babel-plugin-transform-imports[2] to rewrite imports so that they work with webpack's tree shaking logic. See webpack issue #2867[3] for more information.

19.3 Conclusion

Tree shaking is a potentially powerful technique. For the source to benefit from tree shaking, npm packages have to be implemented using the ES6 module syntax, and they have to expose the ES6 version through *package.json* `module` field tools like webpack can pick up.

To recap:

- **Tree shaking** drops unused pieces of code based on static code analysis. Webpack performs this process for you as it traverses the dependency graph.
- To benefit from tree shaking, you have to use ES6 module definition.
- As a package author, you can provide a version of your package that contains ES6 modules, while the rest has been transpiled to ES5.

You'll learn how to manage environment variables using webpack in the next chapter.

---

[2]https://www.npmjs.com/package/babel-plugin-transform-imports
[3]https://github.com/webpack/webpack/issues/2867

20. Environment Variables

Sometimes a part of your code should execute only during development. Or you could have experimental features in your build that are not ready for production yet. This is where controlling **environment variables** becomes valuable as you can toggle functionality using them.

Since JavaScript minifiers can remove dead code (`if (false)`), you can build on top of this idea and write code that gets transformed into this form. Webpack's `DefinePlugin` enables replacing **free variables** so that you can convert `if (process.env.NODE_ENV === 'development')` kind of code to `if (true)` or `if (false)` depending on the environment.

You can find packages that rely on this behavior. React is perhaps the most known example of an early adopter of the technique. Using `DefinePlugin` can bring down the size of your React production build somewhat as a result, and you can see a similar effect with other packages as well.

20.1 The Basic Idea of `DefinePlugin`

To understand the idea of `DefinePlugin` better, consider the example below:

```
var foo;

// Not free due to "foo" above, not ok to replace
if (foo === 'bar') {
  console.log('bar');
}

// Free since you don't refer to "bar", ok to replace
if (bar === 'bar') {
  console.log('bar');
}
```

If you replaced bar with a string like 'foobar', then you would end up with code as below:

```
var foo;

// Not free due to "foo" above, not ok to replace
if (foo === 'bar') {
  console.log('bar');
}

// Free since you don't refer to "bar", ok to replace
if ('foobar' === 'bar') {
  console.log('bar');
}
```

Further analysis shows that 'foobar' === 'bar' equals false so a minifier gives the following:

```
var foo;

// Not free due to "foo" above, not ok to replace
if (foo === 'bar') {
  console.log('bar');
}

// Free since you don't refer to "bar", ok to replace
if (false) {
  console.log('bar');
}
```

A minifier eliminates the `if` statement as it has become dead code:

```
var foo;

// Not free, not ok to replace
if (foo === 'bar') {
  console.log('bar');
}

// if (false) means the block can be dropped entirely
```

Elimination is the core idea of `DefinePlugin` and it allows toggling. A minifier performs analysis and toggles entire portions of the code.

20.2 Setting `process.env.NODE_ENV`

Given you are using React in the project and it happens to use the technique, you can try to enable `DefinePlugin` and see what it does to the production build.

As before, encapsulate this idea to a function. Due to the way webpack replaces the free variable, you should push it through `JSON.stringify`. You end up with a string like `'"demo"'` and then webpack inserts that into the slots it finds:

webpack.parts.js

```
exports.setFreeVariable = (key, value) => {
  const env = {};
  env[key] = JSON.stringify(value);

  return {
    plugins: [
      new webpack.DefinePlugin(env),
    ],
  };
};
```

You can connect this with the configuration:

webpack.config.js

```
const productionConfig = merge([
  ...
  parts.setFreeVariable(
    'process.env.NODE_ENV',
    'production'
  ),
]);
```

Execute npm run build and you should see improved results:

```
Hash: fe11f4781275080dd01a
Version: webpack 2.2.1
Time: 4726ms
         Asset       Size  Chunks             Chunk Names
        app.js  802 bytes       1  [emitted]  app
   ...font.eot     166 kB          [emitted]
 ...font.woff2    77.2 kB          [emitted]
  ...font.woff      98 kB          [emitted]
   ...font.svg     444 kB          [emitted]
      logo.png      77 kB          [emitted]
          0.js  399 bytes       0  [emitted]
   ...font.ttf     166 kB          [emitted]
     vendor.js    24.3 kB       2  [emitted]  vendor
       app.css    2.48 kB       1  [emitted]  app
      0.js.map    2.07 kB       0  [emitted]
    app.js.map    2.32 kB       1  [emitted]  app
   app.css.map   84 bytes       1  [emitted]  app
 vendor.js.map     135 kB       2  [emitted]  vendor
    index.html  274 bytes          [emitted]
   [4] ./~/object-assign/index.js 2.11 kB {2} [built]
  [14] ./app/component.js 461 bytes {1} [built]
  [15] ./app/shake.js 138 bytes {1} [built]
...
```

You went from 150 kB to 45 kB, and finally, to 24 kB. The final build is faster than the previous one as well.

Given the 24 kB can be served gzipped, it's somewhat reasonable. gzipping drops around another 40%, and it's well supported by browsers.

 `webpack.EnvironmentPlugin(['NODE_ENV'])` is a shortcut that allows you to refer to environment variables. It uses `DefinePlugin` underneath and you can achieve the same effect by passing `process.env.NODE_-ENV` to the custom function you made. The documentation covers `EnvironmentPlugin`[1] in greater detail.

20.3 Replacing Free Variables Through Babel

babel-plugin-transform-inline-environment-variables[2] Babel plugin can be used to achieve the same effect. See the official documentation[3] for details.

babel-plugin-transform-define[4] and babel-plugin-minify-replace[5] are other alternatives for Babel.

20.4 Choosing Which Module to Use

The techniques discussed in this chapter can be used to choose entire modules depending on the environment. As seen above, `DefinePlugin` based splitting allows you to choose which branch of code to use and which to discard. This idea can be used to implement branching on module level.

---

[1] https://webpack.js.org/plugins/environment-plugin/

[2] https://www.npmjs.com/package/babel-plugin-transform-inline-environment-variables

[3] https://babeljs.io/docs/plugins/transform-inline-environment-variables/

[4] https://www.npmjs.com/package/babel-plugin-transform-define

[5] https://www.npmjs.com/package/babel-plugin-minify-replace

Consider the file structure below:

```
.
└── store
    ├── index.js
    ├── store.dev.js
    └── store.prod.js
```

The idea is that you choose either dev or prod version of the store depending on the environment. It's that *index.js* which does the hard work:

```
if (process.env.NODE_ENV === 'production') {
  module.exports = require('./store.prod');
} else {
  module.exports = require('./store.dev');
}
```

Webpack can pick the right code based on the DefinePlugin declaration and this code. You have to use CommonJS module definition style here as ES6 imports don't allow dynamic behavior by design.

 A related technique, **aliasing**, is discussed in the *Package Consuming Techniques* chapter.

20.5 Webpack Optimization Plugins

Webpack includes a collection of optimization related plugins:

- compression-webpack-plugin[6] allows you to push the problem of generating compressed files to webpack to potentially save processing time on the server.

---

[6]https://www.npmjs.com/package/compression-webpack-plugin

- `webpack.optimize.UglifyJsPlugin` allows you to minify output using different heuristics. Certain of them break code unless you are careful.
- `webpack.optimize.AggressiveSplittingPlugin` allows you to split code into smaller bundles as discussed in the *Bundle Splitting* chapter. The result is ideal for a HTTP/2 environment.
- `webpack.optimize.CommonsChunkPlugin` makes it possible to extract common dependencies into bundles of their own.
- `webpack.DefinePlugin` allows you to use feature flags in your code and eliminate the redundant code as discussed in this chapter.
- lodash-webpack-plugin[7] creates smaller Lodash builds by replacing feature sets with smaller alternatives leading to more compact builds.

20.6 Conclusion

Setting environment variables is a technique that allows you to control which paths of the source are included in the build.

To recap:

- Webpack allows you to set **environment variables** through `DefinePlugin` and `EnvironmentPlugin`. Latter maps system level environment variables to the source.
- `DefinePlugin` operates based on **free variables** and it replaces them as webpack analyzes the source code. You can achieve similar results by using Babel plugins.
- Given minifiers eliminate dead code, using the plugins allows you to remove the code from the resulting build.
- The plugins enable module level patterns. By implementing a wrapper, you can choose which file webpack includes to the resulting build.
- In addition to these plugins, you can find other optimization related plugins that allow you to control the build result in many ways.

To ensure the build has good cache invalidation behavior, you'll learn to include hashes to the generated filenames in the next chapter. This way the client notices if assets have changed and can fetch the updated versions.

---

[7]https://www.npmjs.com/package/lodash-webpack-plugin

21. Adding Hashes to Filenames

Even though the build generates fine now, the naming it uses is problematic. It doesn't allow to leverage client level cache effectively as there's no way tell whether or not a file has changed. Cache invalidation can be achieved by including a hash to filenames.

21.1 Placeholders

Webpack provides **placeholders** for this purpose. These strings are used to attach specific information to webpack output. The most valuable ones are:

- [path] - Returns the file path.
- [name] - Returns the file name.
- [ext] - Returns the extension. [ext] works for most available fields. Extract-TextPlugin is a notable exception to this rule.
- [hash] - Returns the build hash. If any portion of the build changes, this changes as well.
- [chunkhash] - Returns an entry chunk-specific hash. Each entry defined at the configuration receives a hash of own. If any portion of the entry changes, the hash changes as well. [chunkhash] is more granular than [hash] by definition.
- [contenthash] - Returns a hash specific to content. [contenthash] is available for ExtractTextPlugin only and is the most specific option available.

It's preferable to use particularly hash and chunkhash only for production purposes as hashing doesn't do much good during development.

 It's possible to slice hash and chunkhash using specific syntax: [chunkhash:8]. Instead of a hash like 8c4cbfdb91ff93f3f3c5 this would yield 8c4cbfdb.

There are more options available, and you can even modify the hashing
and digest type as discussed at loader-utils[1] documentation.

Example Placeholders

Assuming you have the following configuration:

```
{
  output: {
    path: PATHS.build,
    filename: '[name].[chunkhash].js',
  },
},
```

Webpack would generate filenames like these:

```
app.d587bbd6e38337f5accd.js
vendor.dc746a5db4ed650296e1.js
```

If the file contents related to a chunk are different, the hash changes as well, thus
invalidating the cache. More accurately, the browser sends a new request for the
new file. If only app bundle gets updated, only that file needs to be requested again.

The same result can be achieved by generating static filenames and invalidating the
cache through a querystring (i.e., app.js?d587bbd6e38337f5accd). The part behind
the question mark invalidates the cache. According to Steve Souders[2], attaching the
hash to the filename is the more performant.

---

[1] https://www.npmjs.com/package/loader-utils#interpolatename
[2] http://www.stevesouders.com/blog/2008/08/23/revving-filenames-dont-use-querystring/

21.2 Setting Up Hashing

The build needs tweaking to generate proper hashes. Images and fonts should receive hash while chunks should use chunkhash in their names to invalidate them correctly:

webpack.config.js

```
const commonConfig = {
  ...
  parts.loadFonts({
    options: {
      name: '[name].[ext]',
      name: '[name].[hash:8].[ext]',
    },
  }),
  ...
};

const productionConfig = merge([
  {
    ...
    output: {
      chunkFilename: '[name].[chunkhash:8].js',
      filename: '[name].[chunkhash:8].js',
    },
  },
  ...
  parts.loadImages({
    options: {
      limit: 15000,
      name: '[name].[ext]',
      name: '[name].[hash:8].[ext]',
    },
  }),
  ...
]);
```

If you used chunkhash for the extracted CSS as well, this would lead to problems as the code points to the CSS through JavaScript bringing it to the same entry. That means if the application code or CSS changed, it would invalidate both. Therefore, instead of chunkhash, you can use contenthash that's generated based on the extracted content:

webpack.parts.js

```
exports.extractCSS = ({ include, exclude, use }) => {
  // Output extracted CSS to a file
  const plugin = new ExtractTextPlugin({
    filename: '[name].css',
    filename: '[name].[contenthash:8].css',
  });

  ...
};
```

 The hashes have been sliced to make the output fit better in the book. In practice, you can skip slicing them.

If you generate a build now (npm run build), you should see something:

```
Hash: 16b92fddd41e579e77ba
Version: webpack 2.2.1
Time: 4258ms
                   Asset       Size  Chunks             Chunk Names
         app.e0f59512.js  811 bytes       1  [emitted]  app
     ...font.674f50d2.eot     166 kB          [emitted]
   ...font.af7ae505.woff2    77.2 kB          [emitted]
    ...font.fee66e71.woff      98 kB          [emitted]
    ...font.912ec66d.svg      444 kB          [emitted]
       logo.85011118.png       77 kB          [emitted]
        0.470796d5.js     408 bytes       0  [emitted]
     ...font.b06871f2.ttf     166 kB          [emitted]
       vendor.f897ca59.js    24.4 kB       2  [emitted]  vendor
        app.bf4d156d.css    2.54 kB       1  [emitted]  app
      0.470796d5.js.map    2.08 kB       0  [emitted]
    app.e0f59512.js.map    2.33 kB       1  [emitted]  app
   app.bf4d156d.css.map   93 bytes       1  [emitted]  app
 vendor.f897ca59.js.map     135 kB       2  [emitted]  vendor
             index.html  301 bytes          [emitted]
  [4] ./~/object-assign/index.js 2.11 kB {2} [built]
 [14] ./app/component.js 461 bytes {1} [built]
 [15] ./app/shake.js 138 bytes {1} [built]
...
```

The files have neat hashes now. To prove that it works for styling, you could try altering *app/main.css* and see what happens to the hashes when you rebuild.

There's one problem, though. If you change the application code, it invalidates the vendor file as well! Solving this requires extracting a **manifest**, but before that, you can improve the way the production build handles module IDs.

21.3 Enabling `HashedModuleIdsPlugin`

Webpack uses number based IDs for the module code it generates. The problem is that they are difficult to work with and can lead to difficult to debug issues, particularly with hashing. This is why webpack provides two plugins. `NamedModulesPlugin` replaces module IDs with paths to the modules making it ideal for development. `HashedModuleIdsPlugin` does the same except it hashes the result and hides the path information.

The process keeps module IDs stable as they aren't derived based on order. You sacrifice a couple of bytes for a cleaner setup, but the trade-off is well worth it.

Tweak the configuration as follows:

webpack.config.js

```
const webpack = require('webpack');
...

const productionConfig = merge([
  {
    ...
    plugins: [
      new webpack.HashedModuleIdsPlugin(),
    ],
  },
  ...
]);
```

As you can see in the build output, the difference is negligible:

```
Hash: 11891d736f3749fb9f8f
Version: webpack 2.2.1
Time: 4115ms
                   Asset     Size  Chunks           Chunk Names
        app.4330d101.js  863 bytes      1  [emitted]  app
   ...font.912ec66d.svg   444 kB          [emitted]
   ...font.674f50d2.eot   166 kB          [emitted]
   ...font.fee66e71.woff   98 kB          [emitted]
   ...font.af7ae505.woff2  77.2 kB        [emitted]
        logo.85011118.png   77 kB        [emitted]
           0.b2a1fec0.js  430 bytes      0  [emitted]
   ...font.b06871f2.ttf   166 kB          [emitted]
       vendor.3c78d233.js  24.8 kB       2  [emitted]  vendor
          app.bf4d156d.css  2.54 kB      1  [emitted]  app
        0.b2a1fec0.js.map  2.08 kB      0  [emitted]
     app.4330d101.js.map   2.34 kB      1  [emitted]  app
    app.bf4d156d.css.map  93 bytes      1  [emitted]  app
   vendor.3c78d233.js.map  135 kB       2  [emitted]  vendor
              index.html  301 bytes        [emitted]
[1Q41] ./app/main.css 41 bytes {1} [built]
[2twT] ./app/index.js 557 bytes {1} [built]
[5W1q] ./~/font-awesome/css/font-awesome.css 41 bytes {1} [built]
...
```

Note how the output has changed, though. Instead of numbers, you can see hashes. But this is expected given the change you made.

 NamedChunksPlugin achieves a similar result for split points. See Predictable long term caching with Webpack[3] by Tim Sebastian for further details.

---

[3]https://medium.com/webpack/predictable-long-term-caching-with-webpack-d3eee1d3fa31

The *Hot Module Replacement* appendix shows how to set up
NamedModulesPlugin as it can be used for debugging HMR.

21.4 Conclusion

Including hashes related to the file contents to their names allows to invalidate them
on the client side. If a hash has changed, the client is forced to download the asset
again.

To recap:

- Webpack's **placeholders** allow you to shape filenames and enable you to
  include hashes to them.
- The most valuable placeholders are [name], [chunkhash], and [ext]. A chunk
  hash is derived based on the entry in which the asset belongs.
- If you are using ExtractTextPlugin, you should use [contenthash]. This way
  the generated assets get invalidated only if their content changes.
- HashedModuleIdsPlugin generates module IDs based on module paths. This is
  more stable than relying on the default order based numeric module IDs.

Even though the project generates hashes now, the output isn't flawless. The problem
is that if the application changes, it invalidates the vendor bundle as well. The next
chapter digs deeper into the topic and shows you how to extract a **manifest** to resolve
the issue.

22. Separating a Manifest

When webpack writes bundles, it maintains a **manifest** as well. You can find it in the generated *vendor* bundle in this project. The manifest describes what files webpack should load. It's possible to extract it and start loading the files of the project faster instead of having to wait for the *vendor* bundle to be loaded.

If the hashes webpack generates change, then the manifest changes as well. As a result, the contents of the vendor bundle change, and become invalidated. The problem can be eliminated by extracting the manifest to a file of its own or by writing it inline to the *index.html* of the project.

 To understand how a manifest is generated in detail, read the technical explanation at Stack Overflow[1].

---

[1]https://stackoverflow.com/questions/39548175/can-someone-explain-webpacks-commonschunkplugin/39600793

22.1 Extracting a Manifest

Most of the work was done already when `extractBundles` was set up in the *Bundle Splitting* chapter. To extract the manifest, a single change is required to capture the remaining code which contains webpack bootstrap:

webpack.config.js

```
const productionConfig = merge([
  ...
  parts.extractBundles([
      {
        ...
      },
      {
        name: 'manifest',
        minChunks: Infinity,
      },
  ]),
  ...
]);
```

The name `manifest` is used by convention. You can use any other name and it will still work. It's important that the definition is after others, though, as it has to capture what has not been extracted yet. `minChunks` is optional in this case and passing `Infinity` tells webpack **not** to move any modules to the resulting bundle.

If you build the project now (npm run build), you should see something:

```
Hash: 73f8c0d53361c3a81ea6
Version: webpack 2.2.1
Time: 4071ms
                    Asset       Size  Chunks             Chunk Names
         app.801b7672.js  865 bytes     2, 3  [emitted]  app
    ...font.912ec66d.svg     444 kB            [emitted]
    ...font.674f50d2.eot     166 kB            [emitted]
    ...font.fee66e71.woff     98 kB            [emitted]
   ...font.af7ae505.woff2   77.2 kB            [emitted]
        logo.85011118.png      77 kB            [emitted]
           0.e7c9bce9.js  432 bytes     0, 3  [emitted]
      vendor.c4ac6d53.js    23.4 kB     1, 3  [emitted]  vendor
     ...font.b06871f2.ttf     166 kB            [emitted]
     manifest.95266dc7.js    1.51 kB        3  [emitted]  manifest
         app.bf4d156d.css    2.54 kB     2, 3  [emitted]  app
       0.e7c9bce9.js.map    2.08 kB     0, 3  [emitted]
    vendor.c4ac6d53.js.map     129 kB     1, 3  [emitted]  vendor
     app.801b7672.js.map    2.34 kB     2, 3  [emitted]  app
     app.bf4d156d.css.map   93 bytes     2, 3  [emitted]  app
 manifest.95266dc7.js.map    5.77 kB        3  [emitted]  manifest
              index.html  368 bytes            [emitted]
[1Q41] ./app/main.css 41 bytes {2} [built]
[2twT] ./app/index.js 557 bytes {2} [built]
[5W1q] ./~/font-awesome/css/font-awesome.css 41 bytes {2} [built]
...
```

This change gave a separate file that contains the manifest. In the output above it has been marked with manifest chunk name. Because the setup is using HtmlWebpack-Plugin, there is no need to worry about loading the manifest ourselves as the plugin adds a reference to *index.html*.

Plugins, such as inline-manifest-webpack-plugin[2] and html-webpack-inline-chunk-

---

[2]https://www.npmjs.com/package/inline-manifest-webpack-plugin

plugin[3], assets-webpack-plugin[4], work with `HtmlWebpackPlugin` and allow you to write the manifest within *index.html* to avoid a request.

 To get a better idea of the manifest contents, comment out `parts.minify()` and examine the resulting manifest. You should see something familiar there.

Try adjusting *app/index.js* and see how the hashes change. This time around it should **not** invalidate the vendor bundle, and only the manifest and app bundle names should become different.

 To integrate with asset pipelines, you can consider using plugins like chunk-manifest-webpack-plugin[5], webpack-manifest-plugin[6], webpack-assets-manifest[7], or webpack-rails-manifest-plugin[8]. These solutions emit JSON that maps the original asset path to the new one.

 The build can be improved further by loading popular dependencies, such as React, through a CDN. That would decrease the size of the vendor bundle even further while adding an external dependency on the project. The idea is that if the user has hit the CDN earlier, caching can kick in like here.

---

[3] https://www.npmjs.com/package/html-webpack-inline-chunk-plugin

[4] https://www.npmjs.com/package/assets-webpack-plugin

[5] https://www.npmjs.com/package/chunk-manifest-webpack-plugin

[6] https://www.npmjs.com/package/webpack-manifest-plugin

[7] https://www.npmjs.com/package/webpack-assets-manifest

[8] https://www.npmjs.com/package/webpack-rails-manifest-plugin

22.2 Using Records

As mentioned in the *Bundle Splitting* chapter, plugins such as `AggressiveSplit-tingPlugin` use **records** to implement caching. The approaches discussed above are still valid, but records go one step further.

Records are used for storing module IDs across separate builds. The problem is that you need to store this file. If you build locally, one option is to include it to your version control.

To generate a *records.json* file, adjust the configuration as follows:

webpack.config.js

```
const productionConfig = merge([
  {
    ...
    recordsPath: path.join(__dirname, 'records.json'),
  },
  ...
]);
```

If you build the project (`npm run build`), you should see a new file, *records.json*, at the project root. The next time webpack builds, it picks up the information and rewrites the file if it has changed.

Records are particularly valuable if you have a complicated setup with code splitting and want to make sure the split parts gain correct caching behavior. The biggest problem is maintaining the record file.

 `recordsInputPath` and `recordsOutputPath` give more granular control over input and output, but often setting only `recordsPath` is enough.

 If you change the way webpack handles module IDs (i.e., remove `HashedModuleIdsPlugin`), possible existing records are still taken into account! If you want to use the new module ID scheme, you have to remove your records file as well.

22.3 Conclusion

The project has basic caching behavior now. If you try to modify *app.js* or *component.js*, the vendor bundle should remain the same.

To recap:

- Webpack maintains a **manifest** containing information needed to run the application.
- If the manifest changes, the change invalidates the containing bundle.
- To overcome this problem, the manifest can be extracted to a bundle of its own using the CommonsChunkPlugin.
- Certain plugins allow you to write the manifest to the generated *index.html*. It's also possible to extract the information to a JSON file. The JSON comes in handy with *Server Side Rendering*.
- **Records** allow you to store module IDs across builds. As a downside you have to track the records file.

You'll learn to analyze the build statistics in the next chapter. This analysis is essential for figuring out how to improve the build result.

23. Analyzing Build Statistics

Analyzing build statistics is a good step towards understanding webpack better. Visualizing them helps you to understand the composition of your bundles.

23.1 Configuring Webpack

To get suitable output, you need to do a couple of tweaks to the configuration. Most importantly, you have to enable two flags:

- `--profile` to capture timing-related information. This is optional, but good to set.
- `--json` to make webpack output statistics.

Here's the line of code you need to pipe the output to a file:

package.json

```
"scripts": {
  "stats": "webpack --env production --profile --json > stats.json",
  ...
},
```

The above is the basic setup you need, regardless of your webpack configuration. Execute `npm run stats` now. After a while you should find *stats.json* at your project root. This file can be pushed through a variety of tools to understand better what's going on.

 Given you piggyback on the production target in the current setup, this process cleans the build directory! If you want to avoid that, set up a separate target where you don't clean.

Node API

Stats can be captured through Node. Since stats can contain errors, so it's a good idea to handle that case separately:

```
const webpack = require('webpack');
const config = require('./webpack.config.js')('production');

webpack(config, (err, stats) => {
  if (err) {
    return console.error(err);
  }

  if (stats.hasErrors()) {
    return console.error(stats.toString('errors-only'));
  }

  console.log(stats);
});
```

This technique can be valuable if you want to do further processing on stats although often the other solutions are enough.

StatsWebpackPlugin and WebpackStatsPlugin

If you want to manage stats through a plugin, check out stats-webpack-plugin[1]. It gives you a bit more control over the output. You can use it to exclude certain dependencies from the output.

webpack-stats-plugin[2] is another option. It allows you to transform the data before outputting it.

---

[1]https://www.npmjs.com/package/stats-webpack-plugin
[2]https://www.npmjs.com/package/webpack-stats-plugin

23.2 Available Analysis Tools

Even though having a look at the file itself gives you idea of what's going on, often it's preferable to use a particular tool for that. Consider the following.

The Official Analyse Tool

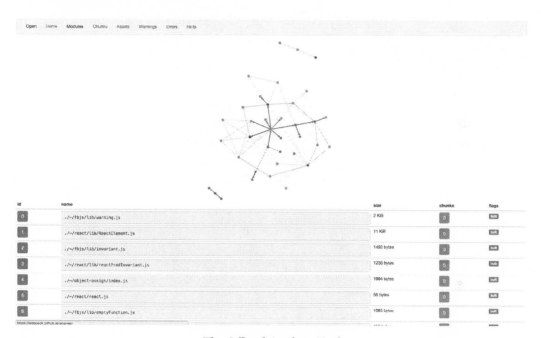

The Official Analyse Tool

The official analyse tool[3] gives you recommendations and a good idea of your application's dependency graph. It can be run locally as well.

---

[3]https://github.com/webpack/analyse

Webpack Visualizer

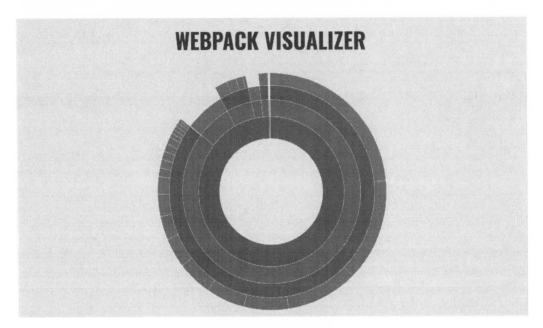

Webpack Visualizer

Webpack Visualizer[4] provides a pie chart showing your bundle composition allowing to understand which dependencies contribute to the size of the overall result.

DuplicatePackageCheckerPlugin

duplicate-package-checker-webpack-plugin[5] warns you if it finds single package multiple times in your build. This situation can be hard to spot otherwise.

---

[4]https://chrisbateman.github.io/webpack-visualizer/

[5]https://www.npmjs.com/package/duplicate-package-checker-webpack-plugin

Webpack Chart

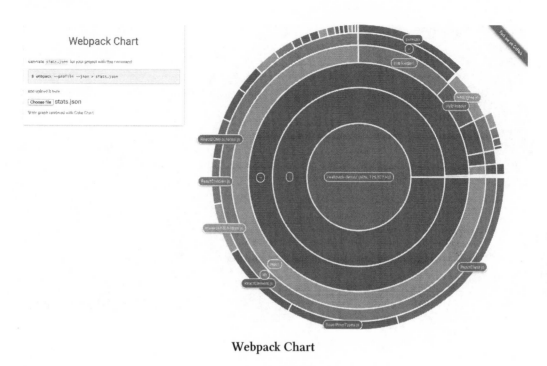

Webpack Chart

Webpack Chart[6] is another similar visualization.

webpack-unused

webpack-unused[7] prints out unused files and can be used to understand which assets are no longer used and can be removed from the project.

---

[6]https://alexkuz.github.io/webpack-chart/

[7]https://www.npmjs.com/package/webpack-unused

Stellar Webpack

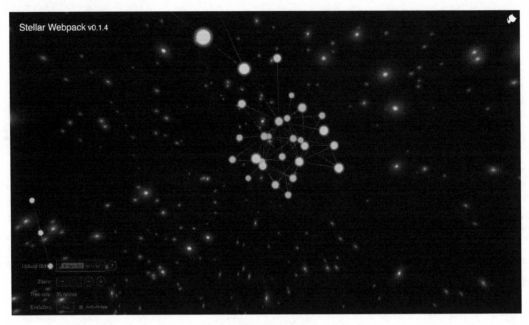

Stellar Webpack

Stellar Webpack[8] gives a universe based visualization and allows you to examine your application in a 3D form.

webpack-bundle-tracker

webpack-bundle-tracker[9] can capture data while webpack is compiling. It uses JSON for this purpose.

---

[8] https://alexkuz.github.io/stellar-webpack/
[9] https://www.npmjs.com/package/webpack-bundle-tracker

webpack-bundle-analyzer

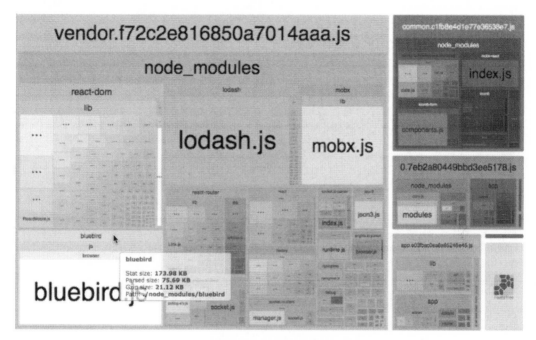

webpack-bundle-analyzer

webpack-bundle-analyzer[10] provides a zoomable treemap.

---

[10]https://www.npmjs.com/package/webpack-bundle-analyzer

webpack-bundle-size-analyzer

webpack-bundle-size-analyzer[11] gives a text based composition.

```
$ webpack-bundle-size-analyzer stats.json
react: 93.99 KB (74.9%)
purecss: 15.56 KB (12.4%)
style-loader: 6.99 KB (5.57%)
fbjs: 5.02 KB (4.00%)
object-assign: 1.95 KB (1.55%)
css-loader: 1.47 KB (1.17%)
<self>: 572 B (0.445%)
```

inspectpack

inspectpack[12] can be used for figuring out specific places of code to improve.

```
$ inspectpack --action=duplicates --bundle=bundle.js
## Summary

* Bundle:
    * Path:                /PATH/TO/bundle.js
    * Bytes (min):         1678533
* Missed Duplicates:
    * Num Unique Files:    116
    * Num Extra Files:     131
    * Extra Bytes (min):   253955
    * Pct of Bundle Size:  15 %
```

---

[11] https://www.npmjs.com/package/webpack-bundle-size-analyzer
[12] https://www.npmjs.com/package/inspectpack

23.3 Independent Tools

In addition to tools that work with webpack output, there are a couple that are webpack agnostic and worth a mention.

source-map-explorer

source-map-explorer[13] is a tool independent from webpack. It allows you to get insight into your build by using source maps. It gives a treemap based visualization showing what code contributes to the result.

madge

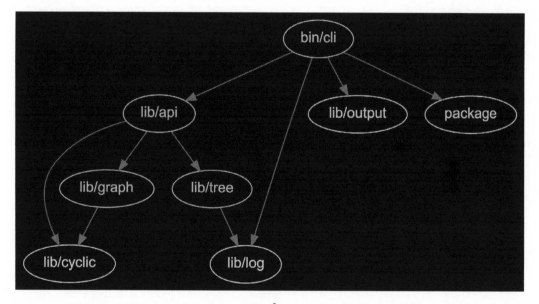

madge

madge[14] is another independent tool that can output a graph based on module input. The graph output allows you to understand the dependencies of your project in greater detail.

---

[13]https://www.npmjs.com/package/source-map-explorer

[14]https://www.npmjs.com/package/madge

23.4 Conclusion

When you are optimizing the size of your bundle output, these tools are invaluable. The official tool has the most functionality, but even a basic visualization can reveal problem spots. You can use the same technique with old projects to understand their composition.

To recap:

- Webpack allows you to extract a JSON file containing information about the build. The information can include the build composition and timing.
- The generated information can be analyzed using various tools that give insight into aspects such as the bundle composition.
- Understanding the bundles is the key to insights on how to optimize the overall size, what to load and when. It can also reveal bigger issues, such as redundant data.
- You can find third party tools that don't depend on webpack but are still valuable for analysis.

You'll learn to tune webpack performance in the next chapter.

24. Performance

Webpack's performance out of the box is often enough for small projects. That said, it begins to hit limits as your project grows in scale. It's a common topic in webpack's issue tracker. Issue 1905[1] is a good example.

There are a couple of ground rules when it comes to optimization:

1. Know what to optimize.
2. Perform fast to implement tweaks first.
3. Perform more involved tweaks after.
4. Measure impact.

Sometimes optimizations come with a cost. They can make your configuration harder to understand or tie it to a particular solution. Often the best optimization is to do less work or do it in a smarter way. The basic directions are covered in the next sections, so you know where to look when it's time to work on performance.

---

[1]https://github.com/webpack/webpack/issues/1905

24.1 High-Level Optimizations

Webpack uses only a single instance by default meaning you aren't able to benefit from a multi-core processor without extra effort. This where third party solutions, such as parallel-webpack[2] and HappyPack[3] come in.

parallel-webpack - Run Multiple Webpack's in Parallel

parallel-webpack allows you to parallelize webpack configuration in two ways. Assuming you have defined your webpack configuration as an array, it can run the configurations in parallel. In addition to this, *parallel-webpack* can generate builds based on given **variants**.

Using variants allows you to generate both production and development builds at once. Variants also allow you to generate bundles with different targets to make them easier to consume depending on the environment. Variants can be used to implement feature flags when combined with DefinePlugin as discussed in the *Environment Variables* chapter.

The underlying idea can be implemented using a worker-farm[4]. In fact, *parallel-webpack* relies on *worker-farm* underneath.

parallel-webpack can be used by installing it to your project as a development dependency and then replacing webpack command with parallel-webpack.

---

[2]https://www.npmjs.com/package/parallel-webpack
[3]https://www.npmjs.com/package/happypack
[4]https://www.npmjs.com/package/worker-farm

HappyPack - File Level Parallelism

Compared to *parallel-webpack*, HappyPack is a more involved option. The idea is that HappyPack intercepts the loader calls you specify and then runs them in parallel. You have to set up the plugin first:

webpack.config.js

```
...
const HappyPack = require('happypack');


...

const commonConfig = merge([{
  {
    plugins: [
      new HappyPack({
        loaders: [
          // Capture Babel loader
          'babel-loader'
        ],
      }),
    ],
  },
}]);
```

To complete the connection, you have to replace the original Babel loader definition with a HappyPack one:

```
exports.loadJavaScript = ({ include, exclude }) => ({
  module: {
    rules: [
      {
        ...
        loader: 'babel-loader',
        loader: 'happypack/loader',
        ...
      },
    ],
  },
});
```

The example above contains enough information for webpack to run the given loader parallel. HappyPack comes with more advanced options, but applying this idea is enough to get started.

Perhaps the problem with HappyPack is that it couples your configuration with it. It would be possible to overcome this issue by design and make it easier to inject. One option would be to build a higher level abstraction that can perform the replacement on top of vanilla configuration.

24.2 Low-Level Optimizations

Certain lower-level optimizations can be good to know. The key is to allow webpack to perform less work. You have already implemented a couple of these, but it's a good idea to enumerate them:

- Consider using faster source map variants during development or skip them. Skipping is possible if you don't process the code in any way.

- Use babel-preset-env[5] during development instead of source maps to transpile fewer features for modern browsers and make the code more readable and easier to debug.
- Skip polyfills during development. Attaching a package, such as babel-polyfill[6], to the development version of an application adds to the overhead.
- Disable the portions of the application you don't need during development. It can be a valid idea to compile only a small portion you are working on as then you have less to bundle.
- Push bundles that change less to **Dynamically Loaded Libraries** (DLL) to avoid unnecessary processing. It's one more thing to worry about, but can lead to speed increases as there is less to bundle. The official webpack example[7] gets to the point while Rob Knight's blog post[8] explains the idea further.

Loader and Plugin Specific Optimizations

There are a series of loader and plugin specific optimizations to consider:

- Perform less processing by skipping loaders during development. Especially if you are using a modern browser, you can skip using *babel-loader* or equivalent altogether.
- Use either `include` or `exclude` with JavaScript specific loaders. Webpack traverses *node_modules* by default and executes *babel-loader* over the files unless it has been configured correctly.
- Utilize caching through plugins like hard-source-webpack-plugin[9] to avoid unnecessary work. The caching idea applies to loaders as well. For example, you can enable cache on *babel-loader*.
- Use equivalent, but lighter alternatives, of plugins and loaders during development. Replacing `HtmlWebpackPlugin` with a HtmlPlugin[10] that does far less is one direction.

---

[5]https://www.npmjs.com/package/babel-preset-env

[6]https://www.npmjs.com/package/babel-polyfill

[7]https://github.com/webpack/webpack/tree/master/examples/dll-user

[8]https://robertknight.github.io/posts/webpack-dll-plugins/

[9]https://www.npmjs.com/package/hard-source-webpack-plugin

[10]https://gist.github.com/bebraw/5bd5ebbb2a06936e052886f5eb1e6874

- Consider using parallel variants of plugins if they are available. webpack-uglify-parallel[11] is one example.

24.3 Optimizing Rebundling Speed During Development

It's possible to optimize rebundling times during development by pointing the development setup to a minified version of a library, such as React. In React's case, you lose propType-based validation. But if speed is more important, this technique is worth a go.

module.noParse accepts a RegExp or an array of RegExps. In addition to telling webpack not to parse the minified file you want to use, you also have to point react to it by using resolve.alias. The aliasing idea is discussed in detail in the *Package Consuming Techniques* chapter.

It's possible to encapsulate the core idea within a function:

```
exports.dontParse = ({ name, path }) => {
  const alias = {};
  alias[name] = path;

  return {
    module: {
      noParse: [
        new RegExp(path),
      ],
    },
    resolve: {
      alias,
    },
  };
};
```

---

[11]https://www.npmjs.com/package/webpack-uglify-parallel

To use the function, you would call it as follows:

```
dontParse({
  name: 'react',
  path: path.resolve(
    __dirname, 'node_modules/react/dist/react.min.js',
  ),
}),
```

After this change, the application should be faster to rebuild depending on the underlying implementation. The technique can also be applied during production.

Given `module.noParse` accepts a regular expression if you wanted to ignore all `*.min.js` files, you could set it to `/\.min\.js/`.

 Not all modules support `module.noParse`. They should not have a reference to `require`, `define`, or similar, as that leads to an `Uncaught ReferenceError: require is not defined` error.

24.4 Conclusion

You can optimize webpack's performance in multiple ways. Often it's a good idea to start with easier techniques before moving to more involved ones. The exact methods you have to use, depend on the project.

To recap:

- Start with higher level techniques that are fast to implement first.
- Lower level techniques are more involved but come with their wins.
- Since webpack runs using a single instance by default, parallelizing is worthwhile.
- Especially during development, skipping work can be acceptable thanks to modern browsers.

VI Output

This part covers different output formats webpack provides. You also see how to manage a multi-page setup and how to handle server side rendering.

25. Build Targets

Even though webpack is used most commonly for bundling web applications, it can do more. You can use it to target Node or desktop environments, such as Electron. Webpack can also bundle as a library while writing an appropriate output wrapper making it possible to consume the library.

Webpack's output target is controlled by the target field. You'll learn about the main targets next and dig into library specific options after that.

25.1 Web Targets

Webpack uses the *web* target by default. This is ideal for a web application like the one you have developed in this book. Webpack bootstraps the application and load its modules. The initial list of modules to load is maintained in a manifest, and then the modules can load each other as defined.

Web Workers

The *webworker* target wraps your application as a web worker[1]. Using web workers is valuable if you want to execute computation outside of the main thread of the application without slowing down the user interface. There are a couple of limitations you should be aware of:

- You cannot use webpack's hashing features when the *webworker* target is used.
- You cannot manipulate the DOM from a web worker. If you wrapped the book project as a worker, it would not display anything.

 Web workers and their usage are discussed in detail in the *Web Workers* chapter.

---

[1]https://developer.mozilla.org/en-US/docs/Web/API/Web_Workers_API

25.2 Node Targets

Webpack provides two Node-specific targets: node and async-node. It uses standard Node require to load chunks unless async mode is used. In that case, it wraps modules so that they are loaded asynchronously through Node fs and vm modules.

The main use case for using the Node target is *Server Side Rendering* (SSR). The idea is discussed in the *Server Side Rendering* chapter.

25.3 Desktop Targets

There are desktop shells, such as NW.js[2] (previously *node-webkit*) and Electron[3] (previously *Atom*). Webpack can target these as follows:

- node-webkit - Targets NW.js while considered experimental.
- atom, electron, electron-main - Targets Electron main process[4].
- electron-renderer - Targets Electron renderer process.

electron-react-boilerplate[5] is a good starting point if you want hot loading webpack setup for Electron and React based development. electron-compile[6] skips webpack entirely and can be a lighter alternative for compiling JavaScript and CSS for Electron. Using the official quick start for Electron[7] is one way.

---

[2] https://nwjs.io/

[3] http://electron.atom.io/

[4] https://github.com/electron/electron/blob/master/docs/tutorial/quick-start.md

[5] https://github.com/chentsulin/electron-react-boilerplate

[6] https://github.com/electron/electron-compile

[7] https://github.com/electron/electron-quick-start

25.4 Conclusion

Webpack supports targets beyond the web. Based on this you can say name "webpack" is an understatement considering its capabilities.

To recap:

- Webpack's output target can be controlled through the `target` field. It defaults to `web`, but accepts other options too.
- Webpack can target the desktop, Node, and web workers in addition to its web target.
- The Node targets come in handy if especially in Server Side Rendering setups.

You'll learn how to bundle libraries in the next chapter.

26. Bundling Libraries

To understand webpack's library targets better, you could set up a small library to bundle. The idea is to end up with a non-minified, a minified version, and a version compatible with *package.json* `module` field. The first two can be used for standalone consumption. You can also point to the non-minified version through *package.json* `main`.

26.1 Setting Up a Library

To have something to build, set up a module as follows:

lib/index.js

```
const add = (a, b) => a + b;

export {
  add,
};
```

The idea is that this file becomes the entry point for the entire library and represents the API exposed to the consumers. If you want to support both CommonJS and ES6, it can be a good idea to use the CommonJS module definition here. If you go with ES6 `export default`, using such an export in a CommonJS environment often requires extra effort.

26.2 Setting Up an npm Script

Given the `build` target of the project has been taken already by the main application, you should set up a separate one for generating the library. It points to a library specific configuration file to keep things nice and tidy.

package.json

```
"scripts": {
  "build:lib": "webpack --config webpack.lib.js",
  ...
},
```

26.3 Setting Up Webpack

Webpack configuration itself can be adapted from the one you built. This time, however, you have to generate two files - a non-minified version and a minified one. This can be achieved by running webpack in so called *multi-compiler mode*. It means you can expose an array of configurations for webpack and it executes each.

webpack.lib.js

```
const path = require('path');
const merge = require('webpack-merge');

const parts = require('./webpack.parts');

const PATHS = {
  lib: path.join(__dirname, 'lib'),
  build: path.join(__dirname, 'dist'),
};

const commonConfig = merge([
  {
    entry: {
```

```
      lib: PATHS.lib,
    },
    output: {
      path: PATHS.build,
      library: 'Demo',
      libraryTarget: 'var', // Default
    },
  },
  parts.attachRevision(),
  parts.generateSourceMaps({ type: 'source-map' }),
  parts.loadJavaScript({ include: PATHS.lib }),
]);

const libraryConfig = merge([
  commonConfig,
  {
    output: {
      filename: '[name].js',
    },
  },
]);

const libraryMinConfig = merge([
  commonConfig,
  {
    output: {
      filename: '[name].min.js',
    },
  },
  parts.minifyJavaScript(),
]);

module.exports = [
  libraryConfig,
  libraryMinConfig,
```

```
];
```

If you execute npm run build:lib now, you should see output:

```
Hash: 760c4d25403432782e1079cf0c3f76bbd168a80c
Version: webpack 2.2.1
Child
    Hash: 760c4d25403432782e10
    Time: 302ms
        Asset      Size   Chunks                  Chunk Names
       lib.js   2.96 kB        0  [emitted]  lib
   lib.js.map   2.85 kB        0  [emitted]  lib
      [0] ./lib/index.js 55 bytes {0} [built]
Child
    Hash: 79cf0c3f76bbd168a80c
    Time: 291ms
            Asset       Size   Chunks                 Chunk Names
       lib.min.js   695 bytes        0  [emitted]  lib
   lib.min.js.map    6.72 kB        0  [emitted]  lib
      [0] ./lib/index.js 55 bytes {0} [built]
```

Webpack ran twice in this case. It can be argued that it would be smarter to minify
the initial result separately. In this case, the overhead is so small that it's not worth
the extra setup.

Examining the build output reveals more:

dist/lib.js

```
/*! 33c69fc */
var Demo =
/******/ (function(modules) { // webpackBootstrap
...
/******/ })
/************************************************************\
*****/
/******/ ([
/* 0 */
/***/ (function(module, __webpack_exports__, __webpack_require__) {

"use strict";
Object.defineProperty(__webpack_exports__, "__esModule", { value: tr\
ue });
/* harmony export (binding) */ __webpack_require__.d(__webpack_expor\
ts__, "add", function() { return add; });
var add = function add(a, b) {
  return a + b;
};


/***/ })
/******/ ]);
//# sourceMappingURL=lib.js.map
```

You can see familiar code there and more. Webpack's bootstrap script is in place, and it starts the entire execution process. It takes the majority of space for a small library, but that's not a problem as the library begins to grow.

 Instead of using the multi-compiler mode, it would be possible to define two targets. One of them would generate the non-minified version while the other would generate the minified one. The other npm script could be called as build:lib:dist and you could define a build:lib:all script to build both.

26.4 Cleaning and Linting Before Building

It's a good idea to clean the build directory and lint the code before building the library. You could expand webpack configuration:

```
...

const libraryConfig = merge([
  commonConfig,
  {
    output: {
      filename: '[name].js',
    },
  },
  parts.clean(PATHS.build),
  parts.lintJavaScript({ include: PATHS.lib }),
]);

...
```

`parts.clean` and `parts.lintJavaScript` were included to `libraryConfig` on purpose as it makes sense to run them only once at the beginning of the execution. This solution would be problematic with *parallel-webpack* though as it can run configurations out of order.

 There's a proposal to improve the situation[1] by introducing the concepts of pre- and post-processing to webpack.

---

[1]https://github.com/webpack/webpack/issues/4271

26.5 Cleaning and Linting Through npm

Another, and in this case a more fitting, way would be to handle the problem through an npm script. As discussing in the *Package Authoring Techniques* chapter, npm provides pre- and post-script hooks. To keep this solution cross-platform, install rimraf[2] first:

```
npm install rimraf --save-dev
```

Then, to remove the build directory and lint the source before building, adjust as follows:

package.json

```
"scripts": {
  "prebuild:lib": "npm run lint:js && rimraf dist",
  ...
},
```

If either process fails, npm doesn't proceed to the lib script. You can verify this by breaking a linting rule and seeing what happens when you build (npm run build:lib). Instead, it gives you an error.

 To get cleaner error output, run either npm run build:lib --silent or npm run build:lib -s.

 The same idea can be used for post-processes, such as deployment. For example, you could set up a postpublish script to deploy the library site after you have published it to npm.

---

[2]https://www.npmjs.com/package/rimraf

26.6 Conclusion

Webpack can be used for bundling libraries. You can use it to generate multiple different output files based on your exact needs.

To recap:

- If you bundle libraries with webpack, you should set the output options carefully to get the result you want.
- Webpack can generate both a non-minified and a minified version of a library through its **multi-compiler** mode. It's possible to minify also as a post-process using an external tool.
- Performing tasks, such as cleaning and linting JavaScript, while using the multi-compiler mode is problematic at the moment. Instead, it can be a good idea to handle these tasks outside of webpack or run multiple webpack instances separately.

If you try to import *./dist/lib.js* through Node, you notice it emits { }. The problem has to do with the output type that was chosen. To understand better which output to use and why, the next chapter covers them in detail.

 The *Package Authoring Techniques* chapter discusses npm specific techniques in detail.

27. Library Output

The example of the previous chapter can be expanded further to study webpack's library output options in detail.

The library target is controlled through the `output.libraryTarget` field. `output.library` comes into play as well and individual targets have additional fields related to them.

27.1 var

The demonstration project of ours uses `var` by default through configuration:

webpack.lib.js

```
const commonConfig = merge([
  {
    ...
    output: {
      path: PATHS.build,
      library: 'Demo',
      libraryTarget: 'var',
    },
  },
  ...
]);
```

The output configuration maps `library` and `libraryTarget` to the following form:

```
var Demo =
/******/ (function(modules) { // webpackBootstrap
...
/******/ })
...
/******/ ([
  ...
/******/ ]);
//# sourceMappingURL=lib.js.map
```

This tells it generates `var <output.library>` = `<webpack bootstrap>` kind of code and also explains why importing the code from Node does not give access to any functionality.

27.2 `window`, `global`, `assign`, `this`

Most of the available options vary the first line of the output as listed below:

- `window` - `window["Demo"]` =
- `global` - `global["Demo"]` =
- `assign` - `Demo` = - If you executed this code in the right context, it would associate it to a global `Demo`.
- `this` - `this["Demo"]` = - Now the code would associate to context `this` and work through Node.

 You can try running the resulting code through Node REPL (use `node` at project root and use `require('./dist/lib')`).

27.3 CommonJS

The CommonJS specific targets are handy when it comes to Node. There are two options: `commonjs` and `commonjs2`. These refer to different interpretations of the CommonJS specification[1]. Let's explore the difference.

commonjs

If you used the `commonjs` option, you would end up with code that expects global `exports` in which to associate:

```
exports["Demo"] =
...
```

If this code was imported from Node, you would get `{ Demo: { add: [Getter] } }`.

commonjs2

`commonjs2` expects a global `module.exports` instead:

```
module.exports =
...
```

The library name, `Demo`, isn't used anywhere. As a result importing the module yields `{ add: [Getter] }`. You lose the extra wrapping.

27.4 AMD

If you remember RequireJS[2], you recognize the AMD format it uses. In case you can use the `amd` target, you get output:

---

[1]http://wiki.commonjs.org/wiki/CommonJS

[2]http://requirejs.org/

```
define("Demo", [], function() { return /******/ (function(modules) {\
 // webpackBootstrap
 ...
```

In other words, webpack has generated a named AMD module. The result doesn't work from Node as there is no support for the AMD format.

27.5 UMD

Universal Module Definition[3] (UMD) was developed to solve the problem of consuming the same code from different environments. Webpack implements two output variants: umd and umd2. To understand the idea better, let's see what happens when the options are used.

umd

Basic UMD output looks complicated:

```
(function webpackUniversalModuleDefinition(root, factory) {
  if(typeof exports === 'object' && typeof module === 'object')
    module.exports = factory();
  else if(typeof define === 'function' && define.amd)
    define("Demo", [], factory);
  else if(typeof exports === 'object')
    exports["Demo"] = factory();
  else
    root["Demo"] = factory();
})(this, function() {
```

The code performs checks based on the environment and figures out what kind of export to use. The first case covers Node, the second is for AMD, the third one for Node again, while the last one includes a global environment.

The output can be modified further by setting output.umdNamedDefine: false:

---

[3]https://github.com/umdjs/umd

```
(function webpackUniversalModuleDefinition(root, factory) {
  if(typeof exports === 'object' && typeof module === 'object')
    module.exports = factory();
  else if(typeof define === 'function' && define.amd)
    define([], factory);
  else if(typeof exports === 'object')
    exports["Demo"] = factory();
  else
    root["Demo"] = factory();
})(this, function() {
...
```

To understand umd2 option, you have to understand *optional externals* first.

Optional Externals

In webpack terms, externals are dependencies that are resolved outside of webpack and are available through the environment. Optional externals are dependencies that can exist in the environment, but if they don't, they get skipped instead of failing hard.

Consider the following example where jQuery is loaded if it exists:

lib/index.js

```
var optionaljQuery;
try {
  optionaljQuery = require('jquery');
} catch(err) {} // eslint-disable-line no-empty

function add(a, b) {
  return a + b;
}

export {
  add,
};
```

To treat jQuery as an external, you should configure as follows:

```
{
  externals: {
    jquery: 'jQuery',
  },
},
```

If libraryTarget: 'umd' is used after these changes, you get output:

```
(function webpackUniversalModuleDefinition(root, factory) {
  if(typeof exports === 'object' && typeof module === 'object')
    module.exports = factory((
      function webpackLoadOptionalExternalModule() {
        try { return require("jQuery"); } catch(e) {}
      }())
    );
  else if(typeof define === 'function' && define.amd)
    define(["jQuery"], factory);
  else if(typeof exports === 'object')
    exports["Demo"] = factory((
      function webpackLoadOptionalExternalModule() {
        try { return require("jQuery"); } catch(e) {}
      }())
    );
  else
    root["Demo"] = factory(root["jQuery"]);
})(this, function(__WEBPACK_EXTERNAL_MODULE_0__) {
return /******/ (function(modules) { // webpackBootstrap
...
```

Webpack wrapped the optional externals in try/catch blocks.

umd2

To understand what the umd2 option does, consider the following output:

```
/*! fd0ace9 */
(function webpackUniversalModuleDefinition(root, factory) {
  if(typeof exports === 'object' && typeof module === 'object')
    module.exports = factory((
      function webpackLoadOptionalExternalModule() {
        try { return require("jQuery"); } catch(e) {}
      }())
    );
  else if(typeof define === 'function' && define.amd)
    define([], function webpackLoadOptionalExternalModuleAmd() {
      return factory(root["jQuery"]);
    });
  else if(typeof exports === 'object')
    exports["Demo"] = factory((
      function webpackLoadOptionalExternalModule() {
        try { return require("jQuery"); } catch(e) {}
      }())
    );
  else
    root["Demo"] = factory(root["jQuery"]);
})(this, function(__WEBPACK_EXTERNAL_MODULE_0__) {
return /******/ (function(modules) { // webpackBootstrap
```

You can see one important difference: the AMD block contains more code than earlier. The output follows non-standard Knockout.js convention as discussed in the related pull request[4].

In most of the cases using output.libraryTarget: 'umd' is enough as optional dependencies and AMD tend to be a rare configuration especially if you use modern technologies.

---

[4]https://github.com/webpack/webpack/pull/362

27.6 JSONP

There's one more output option: `jsonp`. It generates output as below:

```
Demo(/******/ (function(modules) { // webpackBootstrap
...
```

In short, `output.library` maps to the JSONP function name. The idea is that you could load a file across domains and have it call the named function. Specific APIs implement the pattern although there is no official standard for it.

27.7 SystemJS

SystemJS[5] is an emerging standard. webpack-system-register[6] plugin allows you to wrap your output in a `System.register` call making it compatible with the scheme. If you want to support SystemJS this way, set up another build target.

27.8 Conclusion

Webpack supports a large variety of library output formats. `umd` is the most valuable for a package author. The rest are more specialized and require specific use cases to be valuable.

To recap:

- Most often `umd` is all you need. The other library targets exist more specialized usage in mind.
- The CommonJS variants are handy if you target only Node or consume the output through bundlers alone. UMD implements support for CommonJS, AMD, and globals.
- It's possible to target SystemJS through a plugin. Webpack does not support it out of the box.

You'll learn to manage multi-page setups in the next chapter.

---

[5]https://www.npmjs.com/package/systemjs
[6]https://www.npmjs.com/package/webpack-system-register

28. Multiple Pages

Even though webpack is often used for bundling single page applications, it's possible to use it with multiple separate pages as well. The idea is similar to the way you generated multiple output files in the *Targets* chapter. This time, however, you have to generate separate pages. That's achievable through HtmlWebpackPlugin and a bit of configuration.

28.1 Possible Approaches

When generating multiple pages with webpack, you have a couple of possibilities:

- Go through the *multi-compiler mode* and return an array of configurations. The approach would work as long as the pages are separate and there is a minimal need for sharing code across them. The benefit of this approach is that you can process it through parallel-webpack[1] to improve build performance.
- Set up a single configuration and extract the commonalities. The way you do this can differ depending on how you chunk it up.
- If you follow the idea of Progressive Web Applications[2] (PWA), you can end up with either an **app shell** or a **page shell** and load portions of the application as it's used.

In practice, you have more dimensions. For example, you have to generate i18n variants for pages. These ideas grow on top of the basic approaches.

28.2 Generating Multiple Pages

To generate multiple separate pages, they should be initialized somehow. You should also be able to return a configuration for each page, so webpack picks them up and process them through the multi-compiler mode.

---

[1]https://www.npmjs.com/package/parallel-webpack
[2]https://developers.google.com/web/progressive-web-apps/

Abstracting Pages

To initialize a page, it should receive page title, output path, and an optional template at least. Each page should receive optional output path, and a template for customization. The idea can be modeled as a configuration part:

webpack.parts.js

```
...
const HtmlWebpackPlugin = require('html-webpack-plugin');


...


exports.page = ({
  path = '',
  template = require.resolve(
    'html-webpack-plugin/default_index.ejs'
  ),
  title,
} = {}) => ({
  plugins: [
    new HtmlWebpackPlugin({
      filename: `${path && path + '/'}index.html`,
      template,
      title,
    }),
  ],
});
```

Integrating to Configuration

To incorporate the idea to the configuration, the way it's composed has to change. Also, a page definition is required. To get started, let's reuse the same JavaScript logic for each page for now:

webpack.config.js

```
const webpack = require('webpack');
const path = require('path');
const HtmlWebpackPlugin = require('html-webpack-plugin');
...


const commonConfig = merge([
  {
    ...
    plugins: [
      new HtmlWebpackPlugin({
        title: 'Webpack demo',
      }),
    ],
  },
]);


...


module.exports = (env) => {
  if (env === 'production') {
    return merge(commonConfig, productionConfig);
  }

  return merge(commonConfig, developmentConfig);
  const pages = [
    parts.page({ title: 'Webpack demo' }),
    parts.page({ title: 'Another demo', path: 'another' }),
```

```
  ];
  const config = env === 'production' ?
    productionConfig :
    developmentConfig;

  return pages.map(page => merge(commonConfig, config, page));
};
```

After this change you should have two pages in the application: / and /another. It should be possible to navigate to both while seeing the same output.

Injecting Different Script per Page

The question is, how to inject a different script per each page. In the current configuration, the same entry is shared by both. To solve the problem, you should move entry configuration to lower level and manage it per page. To have a script to test with, set up another entry point:

app/another.js

```
import './main.css';
import component from './component';

let demoComponent = component('Another');

document.body.appendChild(demoComponent);
```

The file could go to a directory of its own. Here the existing code is reused to get something to show up. Webpack configuration has to point to this file:

webpack.config.js

```
const commonConfig = merge([
  {
    entry: {
      app: PATHS.app,
    },
    ...
  },
  ...
]);


...


module.exports = (env) => {
  const pages = [
    parts.page({ title: 'Webpack demo' }),
    parts.page({ title: 'Another demo', path: 'another' }),
  ];
  const pages = [
    parts.page({
      title: 'Webpack demo',
      entry: {
        app: PATHS.app,
      },
    }),
    parts.page({
      title: 'Another demo',
      path: 'another',
      entry: {
        another: path.join(PATHS.app, 'another.js'),
      },
    }),
```

```
  ];
  const config = env === 'production' ?
    productionConfig :
    developmentConfig;

  return pages.map(page => merge(commonConfig, config, page));
};
```

The tweak also requires a change at the related part so that entry gets included in the configuration:

webpack.parts.js

```
exports.page = ({
  ...
  entry,
} = {}) => ({
  entry,
  ...
});
```

After these changes /another should show something familiar:

Another

Another page shows up

Pros and Cons

If you build the application (`npm run build`), you should find *another/index.html*. Based on the generated code, you can make the following observations:

- It's clear how to add more pages to the setup.
- The generated assets are directly below the build root. The pages are an exception as those are handled by `HtmlWebpackPlugin`, but they still point to the assets below the root. It would be possible to add more abstraction in the form of *webpack.page.js* and manage the paths by exposing a function that accepts page configuration.
- Records should be written separately per each page in files of their own. Currently, the configuration that writes the last, wins. The above solution would allow solving this.
- Processes like linting and cleaning run twice currently. The *Targets* chapter discussed potential solutions to that problem.

The approach can be pushed to another direction by dropping the multi-compiler mode. Even though it's slower to process this kind of build, it enables code sharing, and the implementation of shells. The first step towards a shell setup is to rework the configuration so that it picks up the code shared between the pages.

28.3 Generating Multiple Pages While Sharing Code

The current configuration shares code by coincidence already due to the usage patterns. Only a small part of the code differs, and as a result only the page manifests, and the bundles mapping to their entries differ.

In a more complicated application, you should apply techniques covered in the *Bundle Splitting* chapter across the pages. Dropping the multi-compiler mode can be worthwhile then.

Adjusting Configuration

To reach a code sharing setup, a minor adjustment is needed. Most of the code can remain the same. The way you expose it to webpack has to change so that it receives a single configuration object. As HtmlWebpackPlugin picks up all chunks by default, you have to adjust it to pick up only the chunks that are related to each page:

webpack.config.js

```
module.exports = (env) => {
  const pages = [
    parts.page({
      title: 'Webpack demo',
      entry: {
        app: PATHS.app,
      },
      chunks: ['app', 'manifest', 'vendor'],
    }),
    parts.page({
      title: 'Another demo',
      path: 'another',
      entry: {
        another: path.join(PATHS.app, 'another.js'),
      },
      chunks: ['another', 'manifest', 'vendor'],
    }),
  ];
  const config = env === 'production' ?
    productionConfig :
    developmentConfig;

  return pages.map(page => merge(commonConfig, config, page));
  return merge([commonConfig, config].concat(pages));
};
```

The page-specific configuration requires a small tweak as well:

webpack.parts.js

```
exports.page = ({
  ...
  chunks,
} = {}) => ({
  entry,
  plugins: [
    new HtmlWebpackPlugin({
      chunks,
      ...
    }),
  ],
});
```

If you generate a build (`npm run build`), you should notice that something is different compared to the first multiple page build you did. Instead of two manifest files, you can find only one. If you examine it, you notice it contains references to all files that were generated.

Studying the entry specific files in detail reveals more. You can see that they point to different parts of the manifest. The manifest runs different code depending on the entry. Multiple separate manifests are not needed.

Pros and Cons

Compared to the earlier approach, something was gained, but also lost:

- Given the configuration isn't in the multi-compiler form anymore, processing can be slower.
- Plugins such as `CleanWebpackPlugin` don't work without additional consideration now.
- Instead of multiple manifests, only one remains. The result is not a problem, though, as the entries use it differently based on their setup.
- `CommonsChunkPlugin` related setup required careful thought to avoid problems with styling. The earlier approach avoided this issue through isolation.

28.4 Progressive Web Applications

If you push the idea further by combining it with code splitting and smart routing, you'll end up with the idea of Progressive Web Applications (PWA). webpack-pwa[3] example illustrates how to implement the approach using webpack either through an app shell or a page shell.

App shell is loaded initially, and it manages the whole application including its routing. Page shells are more granular, and more are loaded as you use the application. The total size of the application is larger but conversely you can load initial content faster.

PWA combines well with plugins like offline-plugin[4] and sw-precache-webpack-plugin[5]. Using Service Workers[6] and improves the offline experience.

28.5 Conclusion

Webpack allows you to manage multiple page setups. The PWA approach allows the application to be loaded progressively as it's used and webpack allows implementing it.

To recap:

- Webpack can be used to generate separate pages either through its multi-compiler mode or by including all the page configuration into one.
- The multi-compiler configuration can run in parallel using external solutions, but it's harder to apply techniques such as bundle splitting against it.
- A multi-page setup can lead to a **Progressive Web Application**. In this case you use various webpack techniques to come up with an application that is fast to load and that fetches functionality as required. Both two flavors of this technique have their own merits.

You'll learn to implement Server Side Rendering in the next chapter.

---

[3]https://github.com/webpack/webpack-pwa

[4]https://www.npmjs.com/package/offline-plugin

[5]https://www.npmjs.com/package/sw-precache-webpack-plugin

[6]https://developer.mozilla.org/en/docs/Web/API/Service_Worker_API

29. Server Side Rendering

Server Side Rendering (SSR) is a technique that allows you to serve an initial payload with HTML, JavaScript, CSS, and even application state. You serve a fully rendered HTML page that would make sense even without JavaScript enabled. In addition to providing potential performance benefits, this can help with Search Engine Optimization (SEO).

Even though the idea does not sound that special, there is a technical cost involved, and you can find sharp corners. The approach was popularized by React. Since then frameworks encapsulating the tricky bits, such as Next.js[1], have appeared. isomorphic-webpack[2] is a good example of a solution designed on top of webpack.

To demonstrate SSR, you can use webpack to compile a client-side build that then gets picked up by a server that renders it using React following the principle. This is enough to understand how it works and also where the problems begin.

29.1 Setting Up Babel with React

The *Loading JavaScript* chapter covers the essentials of using Babel with webpack. There's setup that is particular to React you should perform, though. Given most of React projects rely on JSX[3] format, you have to enable it through Babel.

To get React, and particularly JSX, work with Babel, install the preset first:

```
npm install babel-preset-react --save-dev
```

---

[1]https://www.npmjs.com/package/next
[2]https://www.npmjs.com/package/isomorphic-webpack
[3]https://facebook.github.io/jsx/

Connect the preset with Babel configuration as follows:

.babelrc

```
{
  ...
  "presets": [
    "react",
    ...
  ]
}
```

29.2 Configuring React with ESLint

Using React with ESLint and JSX requires extra work as well. eslint-plugin-react[4] does a part of the work, but also ESLint configuration is needed.

Install *eslint-plugin-react* to get started:

```
npm install eslint-plugin-react --save-dev
```

The suggested minimum configuration is as follows:

.eslintrc.js

---

[4]https://www.npmjs.com/package/eslint-plugin-react

```
module.exports = {
  ...
  extends: 'eslint:recommended',
  extends: ['eslint:recommended', 'plugin:react/recommended'],
  parser: 'babel-eslint',
  parserOptions: {
    sourceType: 'module',
    allowImportExportEverywhere: true,

    // Enable JSX
    ecmaFeatures: {
      jsx: true,
    },
  },
  plugins: [
    'react',
  ],
  ...
};
```

`plugin:react/recommended` gives a good starting point. It's important to remember to enable JSX at the `parserOptions` as otherwise it will fail to parse JSX syntax.

29.3 Setting Up a React Demo

To make sure the project has the dependencies in place, install React and react-dom[5]. The latter package is needed to render the application to the DOM.

```
npm install react react-dom --save
```

Next, the React code needs a small entry point. If you are on the browser side, you should mount `Hello world div` to the document. To prove it works, clicking it should give a dialog with a "hello" message. On server-side the React component is returned so the server can pick it up.

---

[5]https://www.npmjs.com/package/react-dom

Adjust as follows:

app/ssr.js

```
const React = require('react');
const ReactDOM = require('react-dom');

const SSR = <div onClick={() => alert('hello')}>Hello world</div>;

// Render only in the browser, export otherwise
if (typeof document === 'undefined') {
  module.exports = SSR;
} else {
  ReactDOM.render(SSR, document.getElementById('app'));
}
```

You are still missing webpack configuration to turn this file into something the server can pick up.

 Given ES6 style imports and CommonJS exports cannot be mixed, the entry point was written in CommonJS style.

29.4 Configuring Webpack

To keep things nice and tidy, it's possible to push the demo configuration to a file of its own. A lot of the work has been done already. Given you have to consume the same output from multiple environments, using UMD as the library target makes sense:

webpack.ssr.js

```
const path = require('path');
const merge = require('webpack-merge');

const parts = require('./webpack.parts');

const PATHS = {
  build: path.join(__dirname, 'static'),
  ssrDemo: path.join(__dirname, 'app', 'ssr.js'),
};

module.exports = merge([
  {
    entry: {
      index: PATHS.ssrDemo,
    },
    output: {
      path: PATHS.build,
      filename: '[name].js',
      libraryTarget: 'umd',
    },
  },
  parts.loadJavaScript({ include: PATHS.ssrDemo }),
]);
```

To make it convenient to generate a build, add a helper script:

package.json

```
"scripts": {
  "build:ssr": "webpack --config webpack.ssr.js",
  ...
},
```

If you build the SSR demo (`npm run build:ssr`), you should see a new file at *./static/index.js*. The next step is to set up a server to render it.

29.5 Setting Up a Server

To keep things clear to understand, you can set up a standalone Express server that picks up the generated bundle and renders it following the SSR principle. Install Express first:

```
npm install express --save-dev
```

Then, to get something running, implement a server as follows:

server.js

```
const express = require('express');
const { renderToString } = require('react-dom/server');

const SSR = require('./static');

server(process.env.PORT || 8080);

function server(port) {
  const app = express();
```

```
  app.use(express.static('static'));
  app.get('/', (req, res) => res.status(200).send(
    renderMarkup(renderToString(SSR))
  ));

  app.listen(port);
}

function renderMarkup(html) {
  return `<!DOCTYPE html>
<html>
  <head>
    <title>Webpack SSR Demo</title>
    <meta charset="utf-8" />
  </head>
  <body>
    <div id="app">${html}</div>
    <script src="./index.js"></script>
  </body>
</html>`;
}
```

Run the server now (node ./server.js) and go below http://localhost:8080, you should see something familiar:

Hello world

Hello world

Even though there is a basic React application running now, it's difficult to develop. If you try to modify the code, nothing happens. This can be solved running webpack in a multi-compiler mode as earlier in this book. Another option is to run webpack in **watch mode** against the current configuration and set up a watcher for the server. You'll learn the latter setup next.

 If you want to debug output from the server, set export DEBUG=express:application.

 The references to the assets generated by webpack could be written automatically to the server side template if you wrote a manifest as discussed in the *Separating a Manifest* chapter.

 If you get a linting warning like warning 'React' is defined but never used no-unused-vars, make sure the ESLint React plugin has been enabled and its default preset is in use.

29.6 Watching SSR Changes and Refreshing the Browser

The first portion of the problem is fast to solve. Run npm run build:ssr -- --watch in a terminal. That forces webpack to run in a watch mode. It would be possible to wrap this idea within an npm script for convenience, but this is enough for this demo.

The remaining part is harder than what was done so far. How to make the server aware of the changes and how to communicate the changes to the browser?

browser-refresh[6] can come in handy as it solves both of the problems. Install it first:

---

[6]https://www.npmjs.com/package/browser-refresh

```
npm install browser-refresh --save-dev
```

The client portion requires two small changes to the server code:

server.js

```
server(process.env.PORT || 8080);

function server(port) {
  ...

  app.listen(port);
  app.listen(port, () => process.send && process.send('online'));
}

function renderMarkup(html) {
  return `<!DOCTYPE html>
<html>
  ...
  <body>
    ...
    <script src="${process.env.BROWSER_REFRESH_URL}"></script>
  </body>
</html>`;
}
```

The first change tells the client that the application is online and ready to go. The latter change attaches the client script to the output. *browser-refresh* manages the environment variable in question.

Run `node_modules/.bin/browser-refresh ./server.js` in another terminal and open the browser at `http://localhost:8080` as earlier to test the setup. Remember to have webpack running in the watch mode at another terminal. If everything went right, any change you make to the demo client script (*app/ssr.js*) should show up in the browser or cause a failure at the server.

If the server crashes, it loses the WebSocket connection. You have to force a refresh in the browser in this case. If the server was managed through webpack as well, the problem could have been avoided.

To prove that SSR works, check out the browser inspector. You should see something familiar there:

```
⌖ ⬚    Elements  Console  Sources  Network  Timeline  Profiles  Application  Security  Audits  ⊢
<!DOCTYPE html>
<html>
▶ <head>…</head>
▼ <body>
    ▼ <div id="app"> == $0
        <div data-reactroot data-reactid="1" data-react-checksum="1022694294">Hello world</div>
      </div>
      <script type="text/javascript" src="./index.js"></script>
      <script src="http://localhost:62613/browser-refresh.js"></script>
      <span id="buffer-extension-hover-button" style="display: none;position: absolute;z-index: 8
      data/shared/img/buffer-hover-icon@2x.png);background-size: 100px 25px;opacity: 0.9;cursor:
    </body>
▶ <style type="text/css">…</style>
▶ <style type="text/css">…</style>
</html>
```

SSR output

Instead of a `div` where to mount an application, you can see all related HTML there. It's not much in this particular case, but it's enough to showcase the approach.

 The implementation could be refined further by implementing a production mode for the server that would skip injecting the browser refresh script at a minimum. The server could inject initial data payload to the generated HTML. Doing this would avoid queries on the client-side.

29.7 Open Questions

Even though the demo illustrates the basic idea of SSR, it still leaves open questions:

- How to deal with styles? Node doesn't understand CSS related imports.
- How to deal with anything else than JavaScript? If the server side is processed through webpack, this is less of an issue as you can patch it at webpack.

- How to run the server through something else than Node? One option would be to wrap the Node instance in a service you then run through your host environment. Ideally, the results would be cached, and you can find more specific solutions for this particular per platform.

Questions like these are the reason why solutions such as isomorphic-webpack[7] or Next.js[8] exist. They have been designed to solve SSR-specific problems like these.

 Routing is a big problem of its own solved by frameworks like Next.js. Patrick Hund discusses how to solve it with React and React Router 4[9].

29.8 Conclusion

SSR comes with a technical challenge and for this reason specific solutions have appeared around it. Webpack is a good fit for SSR setups.

To recap:

- **Server Side Rendering** can provide more for the browser to render initially. Instead of waiting for the JavaScript to load, you can display markup instantly.
- Server Side Rendering also allows you to pass initial payload of data to the client to avoid unnecessary queries to the server.
- Webpack can manage the client side portion of the problem. It can be used to generate the server as well if more integrated solution is required. Abstractions, such as Next.js, hide these details.
- Server Side Rendering does not come without a cost and it leads to new problems as you need better approaches for dealing with aspects, such as styling or routing. The server and the client environment differ in important manners, so code has to be written so that it does not rely on platform-specific features too much.

[7] https://www.npmjs.com/package/isomorphic-webpack
[8] https://github.com/zeit/next.js
[9] https://ebaytech.berlin/universal-web-apps-with-react-router-4-15002bb30ccb

VII Techniques

In this part, you will learn to use webpack techniques such as dynamic loading, using web workers, internationalization, and deploying.

30. Dynamic Loading

Even though you can get far with webpack's code splitting features covered in the *Code Splitting* chapter, there's more to it. Webpack provides more dynamic ways to deal with code through require.context.

30.1 Dynamic Loading with require.context

require.context[1] provides a general form of code splitting. Let's say you are writing a static site generator on top of webpack. You could model your site contents within a directory structure by having a ./pages/ directory which would contain the Markdown files.

Each of these files would have a YAML frontmatter for their metadata. The url of each page could be determined based on the filename and mapped as a site. To model the idea using require.context, you could end up with code as below:

```
// Process pages through `yaml-frontmatter-loader` and `json-loader`.
// The first one extracts the frontmatter and the body and the latter
// converts it into a JSON structure to use later. Markdown
// hasn't been processed yet.
const req = require.context(
  'json-loader!yaml-frontmatter-loader!./pages',
  true, // Load files recursively. Pass false to skip recursion.
  /^\.\/.*\.md$/ // Match files ending with .md.
);
```

 The loader definition could be pushed to webpack configuration. The inline form is used to keep the example minimal.

---

[1]https://webpack.js.org/configuration/entry-context/#context

`require.context` returns a function to `require` against. It also knows its module `id` and it provides a `keys()` method for figuring out the contents of the context. To give you a better example, consider the code below:

```
req.keys(); // ['./demo.md', './another-demo.md']

req.id; // 42

// {title: 'Demo', body: '# Demo page\nDemo content\n\n'}
const demoPage = req('./demo.md');
```

The technique can be valuable for other purposes, such as testing or adding files for webpack to watch. In that case, you would set up a `require.context` within a file which you then point to through a webpack `entry`.

 The information is enough for generating an entire site. This has been done with Antwar[2].

---

[2]https://github.com/antwarjs/antwar

30.2 Combining Multiple `require.contexts`

Multiple separate `require.contexts` can be combined into one by wrapping them behind a function:

```
const { concat, uniq } from 'lodash';

const combineContexts = (...contexts) => {
  function webpackContext(req) {
    // Find the first match and execute
    const matches = contexts.map(
      context => context.keys().indexOf(req) >= 0 && context
    ).filter(a => a);

    return matches[0] && matches[0](req);
  }
  webpackContext.keys = () => uniq(
    concat.apply(
      null,
      contexts.map(context => context.keys())
    )
  );

  return webpackContext;
}
```

30.3 Dynamic Paths with a Dynamic `import`

The same idea works with dynamic `import`. Instead of passing a complete path, you can pass a partial one. Webpack sets up a context internally. Here's a brief example:

```
// Set up a target or derive this somehow
const target = 'fi';

// Elsewhere in code
import(`translations/${target}.json`).then(...).catch(...);
```

The same idea works with `require` as long as webpack can analyze the situation statically.

 Any time you are using dynamic imports, it's a good idea to specify file extension in the path as that helps with performance by keeping the context smaller than otherwise.

30.4 Dealing with Dynamic Paths

Given the approaches discussed here rely on static analysis and webpack has to find the files in question, it doesn't work for every possible case. If the files you need are on another server or have to be accessed through a particular end-point, then webpack isn't enough.

Consider using browser-side loaders like $script.js[3] or little-loader[4] on top of webpack in this case.

---

[3]https://www.npmjs.com/package/scriptjs
[4]https://www.npmjs.com/package/little-loader

30.5 Conclusion

Even though `require.context` is a niche feature, it's good to be aware of it. It becomes valuable if you have to perform lookups against multiple files available within the file system. If your lookup is more complex than that, you have to resort to other alternatives that allow you to perform loading runtime.

To recap:

- `require.context` is an advanced feature that's often hidden behind the scenes. If you have to perform a lookup against a large amount of files, use it.
- If you write a dynamic `import` in a certain form, webpack generates a `require.context` call. The code reads slightly better in this case.
- The techniques work only against the file system. If you have to operate against urls, you should look into client-side solutions.

The next chapter shows how to use web workers with webpack.

31. Web Workers

Web workers[1] allow you to push work outside of main execution thread of JavaScript making them convenient for long running computations and background work.

Moving data between the main thread and the worker comes with communication-related overhead. The split provides isolation that forces workers to focus on logic only as they cannot manipulate the user interface directly.

The idea of workers is valuable on a more general level. parallel-webpack[2] uses worker-farm[3] underneath to parallelize webpack execution.

As discussed in the *Build Targets* chapter, webpack allows you to build your application as a worker itself. To get the idea of web workers better, you'll learn how to build a small worker using worker-loader[4].

31.1 Setting Up Worker Loader

To get started, install *worker-loader* to the project:

```
npm install worker-loader --save-dev
```

Instead of pushing the loader definition to webpack configuration, you can use inline loader definitions to keep the demonstration minimal. See the *Loader Definitions* chapter for more information about the alternatives.

---

[1] https://developer.mozilla.org/en-US/docs/Web/API/Web_Workers_API

[2] https://www.npmjs.com/package/parallel-webpack

[3] https://www.npmjs.com/package/worker-farm

[4] https://www.npmjs.com/package/worker-loader

31.2 Setting Up a Worker

A worker has to do two things: listen to messages and respond. Between those two actions, it can perform a computation. In this case, you accept text data, append it to itself, and send the result:

app/worker.js

```
self.onmessage = ({ data: { text } }) => {
  self.postMessage({ text: text + text });
};
```

31.3 Setting Up a Host

The host has to instantiate the worker and the communicate with it. The idea is almost the same except the host has the control:

app/component.js

```
import Worker from 'worker-loader!./worker';

export default () => {
  const element = document.createElement('h1');
  const worker = new Worker();
  const state = { text: 'foo' };

  worker.addEventListener(
    'message',
    ({ data: { text } }) => {
      state.text = text;
      element.innerHTML = text;
    }
  );

  element.innerHTML = state.text;
```

```
element.onclick = () => worker.postMessage({ text: state.text });

  return element;
}
```

After you have these two set up, it should work. As you click the text, it should mutate the application state as the worker completes its execution. To demonstrate the asynchronous nature of workers, you could try adding delay to the answer and see what happens.

 webworkify-webpack[5] is an alternative to *worker-loader*. The API allows you to use the worker as a regular JavaScript module as well given you avoid the `self` requirement visible in the example solution.

31.4 Conclusion

The important thing to note is that the worker cannot access the DOM. You can perform computation and queries in a worker, but it cannot manipulate the user interface directly.

To recap:

- Web workers allow you to push work out of the main thread of the browser. This separation is valuable especially if performance is an issue.
- Web workers cannot manipulate the DOM. Instead, it's best to use them for long running computations and requests.
- The isolation provided by web workers can be used for architectural benefit. It forces the programmers to stay within a specific sandbox.
- Communicating with web workers comes with an overhead that makes them less practical. As the specification evolves, this can change in the future.

You'll learn about internationalization in the next chapter.

---

[5] https://www.npmjs.com/package/webworkify-webpack

32. Internationalization

Internationalization (i18n) is a big topic by itself. The broadest definition has to do with translating your user interface to other languages. **Localization** (l10n) is a more specific term, and it describes how to adapt your application to a specific locale or market. Different locales can have the same language, but they still have their customs, like date formatting or measures.

The problem could be solved by pushing the translations behind an end point and loading them dynamically to decouple the problem from webpack. This would also allow you to implement a translation interface within your application to allow your translators, or even users, to translate the application. The downside of this approach is that then you have a translation backend to maintain.

Another approach is to let webpack generate static builds, each per language. The problem is that you have to update your application each time your translations change.

32.1 i18n with Webpack

The basic idea of i18n with webpack is often the same. You have a translation definition that is then mapped to the application through replacements. The result contains a translated version of the application. You can use multiple translation formats through a couple of solutions:

- i18n-webpack-plugin[1] relies on a pure JSON definition and performs the replacement through __('Hello') placeholders.
- po-loader[2] maps GNU gettext PO files[3] to multiple formats including raw JSON and Jed[4].

---

[1] https://www.npmjs.com/package/i18n-webpack-plugin

[2] https://www.npmjs.com/package/po-loader

[3] https://www.gnu.org/software/gettext/manual/html_node/PO-Files.html

[4] https://messageformat.github.io/Jed/

- jed-webpack-plugin[5] is a plugin-based solution for Jed.

To illustrate the setup, *i18n-webpack-plugin* is a good starting point.

32.2 Setting Up a Project

To prove that translation works, set up something to replace:

app/i18n.js

```
console.log(__('Hello world'));
```

To translate that into Finnish, set up a definition:

languages/fi.json

```
{ "Hello world": "Terve maailma" }
```

To make ESLint aware of the global __ function, you should add it to your linting rules:

.eslintrc.js

```
module.exports = {
  ...
  globals: {
    __: true,
  },
  ...
};
```

The next step is to glue the files together using webpack.

---

[5] https://www.npmjs.com/package/jed-webpack-plugin

32.3 Setting Up `I18nWebpackPlugin`

Install *i18n-webpack-plugin* and *glob* helper first. The latter is needed for capturing translation files.

```
npm install glob i18n-webpack-plugin --save-dev
```

On the webpack side, you should iterate through the available languages, and then set up a configuration for each:

webpack.i18n.js

```
const path = require('path');
const glob = require('glob');
const I18nPlugin = require('i18n-webpack-plugin');

const PATHS = {
  build: path.join(__dirname, 'i18n-build'),
  i18nDemo: path.join(__dirname, 'app', 'i18n.js'),
};

const TRANSLATIONS = [{ language: 'en' }].concat(
  glob.sync('./languages/*.json').map((file) => ({
    language: path.basename(file, path.extname(file)),
    translation: require(file),
  }))
);

module.exports = TRANSLATIONS.map(({
  language, translation,
}) => (
  {
    entry: {
      index: PATHS.i18nDemo,
    },
```

```
    output: {
      path: PATHS.build,
      filename: `[name].${language}.js`,
    },
    plugins: [
      new I18nPlugin(translation),
    ],
  }
));
```

To make it convenient to build, set a shortcut:

package.json

```
"scripts": {
  "build:i18n": "webpack --config webpack.i18n.js",
  ...
},
```

If you build now (npm run build:i18n), you should end up with a new directory containing two translated files. If you examine them, you should see webpack bootstrap and the translated code in each.

To take the example further, you could generate a proper page for each translation as described in the *Multiple Pages* chapter. Language selector would be a good addition to the demonstration. You could handle the language definition through webpack's DefinePlugin. A user interface widget could rely on that and load another language based a page or directory naming convention.

 The techniques discussed in the *Code Splitting* chapter are valid with i18n. You could define dynamic imports to load translation files on demand. Doing this would push the problem of loading and maintaining translations elsewhere.

32.4 Conclusion

The other webpack approaches follow a similar idea but require more work on the frontend side. They are also more flexible, and if you go with a loader based solution, then you can set up split points to load languages on demand. You can also consider caching the language data to avoid fetching it altogether or loading it in smaller portions.

To recap:

- **Internationalization** (i18n) and **localization** (l10n) are important problems if you target multiple markets with your application.
- Webpack supports multiple approaches to i18n. The most basic approach is to replace specifically strings with other strings although more sophisticated alternatives are available.
- The problem can be handled by pushing it to a server. This way would be a more dynamic and it would also allow you to handle translating the actual application through the same API.

The next chapter covers various testing setups and tools that work with webpack.

33. Testing

Testing is a vital part of development. Even though techniques, such as linting, can help to spot and solve issues, they have their limitations. Testing can be applied against the code and an application on many different levels.

You can **unit test** specific piece of code, or you can look at the application from the user's point of view through **acceptance testing**. **Integration testing** fits between these ends of the spectrum and is concerned about how separate units of code operate together.

You can find a lot of testing tools for JavaScript. The most popular options work with webpack after you configure it right. Even though test runners work without webpack, running them through it allows you to process code the test runners do not understand while having control over the way modules are resolved. You can also use webpack's watch mode instead of relying on one provided by a test runner.

33.1 Mocha

Mocha

Mocha[1] is a popular test framework for Node. While Mocha provides test infrastructure, you have to bring your asserts to it. Even though Node assert[2] can be enough, there are good alternatives such as power-assert[3], Chai[4], or Unexpected[5].

mocha-loader[6] allows running Mocha tests through webpack. mocha-webpack[7] is another option that aims to provide more functionality. You'll learn the basic *mocha-loader* setup next.

---

[1] https://mochajs.org/

[2] https://nodejs.org/api/assert.html

[3] https://www.npmjs.com/package/power-assert

[4] http://chaijs.com/

[5] http://unexpected.js.org/

[6] https://www.npmjs.com/package/mocha-loader

[7] https://www.npmjs.com/package/mocha-webpack

Configuring *mocha-loader* with Webpack

To get started, include Mocha and *mocha-loader* to your project:

```
npm install mocha mocha-loader --save-dev
```

To make ESLint aware of Mocha globals, tweak as follows:

eslintrc.js

```
module.exports = {
  env: {
    ...
    mocha: true,
  },
  ...
};
```

Setting Up Code to Test

To have something to test, set up a function:

tests/add.js

```
module.exports = (a, b) => a + b;
```

Then, to test that, set up a small test suite:

tests/add.test.js

```javascript
const assert = require('assert');
const add = require('./add');

describe('Demo', () => {
  it('should add correctly', () => {
    assert.equal(add(1, 1), 2);
  });
});
```

Configuring Mocha

To run Mocha against the test, add a script:

package.json

```json
"scripts": {
  "test:mocha": "mocha tests",
  ...
},
```

If you execute `npm run test:mocha` now, you should see output:

```
Demo
  should add correctly


1 passing (10ms)
```

Mocha also provides a watch mode which you can activate through `npm run test:mocha -- --watch`. It runs the test suite as you modify the code.

 `--grep <pattern>` can be used for constraining the behavior if you want to focus only on a particular set of tests.

Configuring Webpack

Webpack can provide similar functionality through a web interface. The hard parts of the problem have been solved earlier in this book, what remain is combining those solutions together through configuration.

To tell webpack which tests to run, they need to be imported somehow. The *Dynamic Loading* chapter discussed `require.context` that allows to aggregate files based on a rule. It's ideal here. Set up an entry point as follows:

tests/index.js

```
// Skip execution in Node
if (module.hot) {
  const context = require.context(
    'mocha-loader!./', // Process through mocha-loader
    false, // Skip recursive processing
    /\.test.js$/ // Pick only files ending with .test.js
  );

  // Execute each test suite
  context.keys().forEach(context);
}
```

To allow webpack to pick this up, a small amount of configuration is required:

webpack.mocha.js

```
const path = require('path');
const merge = require('webpack-merge');

const parts = require('./webpack.parts');

module.exports = merge([
  parts.devServer(),
  parts.page({
    title: 'Mocha demo',
    entry: {
      tests: path.join(__dirname, 'tests'),
    },
  }),
]);
```

 See the *Composing Configuration* chapter for the full devServer setup. The page setup is explained in the *Multiple Pages* chapter.

Add a helper script to make it convenient to run:

package.json

```
"scripts": {
  "test:mocha:watch": "webpack-dev-server --hot --config webpack.moc\
ha.js",
  ...
},
```

 If you want to understand what --hot does better, see the *Hot Module Replacement* appendix.

If you execute the server now and navigate to `http://localhost:8080/`, you should see the test:

passes: *1* failures: *0* duration: *0.01*s   100%

Demo

   ✓ should add correctly

Mocha in browser

Adjusting either the test or the code should lead to a change in the browser. You can grow your specification or refactor the code while seeing the status of the tests.

Compared to the vanilla Mocha setup, configuring Mocha through webpack comes with a couple of advantages:

- It's possible to adjust module resolution. Webpack aliasing and other techniques work now, but this would also tie the code to webpack.
- You can use webpack's processing to compile your code as you wish. With vanilla Mocha that would imply more setup outside of it.

On the downside, now you need a browser to examine the tests. *mocha-loader* is at its best as a development helper. The problem can be solved by running the tests through a headless browser.

33.2 Karma and Mocha

> **||** *On the AngularJS team, we rely on testing and we always seek better tools to make our life easier. That's why we created Karma - a test runner that fits all our needs.*

Karma

Karma[8] is a test runner that allows you to run tests against real devices and PhantomJS[9], a headless browser. karma-webpack[10] is a Karma preprocessor that allows you to connect Karma with webpack. The same benefits as before apply still. This time around, however, there is more control over the test environment.

To get started, install Karma, Mocha, *karma-mocha* reporter, and *karma-webpack*:

```
npm install karma mocha karma-mocha karma-webpack --save-dev
```

---

[8]https://karma-runner.github.io/

[9]http://phantomjs.org/

[10]https://www.npmjs.com/package/karma-webpack

Like webpack, Karma relies on the configuration as well. Set up a file as follows to make it pick up the tests:

karma.conf.js

```
module.exports = (config) => {
  const tests = 'tests/*.test.js';

  config.set({
    frameworks: ['mocha'],

    files: [
      {
        pattern: tests,
      },
    ],

    // Preprocess through webpack
    preprocessors: {
      [tests]: ['webpack'],
    },

    singleRun: true,
  });
};
```

 The file has to be named exactly as *karma.conf.js*. Otherwise Karma doesn't pick it up automatically.

 The setup generates a bundle per each test. If you have a large amount of tests and want to improve performance, set up require.context as for Mocha above. See karma-webpack issue 23[11] for more details.

---

[11] https://github.com/webpack-contrib/karma-webpack/issues/23

Add an npm shortcut:

```
...
"scripts": {
  "test:karma": "karma start",
  ...
},
...
```

If you execute npm run test:karma now, you should see terminal output:

```
...
webpack: Compiled successfully.
...:INFO [karma]: Karma v1.5.0 server started at http://0.0.0.0:9876/
```

This means Karma is in a waiting state and you have to visit that url to run the tests. As per configuration (singleRun: true), Karma terminates execution after that:

```
...
...:INFO [karma]: Karma v1.5.0 server started at http://0.0.0.0:9876/
...:INFO [Chrome 57...]: Connected on socket D...A with id manual-73
Chrome 57...): Executed 1 of 1 SUCCESS (0.003 secs / 0 secs)
```

Given running tests this way can become annoying, it's a good idea to configure alternative ways. Using PhantomJS is one option.

 You can point Karma to specific browsers through the browsers field. Example: browsers: ['Chrome'].

Running Tests Through PhantomJS

Running tests through PhantomJS requires a couple of dependencies:

```
npm install karma-phantomjs-launcher phantomjs-prebuilt --save-dev
```

To make Karma run tests through Phantom, adjust its configuration as follows:

karma.conf.js

```
module.exports = (config) => {
  ...

  config.set({
    ...

    browsers: ['PhantomJS'],
  });
};
```

If you execute the tests again (npm run test:karma), you should get output without having to visit an url:

```
...
webpack: Compiled successfully.
...:INFO [karma]: Karma v1.5.0 server started at http://0.0.0.0:9876/
...:INFO [launcher]: Launching browser PhantomJS with unlimited conc\
urrency
...:INFO [launcher]: Starting browser PhantomJS
...:INFO [PhantomJS ...]: Connected on socket 7...A with id 123
PhantomJS ...: Executed 1 of 1 SUCCESS (0.005 secs / 0.001 secs)
```

Given running tests after the change can get boring after a while, Karma provides a watch mode.

PhantomJS does not support ES6 features yet so you have to preprocess the code for tests using them. The webpack setup is done later in this chapter. ES6 support is planned for PhantomJS 2.5.

Watch Mode with Karma

Accessing Karma's watch mode is possible as follows:

package.json

```
"scripts": {
  "test:karma:watch": "karma start --auto-watch --no-single-run",
  ...
},
```

If you execute npm run test:karma:watch now, you should see watch behavior.

Generating Coverage Reports

To know how much of the code the tests cover, it can be a good idea to generate coverage reports. Doing this requires code-level instrumentation. Also, the added information has to be reported. This can be done through HTML and LCOV reports.

 LCOV integrates well with visualization services. You can send coverage information to an external service through a continuous integration environment and track the status in one place.

isparta[12] is a popular, ES6 compatible code coverage tool. Connecting it with Karma requires configuration. Most importantly the code has to be instrumented through babel-plugin-istanbul[13]. Doing this requires a small amount of webpack configuration as well due to the setup. karma-coverage[14] is required for the reporting portion of the problem.

---

[12] https://www.npmjs.com/package/isparta

[13] https://www.npmjs.com/package/babel-plugin-istanbul

[14] https://www.npmjs.com/package/karma-coverage

Install the dependencies first:

```
npm install babel-plugin-istanbul karma-coverage --save-dev
```

Connect the Babel plugin so that the instrumentation happens when Karma is run:

.babelrc

```
...
"env": {
  "karma": {
    "plugins": [
      [
        "istanbul",
        { "exclude": ["tests/*.test.js"] }
      ]
    ]
  }
}
```

Make sure to set Babel environment, so it picks up the plugin:

karma.conf.js

```
module.exports = (config) => {
  ...

  process.env.BABEL_ENV = 'karma';

  config.set({
    ...
  });
};
```

 If you want to understand the env idea, see the *Loading JavaScript* chapter.

On Karma side, reporting has to be set up and Karma configuration has to be connected with webpack. *karma-webpack* provides two fields for this purpose: webpack and webpackMiddleware. You should use the former in this case to make sure the code gets processed through Babel.

karma.conf.js

```
const path = require('path');

...

module.exports = (config) => {
  ...

  config.set({
    ...

    webpack: require('./webpack.parts').loadJavaScript({
      include: path.join(__dirname, 'tests'),
    }),

    reporters: ['coverage'],

    coverageReporter: {
      dir: 'build',
      reporters: [
        { type: 'html' },
        { type: 'lcov' },
      ],
    },
  });
};
```

 If you want to emit the reports to specific directories below dir, set subdir per each report.

If you execute karma now (`npm run test:karma`), you should see a new directory containing coverage reports. The HTML report can be examined through the browser.

/

100% Statements 2/2   **100%** Branches 0/0   **100%** Functions 1/1   **100%** Lines 1/1

File ▲		Statements			Branches			Functions			Lines		
tests/		100%	2/2		100%	0/0		100%	1/1		100%	1/1	

Coverage in browser

LCOV requires specific tooling to work. You can find editor plugins such as lcov-info[15] for Atom. A properly configured plugin can give you coverage information while you are developing using the watch mode.

33.3 Jest

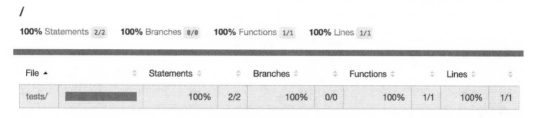

Jest

Painless JavaScript Testing

Jest

Facebook's Jest[16] is an opinionated alternative that encapsulates functionality, including coverage and mocking, with minimal setup. It can capture snapshots of data making it valuable for projects where you have the behavior you would like to record and retain.

Jest tests follow Jasmine[17] test framework semantics, and it supports Jasmine-style assertions out of the box. Especially the suite definition is close enough to Mocha so

---

[15] https://atom.io/packages/lcov-info

[16] https://facebook.github.io/jest/

[17] https://www.npmjs.com/package/jasmine

that the current test should work without any adjustments to the test code itself. Jest provides jest-codemods[18] for migrating more complex projects to Jest semantics.

Install Jest first:

```
npm install jest --save-dev
```

Jest captures tests through *package.json* configuration[19]. It detects tests within a **tests** directory it also happens to capture the naming pattern the project is using by default:

package.json

```
"scripts": {
  "test:jest:watch": "jest --watch",
  "test:jest": "jest",
  ...
},
```

Now you have two new commands: one to run tests once and other to run them in a watch mode. To capture coverage information, you have to set `"collectCoverage"`: `true` at `"jest"` settings in *package.json* or pass `--coverage` flag to Jest. It emits the coverage reports below *coverage* directory by default.

Given generating coverage reports comes with a performance overhead, enabling the behavior through the flag can be a good idea. This way you can control exactly when to capture the information.

Porting a webpack setup to Jest requires more effort especially if you rely on webpack specific features. The official guide[20] covers quite a few of the common problems. You can also configure Jest to use Babel through babel-jest[21] as it allows you to use Babel plugins like babel-plugin-module-resolver[22] to match webpack's functionality.

---

[18] https://www.npmjs.com/package/jest-codemods
[19] https://facebook.github.io/jest/docs/configuration.html
[20] https://facebook.github.io/jest/docs/webpack.html
[21] https://www.npmjs.com/package/babel-jest
[22] https://www.npmjs.com/package/babel-plugin-module-resolver

33.4 AVA

AVA

AVA[23] is a test runner that has been designed to take advantage of parallel execution. It comes with a test suite definition of its own. webpack-ava-recipe[24] covers how to connect it with webpack.

The main idea is to run both webpack and AVA in watch mode to push the problem of processing code to webpack while allowing AVA to consume the processed code. The `require.context` idea discussed with Mocha comes in handy here as you have to capture tests for webpack to process somehow.

---

[23]https://www.npmjs.com/package/ava

[24]https://github.com/greyepoxy/webpack-ava-recipe

33.5 Mocking

Mocking is a technique that allows you to replace test objects. Consider the solutions below:

- Sinon[25] provides mocks, stubs, and spies. It works well with webpack since version 2.0.
- inject-loader[26] allows you to inject code to modules through their dependencies making it valuable for mocking.
- rewire-webpack[27] allows mocking and overriding module globals. babel-plugin-rewire[28] implements rewire[29] for Babel.

33.6 Conclusion

Webpack can be configured to work with a large variety of testing tools. Each tool has its sweet spots, but they also have quite a bit of common ground.

To recap:

- Running testing tools allows you to benefit from webpack's module resolution mechanism.
- Sometimes the test setup can be quite involved. Tools like Jest remove most of the boilerplate and allow you to develop tests with minimal setup.
- You can find multiple mocking tools for webpack. They allow you to shape test environment. Sometimes you can avoid mocking through design, though.

You'll learn to deploy applications using webpack in the next chapter.

---

[25] https://www.npmjs.com/package/sinon

[26] https://www.npmjs.com/package/inject-loader

[27] https://www.npmjs.com/package/rewire-webpack

[28] https://www.npmjs.com/package/babel-plugin-rewire

[29] https://www.npmjs.com/package/rewire

34. Deploying Applications

A project built with webpack can be deployed to a variety of environments. A public project that doesn't rely on a backend can be pushed to GitHub Pages using the *gh-pages* package. Also, there are a variety of webpack plugins that can target other environments, such as S3.

34.1 Deploying with *gh-pages*

gh-pages[1] allows you to host stand-alone applications on GitHub Pages easily. It has to be pointed to a build directory first. It picks up the contents and pushes them to the gh-pages branch.

Despite its name, the package works with other services that support hosting from a Git repository as well. But given GitHub is so popular, it can be used to demonstrate the idea. In practice, you would likely have more complicated setup in place that would push the result to other service through a Continuous Integration system.

Setting Up *gh-pages*

To get started, execute

```
npm install gh-pages --save-dev
```

---

[1]https://www.npmjs.com/package/gh-pages

You are also going to need a script in *package.json*:

package.json

```
"scripts": {
  "deploy": "gh-pages -d build",
  ...
},
```

To make the asset paths work on GitHub Pages, `output.publicPath` field has to be adjusted. Otherwise, the asset paths end up pointing at the root, and that doesn't work unless you are hosting behind a domain root (say `survivejs.com`) directly.

`publicPath` gives control over the resulting urls you see at *index.html* for instance. If you are hosting your assets on a CDN, this would be the place to tweak.

In this case, it's enough to set it to point the GitHub project as below:

webpack.config.js

```
const productionConfig = merge([
  {
    ...
    output: {
      ...
      // Tweak this to match your GitHub project name
      publicPath: '/webpack-demo/',
    },
  },
  ...
]);
```

After building (`npm run build`) and deploying (`npm run deploy`), you should have your application from the `build/` directory hosted through GitHub Pages. You should find it at `https://<name>.github.io/<project>` assuming everything went fine.

 If you need a more elaborate setup, use the Node API that *gh-pages* provides. The default command line tool it provides is enough for basic purposes, though.

GitHub Pages allows you to choose the branch where you deploy. It's possible to use the master branch even as it's enough for minimal sites that don't need bundling. You can also point below the *./docs* directory within your master branch and maintain your site.

Archiving Old Versions

gh-pages provides an add option for archival purposes. The idea goes as follows:

1. Copy the old version of the site in a temporary directory and remove *archive* directory from it. You can name the archival directory as you want.
2. Clean and build the project.
3. Copy the old version below *build/archive/<version>*
4. Set up a script to call *gh-pages* through Node as below and capture possible errors in the callback:

```
ghpages.publish(path.join(__dirname, 'build'), { add: true }, cb);
```

34.2 Deploying to Other Environments

Even though you can push the problem of deployment outside of webpack, there are a couple of webpack specific utilities that come in handy:

- webpack-deploy[2] is a collection of deployment utilities and works even outside of webpack.
- webpack-s3-sync-plugin[3] and webpack-s3-plugin[4] sync the assets to Amazon S3.
- ssh-webpack-plugin[5] has been designed for deployments over SSH.

---

[2]https://www.npmjs.com/package/webpack-deploy

[3]https://www.npmjs.com/package/webpack-s3-sync-plugin

[4]https://www.npmjs.com/package/webpack-s3-plugin

[5]https://www.npmjs.com/package/ssh-webpack-plugin

34.3 Resolving `output.publicPath` Dynamically

If you don't know `publicPath` beforehand, it's possible to resolve it based on the environment by following these steps:

1. Set `__webpack_public_path__ = window.myDynamicPublicPath;` in the application entry point and resolve it as you see fit.
2. Remove `output.publicPath` setting from your webpack configuration.
3. If you are using ESLint, set it to ignore the global.

.eslintrc.js

```
module.exports = {
  ...
  globals: {
    __webpack_public_path__: true
  },
  ...
};
```

When you compile, webpack picks up `__webpack_public_path__` and rewrites it so that it points to webpack logic.

34.4 Conclusion

Even though webpack isn't a deployment tool, you can find plugins for it.

To recap:

- It's possible to handle the problem of deployment outside of webpack. You can achieve this in an npm script for example.
- You can configure webpack's `output.publicPath` dynamically. This technique is valuable if you don't know it compile-time and want to decide it later. This is possible through the `__webpack_public_path__` global.

VIII Packages

In this part, you will learn to understand npm packaging and related webpack techniques.

35. Consuming Packages

Consuming npm packages through webpack is often convenient but there are certain special considerations to take into account. Sometimes the packages don't play with you nicely, or they can require special tweaking to work properly. At the core of this is the concept of SemVer.

35.1 Understanding SemVer

Most popular packages out there comply with SemVer. It's problematic as sometimes packages inadvertently break it, but there are ways around this. Roughly, SemVer states that you should not break backward compatibility, given certain rules[1] are met:

1. The MAJOR version increments when incompatible API changes are made.
2. The MINOR version increments when backwards-compatible features are added.
3. The PATCH version increments when backwards-compatible bugs are fixed.

The rules are different for 0.x versions. There the rule is 0.<MAJOR>.<MINOR>. For packages considered stable and suitable for public usage (1.0.0 and above), the rule is <MAJOR>.<MINOR>.<PATCH>. For example, if the current version of a package is 0.1.4 and a breaking change is performed, it should bump to 0.2.0.

Given SemVer can be tricky to manage, ComVer[2] exists as an alternative. ComVer can be described as a binary decision <not compatible>.<compatible>.

 You can understand SemVer much better by studying the online tool[3] and how it behaves.

---

[1] http://semver.org/

[2] https://github.com/staltz/comver

[3] http://semver.npmjs.com/

35.2 Dependency Types

An npm package comes with different types of dependencies:

- `dependencies` refer to the direct dependencies a package needs to work. On application level you could list the dependencies of the application code itself. This excludes dependencies needed to build it.
- `devDependencies` are dependencies you need to develop the package. They include packages related to building, testing, and similar tasks. When you install a package from npm, they won't be installed by default. If you run `npm install` on a project locally, npm will install them.
- `peerDependencies` are usually given as version ranges. The idea is to allow the user to decide the exact versions of these dependencies without fixing it to a specific one. The behavior was changed in npm 3. Before that npm install peer dependencies automatically. Now you have to install and include them to your project explicitly.
- `bundledDependencies` refer to dependencies that are bundled with the package itself. They are used rarely, though.
- `optionalDependencies` are dependencies that the user can install but aren't required for the package to work. This is another rare field.

35.3 Consumption Workflow

Often npm consumption workflow resolves around two commands:

- `npm install <package> --save` or `npm i <package> -S`.
- `npm install <package> --save-dev` or `npm i <package> -D`

To install a specific version, you should pass it through `@<version>`. npm will set the version prefix based on ~/*.npmrc*. The related ranges are discussed later in this chapter.

You can refer to a package by its name and version but that is not the only way. Consider the following alternatives:

- `<git repository>#<reference>` points to a Git repository and a Git reference.
- `<github user>/<project>#<reference>` shortcut points to GitHub in a similar manner.
- `<github user>/<project>#pull/<id>/head` points to a specific GitHub pull request.

`<reference>` can be either commit hash, tag, or a branch. The technique does not work unless the package has been set up to support consumption outside of Git. The *Package Authoring Techniques* chapter shows how to achieve this.

 To avoid sharing all your packages in public, npm allows you to maintain private packages through their commercial offering. Another option is to use a package like verdaccio[4]. verdaccio allows you to maintain a private server that can also work as a cache for npm. You can also override public packages using it.

35.4 Understanding npm Lookup

npm's lookup algorithm is another aspect that's good to understand. Sometimes this can explain certain errors, and it also leads to good practices, such as preferring local dependencies over global ones. The basic algorithm goes as below:

1. Look into immediate packages. If there is *node_modules*, crawl through that and also check the parent directories until the project root is reached. You can check that using `npm root`.
2. If nothing was found, check globally installed packages. If you are using Unix, look into */usr/local/lib/node_modules* to find them. You can figure out the specific directory using `npm root -g`.
3. If the global lookup fails, it fails hard. You should get an error now.

---

[4]https://www.npmjs.com/package/verdaccio

On a package level, npm resolves to a file through the following process:

1. Look up *package.json* of the package.
2. Get the contents of the `main` field. If it doesn't exist, default to *<package>/index.js*.
3. Resolve to the `main` file.

The general lookup algorithm respects an environment variable `NODE_PATH`. If you are using Unix, you can patch it through `NODE_PATH=$NODE_PATH:./demo`. The call can be included at the beginning of a *package.json* scripts to tweak `NODE_PATH` temporarily.

You can tweak webpack's module resolution through the `resolve.modules` field:

```
{
  resolve: {
    modules: [
      path.join(__dirname, 'demo'),
      'node_modules',
    ],
  },
},
```

Compared to npm environment, webpack provides more flexibility, although you can mimic a lot of webpack's functionality using terminal based tricks.

 Installing global packages can lead to surprising behavior. If you have a package installed both globally and it a project happens to contain it, executing associated terminal command (say `webpack`) points to the version of the project. It doesn't work unless the global package exists.

 app-module-path[5] allows you adjust Node module lookup within JavaScript and this can be an alternative to patching `NODE_PATH`.

---

[5]https://www.npmjs.com/package/app-module-path

35.5 Version Ranges

npm supports multiple version ranges as listed below:

- ~ - Tilde matches only patch versions. For example, ~1.2 would be equal to 1.2.x.
- ^ - Caret is the default you get using --save or --save-dev. It matches minor versions, and this means ^0.2.0 would be equal to 0.2.x.
- * - Asterisk matches major releases, and it's the most dangerous of the ranges. Using this recklessly can easily break your project in the future.
- >= 1.3.0 < 2.0.0 - Ranges between versions come in handy with peerDependencies.

You can set the default range using npm config set save-prefix='^' in case you prefer something else than caret. Alternately, you can modify ~/.npmrc directly. Especially defaulting to tilde can be a good idea that can help you to avoid trouble with dependencies, although it doesn't remove potential problems entirely. That's where shrinkwrapping comes in.

35.6 Shrinkwrapping Versions

Using version ranges can feel dangerous as it doesn't take much to break an application. A single change in the wrong place is enough. npm shrinkwrap[6] allows you to fix your dependency versions and have stricter control over the versions you are using in a production environment. Most importantly it fixes the dependencies of your dependencies avoiding accidental breakage due to version changes and SemVer.

lockdown[7] goes further and gives guarantees about dependency content, not version alone. shrinkpack[8] is another complementary option.

Yarn[9], an npm alternative, goes a step further as it introduces the idea of a *lockfile*. Yarn is worth a look, as it fixes certain shortcomings of npm.

---

[6] https://docs.npmjs.com/cli/shrinkwrap

[7] https://www.npmjs.com/package/lockdown

[8] https://www.npmjs.com/package/shrinkpack

[9] https://yarnpkg.com/

35.7 Keeping Dependencies Up to Date

An important part of maintaining a project is keeping their dependencies up to date. How to do this depends a lot of on the maturity of your project. Ideally, you have an excellent set of tests covering the functionality to avoid problems with updates. Consider the following approaches:

- You can update all dependencies at once and hope for the best. Tools, such as npm-check-updates[10], npm-check[11], npm-upgrade[12], or updtr[13], can do this for you.
- Install the newest version of a specific dependency, e.g., `npm install lo-dash@* --save` as a more controlled approach.
- Patch version information by hand by modifying *package.json* directly.

It's important to remember that your dependencies can introduce backward incompatible changes. Remember how SemVer works and study the release notes of dependencies. They don't exist always, so you have to go through the project commit history.

 `npm ls`, and more specifically `npm ls <package name>`, allow you to figure out which versions you have installed. `npm ls -g` performs a similar lookup against the globally installed packages.

---

[10] https://www.npmjs.com/package/npm-check-updates
[11] https://www.npmjs.com/package/npm-check
[12] https://www.npmjs.com/package/npm-upgrade
[13] https://www.npmjs.com/package/updtr

35.8 Tracking Dependencies

Certain services can help you to keep track of your dependencies:

- David[14]
- versioneye[15]
- Gemnasium[16]

These services provide badges you can integrate into your project *README.md*, and they email you about important changes. They can also point out possible security issues that have been fixed.

For testing your project, you can consider solutions, such as Travis CI[17] or Sauce-Labs[18]. They can test your project against different environments and browsers. The advantage of doing this is that it allows you to detect regressions. If you accept pull requests to your project, these services can help to keep their quality higher as it forces the authors to maintain their code on a higher level.

Codecov[19] and Coveralls[20] provide code coverage information and a badge to include in your README. It's a part of improving the quality of your pull requests as they should maintain the current coverage at a minimum and ideally improve it.

 shields.io[21] lists a large number of available badges. NodeICO[22] provides badges that aggregate package related information.

 There's a Codecov extension[23] for Chrome that allows you to see code coverage through GitHub user interface.

---

[14] https://david-dm.org/

[15] https://www.versioneye.com/

[16] https://gemnasium.com

[17] https://travis-ci.org/

[18] https://saucelabs.com/

[19] https://codecov.io/

[20] https://coveralls.io/

[21] http://shields.io/

[22] https://nodei.co/

[23] https://chrome.google.com/webstore/detail/codecov-extension/keefkhehidemnokodkdkejapdgfjmijf

35.9 Conclusion

To consume npm packages, you should be aware of SemVer and its implications. Lock down your dependencies to avoid surprises. Use services to track changes.

To recap:

- npm packages can be grouped based on their purpose. Often you split them between `dependencies` and `devDependencies`. `peerDependencies` allow you to control the exact version on the consumer side.
- To consume packages effectively, you should understand SemVer. To keep your build repeatable, use shrinkwrapping or Yarn lockfiles.
- To understand your dependencies better, use available tooling and service to study them.

In the next chapter, you'll learn about consuming specific techniques.

36. Package Consuming Techniques

Sometimes packages have not been packaged the way you expect and you have to tweak the way webpack interprets them. Webpack provides multiple ways to achieve this.

36.1 Tweaking Module Resolution

Sometimes packages do not follow the standard rules and their *package.json* contains a faulty main field. It can be missing altogether. resolve.alias is the field to use here as in the example below:

```
{
  resolve: {
    alias: {
      demo: path.resolve(
        __dirname, 'node_modules/demo/dist/demo.js'
      ),
    },
  },
},
```

The idea is that if webpack resolver matches demo in the beginning, it resolves from the target. You can constrain the process to an exact name by using a pattern like demo$.

Light React alternatives, such as Preact[1], react-lite[2], or Inferno[3], offer smaller size while trading off functionality like propTypes and synthetic event handling. Replac-

---

[1]https://www.npmjs.com/package/preact

[2]https://www.npmjs.com/package/react-lite

[3]https://www.npmjs.com/package/inferno

ing React with a lighter alternative can save a significant amount of space but you should test well if you do this.

If you are using *react-lite*, configure it as below:

```
{
  resolve: {
    alias: {
      // Swap the target based on your need.
      'react': 'react-lite',
      'react-dom': 'react-lite',
    },
  },
},
```

 The same technique works with loaders too. You can use `resolveLoader.alias` similarly. You can use the technique to adapt a RequireJS project to work with webpack.

 Specific plugins like directory-named-webpack-plugin[4] allow you to enhance webpack's module resolution. You can attach these to your setup through the `resolve.plugins` field.

36.2 Consuming Packages Outside of Webpack

Browser dependencies, like jQuery, are often served through publicly available Content Delivery Networks (CDN). CDNs allow you to push the problem of loading popular packages elsewhere. If a package has been already loaded from a CDN and it's in the user cache, there is no need to load it.

---

[4]https://www.npmjs.com/package/directory-named-webpack-plugin

To use this technique, you should first mark the dependency in question as an external:

```
externals: {
  'jquery': 'jquery',
},
```

You still have to point to a CDN and ideally provide a local fallback so there is something to load if the CDN does not work for the client:

```
<script src="//ajax.googleapis.com/ajax/libs/jquery/3.1.1/jquery.min\
.js"></script>
<script>
    window.jQuery || document.write('<script src="js/jquery-3.1.1.mi\
n.js"><\/script>')
</script>
```

 html-webpack-cdn-plugin[5] is one option if you are using HtmlWebpackPlugin and want to inject a script tag automatically.

36.3 Dealing with Globals

Sometimes modules depend on globals. $ provided by jQuery is a good example. Webpack provides a few ways that allow you to handle them.

---

[5]https://www.npmjs.com/package/html-webpack-cdn-plugin

Injecting Globals

imports-loader[6] allows you to inject globals as below:

```
{
  module: {
    rules: {
      // Resolve against package path.
      // require.resolve returns a path to it.
      test: require.resolve('jquery-plugin'),
      loader: 'imports-loader?$=jquery',
    },
  },
},
```

Resolving Globals

Webpack's ProvidePlugin allows webpack to resolve globals as it encounters them:

```
{
  plugins: [
    new webpack.ProvidePlugin({
      $: 'jquery',
    }),
  ],
},
```

---

[6]https://www.npmjs.com/package/imports-loader

Exposing Globals to the Browser

Sometimes you have to expose packages to third party scripts. expose-loader[7] allows this as follows:

```
{
  test: require.resolve('react'),
  use: 'expose-loader?React',
},
```

With the small extra tweak, the technique can be used to expose React performance utilities to the browser through React.Perf global. You have to insert the following code to your application entry point for this to work:

```
if (process.env.NODE_ENV !== 'production') {
  React.Perf = require('react-addons-perf');
}
```

It can be a good idea to install React Developer Tools[8] to Chrome for even more information as it allows you to inspect *props* and *state* of your application.

script-loader[9] allows you to execute scripts in a global context. You have to do this if the scripts you are using rely on a global registration setup.

36.4 Removing Unused Modules

Even though packages can work well out of the box, they bring too much code to your project sometimes. Moment.js[10] is a popular example. It brings locale data to your project by default.

---

[7] https://www.npmjs.com/package/expose-loader

[8] https://github.com/facebook/react-devtools

[9] https://www.npmjs.com/package/script-loader

[10] https://www.npmjs.com/package/moment

The easiest method to disable that behavior is to use `IgnorePlugin` to ignore locales:

```
{
  plugins: [
    new webpack.IgnorePlugin(
      /^\.\/locale$/,
      /moment$/
    ),
  ],
},
```

 You can use the same mechanism to work around problematic dependencies. Example: `new webpack.IgnorePlugin(/^(buffertools)$/)`.

To bring specific locales to your project, you should use `ContextReplacementPlugin`:

```
{
  plugins: [
    new webpack.ContextReplacementPlugin(
      /moment[\/\\]locale$/,
      /de|fi/
    ),
  ],
},
```

 There's a Stack Overflow question[11] that covers these ideas in detail.

---

[11] https://stackoverflow.com/questions/25384360/how-to-prevent-moment-js-from-loading-locales-with-webpack/25426019

36.5 Managing Pre-built Dependencies

It's possible webpack gives the following warning with certain dependencies:

```
WARNING in ../~/jasmine-promises/dist/jasmine-promises.js
Critical dependencies:
1:113-120 This seems to be a pre-built javascript file. Though this \
is possible, it's not recommended. Try to require the original sourc\
e to get better results.
 @ ../~/jasmine-promises/dist/jasmine-promises.js 1:113-120
```

The warning can happen if a package points at a pre-built (i.e., minified and already processed) file. Webpack detects this case and warns against it.

The warning can be eliminated by aliasing the package to a source version as discussed above. Given sometimes the source is not available, another option is to tell webpack to skip parsing the files through module.noParse. It accepts either a RegExp or an array of RegExps and can be configured as below:

```
{
  module: {
    noParse: /node_modules\/demo-package\/dist\/demo-package.js/,
  },
},
```

 Take care when disabling warnings as it can hide underlying issues. Consider alternatives first. There's a webpack issue[12] that discusses the problem in detail.

---

[12] https://github.com/webpack/webpack/issues/1617

36.6 Managing Symbolic Links

Symbolic links, or symlinks, are an operating system level feature that allow you to point to other files through a file system without copying them. You can use `npm link` to create global symlinks for packages under development and then use `npm unlink` to remove the links.

Webpack resolves symlinks to their full path like Node does. The problem is that if you are unaware of this fact, the behavior can surprise you especially if you rely on webpack processing. It's possible to work around the behavior as discussed in webpack issues #1643[13] and #985[14]. Webpack core behavior may improve in the future to make these workarounds unnecessary.

 You can disable webpack's symlink handling by setting `resolve.symlinks` as `false`.

36.7 Getting Insights on Packages

To get more information about packages, npm provides `npm info <package>` command for basic queries. You can use it to check the metadata associated with packages while figuring out version related information.

package-config-checker[15] goes a step further. It allows you to understand better which packages of your project have updated recently and it provides means to get insight into your dependencies. It can reveal which packages could use download size related improvements for example.

slow-deps[16] can reveal which dependencies of a project are the slowest to install.

weigh[17] can be used figure out the approximate size of a package when it's served to a browser in different ways (uncompressed, minified, gzipped).

---

[13] https://github.com/webpack/webpack/issues/1643

[14] https://github.com/webpack/webpack/issues/985

[15] https://www.npmjs.com/package/package-config-checker

[16] https://www.npmjs.com/package/slow-deps

[17] https://www.npmjs.com/package/weigh

36.8 Conclusion

Webpack can consume most npm packages without a problem. Sometimes, though, patching is required using webpack's resolution mechanism.

To recap:

- Use webpack's module resolution to your benefit. Sometimes you can work around issues by tweaking resolution. Often it's a good idea to try to push improvements upstream to the projects themselves, though.
- Webpack allows you to patch resolved modules. Given certain dependencies expect globals, you can inject them. You can also expose modules as globals as this is necessary for certain development tooling to work.

In the next chapter, you'll learn to author npm packages. It's the other side of the same coin and worth understanding even if you don't end up authoring packages of your own.

37. Authoring Packages

Even though webpack is handy for bundling applications, it has its uses for package authors as well. It allows you to generate the distribution bundles required by npm. You can also generate the package site through webpack.

In this chapter, you'll learn basic ideas behind authoring npm packages and a couple of webpack specific techniques.

37.1 Anatomy of an npm Package

Most of the available npm packages are small and include only a couple of files:

- *index.js* - On small projects, it's enough to have the code at the root. On larger ones, you likely want to start splitting it up further.
- *package.json* - npm metadata in JSON format.
- *README.md* - README is the most important document of your project. It's written in Markdown format and provides an overview. For smallest projects, the full documentation can fit there. It's shown on the package page at *npmjs.com.*
- *LICENSE* - You can include licensing information within your project. You should refer to the license by name from *package.json* as otherwise, npm gives a warning. If you are using a custom license, you can link to it instead. In commercial projects, you should to set `"private":  true` to avoid pushing your work to public inadvertently.

In larger projects, you often find the following:

- *CONTRIBUTING.md* - A guide for potential contributors describing how the code should be developed.

- *CHANGELOG.md* - This document describes major changes per version. If you do significant API changes, it can be a good idea to cover them here. It's possible to generate the file based on Git commit history, provided you write nice enough commits.
- *.travis.yml* - Travis CI[1] is a popular continuous integration platform that is free for open source projects. You can run the tests of your package over multiple systems using it.
- *.gitignore* - Ignore patterns for Git, i.e., which files shouldn't go under version control. You can ignore npm distribution files here, so they don't clutter your repository.
- *.npmignore* - Ignore patterns for npm describe which files shouldn't go to your distribution version. A good alternative is to use the files[2] field at *package.json*. It allows you to maintain a whitelist of files to include into your distribution version.
- *.eslintignore* - Ignore patterns for ESLint. Again, tool specific.
- *.eslintrc* - Linting rules. You can use *.jshintrc* and such based on your preferences.
- *webpack.config.js* - If you are using a basic setup, you can have the configuration at project root.

Also, you likely have separate directories for the source, tests, demos, documentation, and so on.

 If you want to decrease the size of your dependencies, consider using a tool like package-config-checker[3]. It can pinpoint packages not using the `files` field correctly. Once you know which ones haven't set it, you can consider making Pull Requests (PRs) to those projects.

---

[1] https://travis-ci.org/

[2] https://docs.npmjs.com/files/package.json#files

[3] https://www.npmjs.com/package/package-config-checker

37.2 Understanding *package.json*

All packages come with a *package.json* that describes metadata related to them and includes information about the author, links, dependencies, and so on. The official documentation[4] covers them in detail.

The example below contains an annotated a part of *package.json* from my React component boilerplate[5]:

```
{
  /* Name of the project */
  "name": "react-component-boilerplate",

  /* Brief description */
  "description": "Boilerplate for React.js components",

  /* Who is the author + optional email + optional site */
  "author": "Juho Vepsäläinen <email goes here> (site goes here)",

  /* Version of the package */
  "version": "0.0.0",

  /* `npm run <name>` - `npm run` to get the available commands */
  "scripts": {
    "start": "webpack-dev-server --env development",

    "test": "jest",
    "test:coverage": "jest --coverage",
    "test:watch": "jest --watch",

    "lint:js": "eslint . --ext .js --ext .jsx --ignore-path .gitigno\
re --ignore-pattern dist --cache",
```

---

[4]https://docs.npmjs.com/files/package.json
[5]https://github.com/survivejs/react-component-boilerplate

```
  "gh-pages": "webpack --env gh-pages",
  "gh-pages:deploy": "gh-pages -d gh-pages",
  "gh-pages:stats": "webpack --env gh-pages --json > stats.json",

  "dist:all": "npm run dist && npm run dist:min",
  "dist": "webpack --env dist",
  "dist:min": "webpack --env dist:min",
  "dist:modules": "rimraf ./dist-modules && babel ./src --out-dir \
./dist-modules",

  "pretest": "npm run lint:js",
  "preversion": "npm run test && npm run dist:all && git commit --\
allow-empty -am \"Update dist\"",
  "prepublish": "npm run dist:modules",
  "postpublish": "npm run gh-pages && npm run gh-pages:deploy",

  /* If your library is installed through Git, transpile it */
  "postinstall": "node lib/postinstall.js"
},

/* Entry point for terminal (i.e., <package name>). */
/* Don't set this unless you intend to allow Command line usage */
"bin": "bin/index.js",

/* Entry point (defaults to index.js) */
"main": "dist-modules/",

/* ES6 module based entry point for tree shaking bundlers to pick \
up. */
/* Apart from the module format, the code should use ES5 otherwise\
. */
"module": "dist/",

/* Files to include to npm distribution. */
/* Relative patterns like "./src" fail! */
```

```
  "files": [
    "dist/"
  ],

  /* Package dependencies needed to use it. */
  /* Peer dependencies can work too, see below. */
  "dependencies": { ... },

  /* Package development dependencies needed to develop/compile it */
  "devDependencies": { ... },

  /* Package peer dependencies. The consumer fixes exact versions. */
  /* In npm3 these don't get installed automatically and it's */
  /* up to the user to define which versions to use. */
  /* If you want to include RC versions to the range, consider */
  /* using a pattern such as ^4.0.0-0 */
  "peerDependencies": {
    "lodash": ">= 3.5.0 < 4.0.0",
    "react": ">= 0.11.2 < 16.0.0"
  },

  /* Links to repository, homepage, and issue tracker */
  "repository": {
    "type": "git",
    "url": "https://github.com/survivejs/react-component-boilerplate\
.git"
  },
  "homepage": "https://survivejs.github.io/react-component-boilerpla\
te/",
  "bugs": {
    "url": "https://github.com/survivejs/react-component-boilerplate\
/issues"
  },

  /* Keywords related to package. */
```

```
/* Fill this well to make the package findable. */
"keywords": [
  "react",
  "reactjs",
  "boilerplate"
],

/* Which license to use */
"license": "MIT"
}
```

As you can see, *package.json* can contain a lot of information. You can attach non-npm specific metadata there that can be used by tooling. Given this can bloat *package.json*, it's preferable to keep metadata in files of their own.

   JSON doesn't support comments even though I'm using them above. There are extended notations, such as Hjson[6], that do.

37.3 npm Workflow

To get started, you have to use npm adduser[7]. It allows you to set up an account. After this process has completed, it creates a ∼/.npmrc file and use that data for authentication. There's also npm logout[8] that clears the credentials.

   When creating a project, npm init respects the values set at ∼/.npmrc. Hence, it's worth your while to set reasonable defaults there to save time. If you want to limit your package to a particular scope, use npm init --scope=<scope>. As a result, you get @<scope>/<package> which is handy especially for personal packages since the default namespace of npm is so crowded.

---

[6] http://hjson.org/
[7] https://docs.npmjs.com/cli/adduser
[8] https://docs.npmjs.com/cli/logout

npm organizations[9] give your project a scope (@<scope>/<package>) and make it easier to manage rights across the organization. They are free if your organization contains only public packages.

Publishing a Package

Provided you have logged in, creating new packages is only npm publish away. Given that the package name is still available and everything goes fine, you should have something out there! After this, you can install your package through npm install or npm i.

If you want to see what files are published to npm, consider using npm pack[10] generates a tarball you can examine. irish-pub[11] is another option, and it gives you a listing to review. You can also use publish-diff[12] to get a better of the changes that are going to be published.

 np[13] gives an interactive UI for publishing packages. semantic-release[14] takes the idea one step further and automates the entire process.

What Files to Publish

Even though a project can contain a lot of files, not all of them should be published. Besides wasting bandwidth, this can leak personal files to a public registry and is the reason why it's a good idea to maintain a files[15] array at *package.json* and enumerate which files and directories you want to publish.

You can't find an official recommendation on what files to publish. That said, there are points to consider as discussed in Stack Overflow[16].

---

[9] https://www.npmjs.com/docs/orgs/

[10] https://docs.npmjs.com/cli/pack

[11] https://www.npmjs.com/package/irish-pub

[12] https://www.npmjs.com/package/publish-diff

[13] https://www.npmjs.com/package/np

[14] https://www.npmjs.com/package/semantic-release

[15] https://docs.npmjs.com/files/package.json#files

[16] https://stackoverflow.com/questions/25124844/should-i-npmignore-my-tests

At a minimum, you should distribute the source code needed to run the package. If you have code written using the ES6 standard, you should transpile the code so that it does not lose the ES6 module definitions while everything else is converted to ES5. For the tooling to pick it up, you should point to this version of code through *package.json* `module` field. See the *Loading JavaScript* chapter for the Babel setup.

You should point package `main` to a fully compiled version that's compatible with Node.

In addition to the source, you can consider distributing package *README.md* and *LICENSE*. Any metadata that's required by third-party systems, like Travis, can be safely skipped. Full documentation of the package doesn't have to be included as you can point to the package homepage through its metadata instead.

 Even though it's possible to tell npm what to exclude from `files` through `!src/*.test.js` kind of definitions, using negation patterns is not recommended[17]. Instead, you should use *.npmignore* and include `src/*.test.js` kind of pattern there.

Increasing a Version

To increase the version of your package, you need to invoke one of these commands:

- `npm version <x.y.z>` - Define version yourself.
- `npm version <major|minor|patch>` - Let npm bump the version for you based on SemVer.
- `npm version <premajor|preminor|prepatch|prerelease>` - Same as previous expect this time it generates `-<prerelease number>` suffix. Example: `v2.1.2-2`.

Invoking any of these updates *package.json* and creates a version commit to git automatically. If you execute `npm publish` after doing this, you should have something new out there.

---

[17] https://github.com/npm/npm/wiki/Files-and-Ignores#details

In the example above, `version`-related hooks have been set to make sure a version contains a fresh version of a distribution build. Tests are run to catch potential issues early on.

 Consider using semantic-release[18] if you prefer a more structured approach. It can take pain out of the release process while automating a part of it. For instance, it can detect possible breaking changes and generate change logs.

 dont-break[19] allows you to run the unit tests of dependent projects against your current code to see if it breaks anything. Sometimes it's possible to overlook a use case that is not a part of the public API even and break a dependency. *dont-break* helps with that particular problem.

Respect the SemVer

When publishing new versions, it's important to respect the SemVer. Roughly, it states that you should not break backward compatibility, given certain rules are met. The exact rules were covered in the previous chapter.

To make it easier to comply with SemVer, next-ver[20] can compute the next version you should use and update it for you. commitizen[21] goes further and allows change log generation and automated releases.

Both these tools rely on commit message annotations. On small projects, you can have `fix` or `feat` prefix at your commit titles (e.g., `fix - Allow doodad to work with zero`). You can also communicate the context using `chore(docs)` kind of style to document which part of the project was touched.

This metadata lets the tooling to figure out the types of the changes you made. It can help even with change log generation and allow automated releases over manual

[18] https://www.npmjs.com/package/semantic-release

[19] https://www.npmjs.com/package/dont-break

[20] https://www.npmjs.com/package/next-ver

[21] https://www.npmjs.com/package/commitizen

ones. Annotating your commits well is a good practice in any case as it makes it easier to debug your code later.

 The *Consuming Packages* explains the idea of SemVer in detail.

Publishing a Pre-Release Version

Sometimes, you want to publish something preliminary to test. Tag your release as below:

- v0.5.0-alpha1
- v0.5.0-beta1
- v0.5.0-beta2
- v0.5.0-rc1
- v0.5.0-rc2
- v0.5.0

The initial alpha release allows the users to try out the upcoming functionality and provide feedback. The beta releases can be considered more stable.

The release candidates (RC) are close to an actual release and don't introduce any new functionality. They are all about refining the release till it's suitable for general consumption.

The workflow has two steps:

1. `npm version 0.5.0-alpha1` - Update *package.json* as discussed earlier.
2. `npm publish --tag alpha` - Publish the package under *alpha* tag.

To consume the test version, your users have to use `npm install <your package name>@alpha`.

npm link[22] allows you to link a package as a globally available symbolic link. Node resolves to the linked version unless local `node_modules` exists. Use `npm unlink` or `npm unlink <package>` to remove the link.

On Naming Packages

Before starting to develop, it can be a good idea to spend time on figuring out a good name for your package. It's not fun to write an excellent package only to notice the name has been taken. A good name is possible to find through a search engine, and most importantly, is available at npm. If you find a good name that appears to be abandoned, contact npm. They can give it to you.

As of npm 2.7.0, it's possible to create scoped packages[23]. They follow format `@username/project-name`. Simply follow that when naming your project.

37.4 Conclusion

Authoring packages takes care and patience. Publishing a package is fast but maintenance comes with its own challenges.

To recap:

- It's good to understand what kind of metadata packages contains. They give you insight on their licensing, guidelines, and even quality.
- When publishing packages to npm, remember to respect the SemVer or an equivalent scheme to keep your consumers happy.
- Document the main changes made to your packages using a change log. Documentation comes in handy later as you have to understand when a specific feature was introduced. It also makes it easier to upgrade projects to the most recent features.

In the next chapter, you'll learn about authoring specific techniques.

---

[22]https://docs.npmjs.com/cli/link

[23]https://docs.npmjs.com/getting-started/scoped-packages

38. Package Authoring Techniques

To get most out of npm and webpack, consider the techniques below. Webpack can help you here.

38.1 npm Lifecycle Hooks

npm provides a collection of lifecycle hooks. Suppose you are authoring a React component using Babel. In that case, you should generate an ES5 compatible version of the package for npm consumers and point to it through *package.json* main. You can achieve this using **babel** command line tool:

```
babel ./lib --out-dir ./dist-modules
```

The command walks through the ./lib directory and writes a processed file to ./dist-modules for each module it encounters.

Since running that command each time you publish is tedious, you can set up a prepublish hook:

package.json

```
"scripts": {
  ...
  "prepublish": "babel ./lib --out-dir ./dist-modules"
},
"main": "dist-modules/",
```

Make sure you execute `npm install babel-cli --save-dev` to include the tool into your project.

To avoid versioning the directory and to keep your `git status` clean, consider adding `dist-modules/` to your *.gitignore*.

Besides `prepublish`, npm provides a set of other hooks. The naming is always the same and follows the pattern `pre<hook>`, `<hook>`, `post<hook>` where `<hook>` can be `publish`, `install`, `test`, `stop`, `start`, `restart`, or `version`. Even though npm triggers scripts bound to these automatically, you can trigger them explicitly through `npm run` for testing (i.e., `npm run prepublish`).

The the official documentation[1] covers a lot of smaller tips related to these hooks. However, often all you need is a `prepublish` script for build automation.

Working Around `prepublish` in npm 3

In npm 3 `prepublish` hook gets also triggered when you run `npm install` on the project locally. Sometimes this can be surprising and counter-productive even.

in-publish[2] allows you to tune the behavior and skip the installation step. You need to prepend your script with `in-publish && babel ...` kind of line for this to work. npm 4 and the following versions fix this confusing behavior.

---

[1]https://docs.npmjs.com/misc/scripts
[2]https://www.npmjs.com/package/in-publish

38.2 Avoiding Bundling Dependencies

Since it's not a good idea to bundle your package dependencies, such as React, within the distribution bundle itself, you should let the user inject them. You can configure external dependencies using the `externals` configuration:

webpack.config.js

```
externals: {
  // Adapt `import merge from 'lodash/merge';` to different environm\
ents.
  'lodash/merge': {
    commonjs: 'lodash/merge',
    commonjs2: 'lodash/merge',
    // Look up lodash.merge below ['lodash', 'merge'] for AMD.
    amd: ['lodash', 'merge'],
    // Look up lodash.merge through `_.merge` in global environment.
    root: ['_', 'merge'],
  },
  // Adapt React to different environments.
  'react': {
    commonjs: 'react',
    commonjs2: 'react',
    amd: 'React',
    root: 'React',
  },
  'jquery': 'jquery',
},
```

If you want to include all modules in *node_modules* by default, it's possible to use webpack-node-externals[3] instead. In this case would end up with `externals: [nodeExternals()]` kind of declaration.

---

[3]https://www.npmjs.com/package/webpack-node-externals

Given bundling is still be required sometimes, consider using the bun-
dledDependencies[4] field for sharing third-party files not available through
npm. There's a great Stack Overflow answer[5] discussing the topic further.

38.3 Processing Node Version through Babel

If you are processing your code through Babel, you can skip webpack. The advantage
of doing this is that it gives you separate modules that are easier to consume one by
one if needed.

In this case, a setup as below works:

package.json

```
/* `npm run <name>` */
"scripts": {
  ...
  "dist": "webpack --env dist",
  "dist:min": "webpack --env dist:min",

  /* Process source through Babel! */
  "dist:modules": "babel ./src --out-dir ./dist-modules",
  ...
  "preversion": "npm run test && npm run dist:all && git commit --al\
low-empty -am \"Update dist\"",
  "prepublish": "npm run dist:modules",
  ...
},
/* Point to the Node specific version */
"main": "dist-modules",
```

What if someone points to a development version of your package directly through
GitHub, though? It doesn't work as the `dist-modules` directory is missing. The
problem can be fixed using a hook that generates the needed source.

---

[4]https://docs.npmjs.com/files/package.json#bundleddependencies
[5]http://stackoverflow.com/a/25044361/228885

38.4 Generating a Distribution for Development Usage

To solve the development distribution problem, a custom script is required. First, connect the hook with a custom script:

package.json

```
"scripts": {
  ...
  /* Point to the script that generates the missing source. */
  "postinstall": "node lib/postinstall.js"
},
```

Secondly, define a script:

lib/postinstall.js

```
/* eslint-disable */
// adapted based on rackt/history (MIT)
// Node 4+
const execSync = require('child_process').execSync;
const fs = require('fs');

// This could be read from package.json
const distDirectory = 'dist-modules';

fs.stat(distDirectory, (error, stat) => {
  // Skip building on Travis
  if (process.env.TRAVIS) {
    return;
  }

  if (error || !stat.isDirectory()) {
    // Create a directory to avoid getting stuck
```

```
    // in postinstall loop
    fs.mkdirSync(distDirectory);
    exec('npm install --only=dev');
    exec('npm run build');
  }
});

function exec(command) {
  execSync(command, {
    // Print stdin/stdout/stderr
    stdio: 'inherit'
  });
}
```

The script needs tweaking to fit your purposes. But it's enough to give you a rough idea. If the dist-modules directory is missing, you generate it here.

For the build script to work, you have to remember to include the source of the package to the distribution version and to tweak *package.json* files field accordingly.

 Relying on postinstall scripts can be potentially dangerous[6]. Security-minded developers want to use npm install --ignore-scripts. You can set that default through npm config set ignore-scripts true if you want. Being cautious does not hurt.

---

[6]http://blog.npmjs.org/post/141702881055/package-install-scripts-vulnerability

38.5 Deprecating, Unpublishing, and Renaming Packages

It's possible that your package reaches the end of its life. Another package could replace it, or it can become obsolete. For this purpose, npm provides npm deprecate[7] command. You can state `npm deprecate foo@"< 0.4.0" "Use bar package instead"`.

You can deprecate a range or a whole package by skipping the range. Given mistakes happen, you can undeprecate a package by providing an empty message.

Deprecation can be handy if you have to rename a package. You can publish the package under a new name and let the users know of the new name in your deprecation message.

There is a heavier duty option in the form of npm unpublish[8]. Using `npm unpublish` you can pull a package out of the registry. Given this can be potentially dangerous and break the code for a lot of people, it has been restricted to versions that are less than 24 hours old[9]. Most likely you don't need the feature at all, but it's nice to know it exists.

38.6 Sharing Authorship

As packages evolve, you likely want to start developing with others. You could become the new maintainer of a project, or pass the torch to someone else. These things happen as packages evolve.

npm provides certain commands for these purposes. It's all behind `npm owner` namespace. More specifically, there are `npm owner ls <package name>`, `npm owner add <user> <package name>` and `npm owner rm <user> <package name>`. That's about it.

See npm documentation[10] for the most up to date information about the topic.

---

[7] https://docs.npmjs.com/cli/deprecate

[8] https://docs.npmjs.com/cli/unpublish

[9] http://blog.npmjs.org/post/141905368000/changes-to-npms-unpublish-policy

[10] https://docs.npmjs.com/cli/owner

38.7 Conclusion

Both npm and webpack come with techniques of their own. It's possible to bundle packages without webpack. Webpack can generate standalone bundles and project site easily. You can leave a part of the work to Babel and similar tools.

To recap:

- Consider publishing differently packaged versions of the source to account for different usage patterns. Packaged right, your consumers can benefit from features, such as **tree shaking**.
- To make it possible to consume a work in progress package, implement an npm `postinstall` script that builds the project if a distribution version does not exist in the source.
- If a package becomes obsolete, consider deprecating it and let your users know how to upgrade to another solution.

The covered options are valuable beyond package authoring. Mainly `externals` comes in handy when you want to exclude certain dependencies outside of your bundles and load them using another way.

IX Extending

Even though there are a lot of available loaders and plugins for webpack, it's good to be able to extend it. In this part, you go through a couple of short examples to understand how to get started.

39. Extending with Loaders

As you have seen so far, loaders are one of the building blocks of webpack. If you want to load an asset, you most likely need to set up a matching loader definition. Even though there are a lot of available loaders[1], it's possible you are missing one fitting your purposes.

You'll learn to develop a couple of small loaders next. But before that, it's good to understand how to debug them in isolation.

 If you want a good starting point for a standalone loader or plugin project, consider using webpack-defaults[2]. It provides an opinionated starting point that comes with linting, testing, and other goodies.

39.1 Debugging Loaders with *loader-runner*

loader-runner[3] allows you to run loaders without webpack making it a good tool for learning more about loader development. Install it first:

```
npm install loader-runner --save-dev
```

---

[1]https://webpack.js.org/loaders/

[2]https://github.com/webpack-contrib/webpack-defaults

[3]https://www.npmjs.com/package/loader-runner

To have something to test with, set up a loader that returns twice what's passed to it:

loaders/demo-loader.js

```
module.exports = (input) => input + input;
```

Set up a file to process:

demo.txt

```
foobar
```

There's nothing webpack specific in the code yet. The next step is to run the loader through *loader-runner*:

run-loader.js

```
const fs = require('fs');
const path = require('path');
const { runLoaders } = require('loader-runner');

runLoaders({
  resource: './demo.txt',
  loaders: [
    path.resolve(__dirname, './loaders/demo-loader'),
  ],
  readResource: fs.readFile.bind(fs),
},
(err, result) => err ?
  console.error(err) :
  console.log(result)
);
```

If you run the script now (`node run-loader.js`), you should see output:

```
{ result: [ 'foobar\nfoobar\n' ],
  resourceBuffer: <Buffer 66 6f 6f 62 61 72 0a>,
  cacheable: true,
  fileDependencies: [ './demo.txt' ],
  contextDependencies: [] }
```

The output tells the `result` of the processing, the resource that was processed as a buffer, and other meta information. This is enough to develop more complicated loaders.

 If you want to capture the output to a file, use either `fs.writeFileSync('./output.txt', result.result)` or its asynchronous version as discussed in Node documentation[4].

 It's possible to refer to loaders installed to the local project by name instead of resolving a full path to them. Example: `loaders: ['raw-loader']`.

39.2 Implementing an Asynchronous Loader

Even though you can implement a lot of loaders using the synchronous interface, there are times when asynchronous calculation is required. Wrapping a third party package as a loader can force you to this.

The example above can be adapted to asynchronous form by using webpack specific API through `this.async()`. Webpack sets this and the function returns a callback following Node conventions (error first, result second).

---

[4]https://nodejs.org/api/fs.html

Tweak as follows:

loaders/demo-loader.js

```
module.exports = function(input) {
  const callback = this.async();

  // No callback -> return synchronous results
  // if (callback) { ... }

  callback(null, input + input);
};
```

 Given webpack injects its API through this, the shorter function form (()
=> ...) cannot be used here.

 If you want to pass a source map to webpack, pass it as the third parameter
of the callback.

Running the demo script (node run-loader.js) again should give exactly the same
result as before. To raise an error during execution, try the following:

loaders/demo-loader.js

```
module.exports = function(input) {
  const callback = this.async();

  callback(new Error('Demo error'));
};
```

The result should contain Error: Demo error with a stack trace showing where the
error originates.

39.3 Returning Only Output

Loaders can be used to output code alone. You could have implementation as below:

loaders/demo-loader.js

```
module.exports = function() {
  return 'foobar';
};
```

But what's the point? You can pass to loaders through webpack entries. Instead of pointing to pre-existing files as you would in majority of the cases, you could pass to a loader that generates code dynamically.

 If you want to return Buffer output, set module.exports.raw = true. The flag overrides the default behavior which expects a string is returned.

39.4 Writing Files

Loaders, like *file-loader*, emit files. Webpack provides a single method, this.emitFile, for this. Given *loader-runner* does not implement it, you have to mock it:

run-loader.js

```
const fs = require('fs');
const path = require('path');
const { runLoaders } = require('loader-runner');

runLoaders({
  resource: './demo.txt',
  loaders: [
    path.resolve(__dirname, './loaders/demo-loader'),
  ],
```

```
  context: {
    emitFile: () => {},
  },
  readResource: fs.readFile.bind(fs),
},
(err, result) => err ?
  console.error(err) :
  console.log(result)
);
```

To implement the essential idea of *file-loader*, you have to do two things: emit the file and return path to it. You could implement it as below:

loaders/demo-loader.js

```
const loaderUtils = require('loader-utils');

module.exports = function(content) {
  const url = loaderUtils.interpolateName(
    this, '[hash].[ext]', { content }
  );

  this.emitFile(url, content);

  const path = `__webpack_public_path__ + ${JSON.stringify(url)};`;

  return `export default ${path}`;
};
```

Webpack provides two additional emit methods:

- this.emitWarning(<string>)
- this.emitError(<string>)

These calls should be used over console based alternatives. As with this.emitFile, you have to mock them for *loader-runner* to work.

The next question is, how to pass file name to the loader.

39.5 Passing Options to Loaders

To demonstrate passing options, the runner needs a small tweak:

run-loader.js

```
runLoaders({
  resource: './demo.txt',
  loaders: [
    path.resolve(__dirname, './loaders/demo-loader')
    {
      loader: path.resolve(__dirname, './loaders/demo-loader'),
      options: {
        name: 'demo.[ext]',
      },
    },
  ],
  ...
},
...
);
```

To capture the option, you need to use loader-utils[5]. It has been designed to parse loader options and queries. Install it:

```
npm install loader-utils --save-dev
```

---

[5]https://www.npmjs.com/package/loader-utils

To connect it to the loader, set it to capture name and pass it through webpack's interpolator:

loaders/demo-loader.js

```
const loaderUtils = require('loader-utils');

module.exports = function(content) {
  const { name } = loaderUtils.getOptions(this);
  const url = loaderUtils.interpolateName(
    this, '[hash].[ext]', { content }
    this, name, { content }
  );

  this.emitFile(url, content);

  const filePath = `__webpack_public_path__+${JSON.stringify(url)};`;

  return `export default ${filePath}`;
};
```

After running (node ./run-loader.js), you should see something:

```
{ result: [ 'export default __webpack_public_path__+"demo.txt";' ],
  resourceBuffer: <Buffer 66 6f 6f 62 61 72 0a>,
  cacheable: true,
  fileDependencies: [ './demo.txt' ],
  contextDependencies: [] }
```

You can see that the result matches what the loader should have returned. You can try to pass more options to the loader or use query parameters to see what happens with different combinations.

 It's a good idea to validate options and rather fail hard than silently if the options aren't what you expect. schema-utils[6] has been designed for this purpose.

---

[6]https://www.npmjs.com/package/schema-utils

39.6 Connecting Custom Loaders with Webpack

To get most out of loaders you have to connect them with webpack. To achieve this, you can go through imports:

app/component.js

```
import '!../loaders/demo-loader?name=foo!./main.css';
```

Given the definition is verbose, the loader can be aliased:

webpack.config.js

```
const commonConfig = merge([
  {
  ...
    resolveLoader: {
      alias: {
        'demo-loader': path.resolve(
          __dirname, 'loaders/demo-loader.js'
        ),
      },
    },
  },
  ...
]);
```

With this change the import can be simplified:

```
import '!../loaders/demo-loader?name=foo!./main.css';
import '!demo-loader?name=foo!./main.css';
```

You could also handle the loader definition through `rules`. Once the loader is stable enough, set up a project based on *webpack-defaults*, push the logic there, and begin to consume the loader as a package.

 Although using *loader-runner* can be convenient for developing and testing loaders, implement integration tests that run against webpack. Subtle differences between environments make this essential.

39.7 Pitch Loaders

Webpack evaluates loaders in two phases: pitching and running. If you are used to web event semantics, these map to capturing and bubbling. The idea is that webpack allows you to intercept execution during the pitching (capturing) phase. It goes through the loaders left to right first and executes them from right to left after that.

A pitch loader allows you shape the request and even terminate it. Set it up:

loaders/pitch-loader.js

```
const loaderUtils = require('loader-utils');

module.exports = function(input) {
  const { text } = loaderUtils.getOptions(this);

  return input + text;
};
module.exports.pitch = function(remainingReq, precedingReq, input) {
  console.log(`
Remaining request: ${remainingReq}
Preceding request: ${precedingReq}
Input: ${JSON.stringify(input, null, 2)}
  `);

  return 'pitched';
};
```

To connect it to the runner, add it to the loader definition:

run-loader.js

```
runLoaders({
  resource: './demo.txt',
  loaders: [
    ...
    path.resolve(__dirname, './loaders/pitch-loader'),
  ],
  ...
},
...
);
```

If you run (`node ./run-loader.js`) now, the pitch loader should log intermediate data and intercept the execution:

```
Remaining request: ./demo.txt
Preceding request: .../webpack-demo/loaders/demo-loader?{"name":"dem\
o.[ext]"}
Input: {}

{ result: [ 'export default __webpack_public_path__ + "demo.txt";' ],
  resourceBuffer: null,
  cacheable: true,
  fileDependencies: [],
  contextDependencies: [] }
```

 The official documentation[7] covers the loader API in detail. You can see all fields available through `this` there.

---

[7]https://webpack.js.org/api/loaders/

39.8 Caching with Loaders

Although webpack caches loaders by default unless they set this.cacheable(false),
writing a caching loader can be a good exercise as it helps you to understand how
loader stages can work together. The example below shows how to achieve this
(courtesy of Vladimir Grenaderov):

```
const cache = new Map();

module.exports = function(content) {
  // Calls only once for given resourcePath
  const callbacks = cache.get(this.resourcePath);
  callbacks.forEach(callback => callback(null, content));

  cache.set(this.resourcePath, content);

  return content;
};
module.exports.pitch = function() {
  if (cache.has(this.resourcePath)) {
    const item = cache.get(this.resourcePath);

    if (item instanceof Array) {
      // Load to cache
      item.push(this.async());
    } else {
      // Hit cache
      return item;
    }
  } else {
    // Missed cache
    cache.set(this.resourcePath, []);
  }
};
```

A pitch loader can be used to attach metadata to the input to use later. In this example, cache was constructed during the pitching stage and it was accessed during normal execution.

39.9 Conclusion

Writing loaders is fun in the sense that they describe transformations from a format to another. Often you can figure out how to achieve something specific by either studying either the API documentation or the existing loaders.

To recap:

- *loader-runner* is a valuable tool for understanding how loaders work. Use it for debugging how loaders work.
- Webpack **loaders** accept input and produce output based on it.
- Loaders can be either synchronous or asynchronous. In the latter case, you should use `this.async()` webpack API to capture the callback exposed by webpack.
- If you want to generate code dynamically for webpack entries, that's where loaders can come in handy. A loader does not have to accept input. It's acceptable that it returns only output in this case.
- Use **loader-utils** to parse possible options passed to a loader and consider validating them using **schema-utils**.
- When developing loaders locally, consider setting up a `resolveLoader.alias` to clean up references.
- Pitching stage complements the default behavior allowing you to intercept and to attach metadata.

You'll learn to write plugins in the next chapter. Plugins allow you to intercept webpack's execution process and they can be combined with loaders to develop more advanced functionality.

40. Extending with Plugins

Compared to loaders, plugins are a more flexible means to extend webpack. You have access to webpack's **compiler** and **compilation** processes. It's possible to run child compilers and plugins can work in tandem with loaders as `ExtractTextPlugin` shows.

Plugins allow you to intercept webpack's execution through hooks. Webpack itself has been implemented as a collection of plugins. Underneath it relies on tapable[1] plugin interface that allows webpack to apply plugins in different ways.

You'll learn to develop a couple of small plugins next. Unlike for loaders, there is no separate environment where you can run plugins so you have to run them against webpack itself. It's possible to push smaller logic outside of the webpack facing portion, though, as this allows you to unit test it in isolation.

40.1 The Basic Flow of Webpack Plugins

A webpack plugin is expected to expose an `apply(compiler)` method. JavaScript allows multiple ways to do this. You could use a function and then attach methods to its `prototype`. To follow the newest syntax, you could use a `class` to model the same idea.

Regardless of your approach, you should capture possible options passed by a user at the constructor. It's a good idea to declare a schema to communicate them to the user. schema-utils[2] allows validation and works with loaders too.

When the plugin is connected to webpack configuration, webpack will run its constructor and call `apply` with a compiler object passed to it. The object exposes webpack's plugin API and allows you to use its hooks as listed by the official compiler reference[3].

---

[1]https://www.npmjs.com/package/tapable

[2]https://www.npmjs.com/package/schema-utils

[3]https://webpack.js.org/api/plugins/compiler/

webpack-defaults[4] works as a starting point for webpack plugins. It contains the infrastructure used to develop official webpack loaders and plugins.

40.2 Setting Up a Development Environment

Since plugins have to be run against webpack, you have to set up one to run a demo plugin that will be developed further:

webpack.plugin.js

```
const path = require('path');

const DemoPlugin = require('./plugins/demo-plugin.js');

const PATHS = {
  lib: path.join(__dirname, 'lib'),
  build: path.join(__dirname, 'build'),
};

module.exports = {
  entry: {
    lib: PATHS.lib,
  },
  output: {
    path: PATHS.build,
    filename: '[name].js',
  },
  plugins: [
    new DemoPlugin(),
  ],
};
```

---

[4]https://www.npmjs.com/package/webpack-defaults

If you don't have a lib entry file set up yet, write one. The contents doesn't matter as long as it's JavaScript that webpack can parse.

To make it convenient to run, set up a build shortcut:

package.json

```
"scripts": {
  "build:plugin": "webpack --config webpack.plugin.js",
  ...
},
```

Executing it should result in an Error: Cannot find module failure as the actual plugin is still missing.

 If you want an interactive development environment, consider setting up nodemon[5] against the build. Webpack's own watcher won't work in this case.

40.3 Implementing a Basic Plugin

The simplest plugin should do two things: capture options and provide apply method:

plugins/demo-plugin.js

```
module.exports = class DemoPlugin {
  apply() {
    console.log('applying ');
  }
};
```

If you run the plugin (npm run build:plugin), you should see applying message at console. Given most plugins accept options, it's a good idea to capture those and pass them to apply.

---

[5]https://www.npmjs.com/package/nodemon

40.4 Capturing Options

Options can be captured through a constructor:

plugins/demo-plugin.js

```
module.exports = class DemoPlugin {
  constructor(options) {
    this.options = options;
  }
  apply() {
    console.log('apply', this.options);
  }
};
```

Running the plugin now would result in apply undefined kind of message given no options were passed.

Adjust the configuration to pass an option:

webpack.plugin.js

```
module.exports = {
  ...
  plugins: [
    new DemoPlugin(),
    new DemoPlugin({ name: 'demo' }),
  ],
};
```

Now you should see apply { name: 'demo' } after running.

40.5 Understanding Compiler and Compilation

`apply` receives webpack's compiler as a parameter. Printing reveals more:

plugins/demo-plugin.js

```
module.exports = class DemoPlugin {
  constructor(options) {
    this.options = options;
  }
  apply(compiler) {
    console.log(compiler);
  }
};
```

After running, you should see a lot of data. Especially `options` should look familiar as it contains webpack configuration. You can also see familiar names like `records`.

If you go through webpack's plugin development documentation[6], you'll see a compiler provides a large amount of hooks. Each hook corresponds with a specific stage. For example, to emit files, you could listen to the `emit` event and then write.

Change the implementation to listen and capture `compilation`:

plugins/demo-plugin.js

```
module.exports = class DemoPlugin {
  constructor(options) {
    this.options = options;
  }
  apply(compiler) {
    console.log(compiler);
    compiler.plugin('emit', (compilation, cb) => {
      console.log(compilation);
```

---

[6]https://webpack.js.org/api/plugins/

```
      cb();
    });
  }
};
```

Forgetting the callback and running the plugin makes webpack fail silently!

Running the build should show more information than before. This is because a compilation object contains whole dependency graph traversed by webpack. You have access to everything related to it here including entries, chunks, modules, assets, and more.

Many of the available hooks expose compilation, but sometimes they expose a more specific structure and it takes more specific study to understand those.

Loaders have a dirty access to `compiler` and `compilation` through underscore (`this._compiler`/`this._compilation`).

40.6 Writing Files Through Compilation

The `assets` object of compilation can be used for writing new files. You can also capture already created assets, manipulate them, and write them back.

To write an asset, you have to use webpack-sources[7] file abstraction. Install it first:

```
npm install webpack-sources --save-dev
```

---

[7] https://www.npmjs.com/package/webpack-sources

Adjust the code as follows to write through RawSource:

plugins/demo-plugin.js

```
const { RawSource } = require('webpack-sources');

module.exports = class DemoPlugin {
  constructor(options) {
    this.options = options;
  }
  apply(compiler) {
    const { name } = this.options;

    compiler.plugin('emit', (compilation, cb) => {
      console.log(compilation);
      compilation.assets[name] = new RawSource('demo');

      cb();
    });
  }
};
```

After building, you should see output:

```
Hash: 62abc7fe06a7360b9735
Version: webpack 2.2.1
Time: 58ms
 Asset     Size  Chunks            Chunk Names
lib.js  2.89 kB       0  [emitted]  lib
  demo  4 bytes          [emitted]
   [0] ./lib/index.js 49 bytes {0} [built]
```

If you examine *build/demo* file, you'll see it contains the word *demo* as per code above.

Compilation has a set of hooks of its own as covered in the official
compilation reference[8].

40.7 Managing Warnings and Errors

Plugin execution can be caused to fail by throwing (`throw new Error('Message')`).
If you validate options, you can use this method.

In case you want to give the user a warning or an error message during compilation,
you should use `compilation.warnings` and `compilation.errors`. Example:

```
compilation.warnings.push('warning');
compilation.errors.push('error');
```

There is no way pass information messages to webpack yet although there is a logging
proposal[9]. If you want to use `console.log` for this purpose, push it behind a `verbose`
flag. The problem is that `console.log` will print to stdout and it will end up in
webpack's `--json` output as a result. A flag will allow the user to work around this
problem.

40.8 Plugins Can Have Plugins

A plugin can provide hooks of its own. html-webpack-plugin[10] uses plugins to extend
itself as discussed in the *Getting Started* chapter.

40.9 Plugins Can Run Compilers of Their Own

In special cases, like offline-plugin[11], it makes sense to run a child compiler. This gives
full control over related entries and output. Arthur Stolyar, the author of the plugin
has explained the idea of child compilers at Stack Overflow[12].

---

[8]https://webpack.js.org/api/plugins/compiler/

[9]https://github.com/webpack/webpack/issues/3996

[10]https://www.npmjs.com/package/html-webpack-plugin

[11]https://www.npmjs.com/package/offline-plugin

[12]https://stackoverflow.com/questions/38276028/webpack-child-compiler-change-configuration

40.10 Conclusion

When you begin to design a plugin, spend time studying existing plugins that are close enough. Develop plugins piece-wise so that you validate one piece at a time. Studying webpack source can give more insight given it's a collection of plugins itself.

To recap:

- **Plugins** can intercept webpack's execution and extend it making them more flexible than loaders.
- Plugins can be combined with loaders. `ExtractTextPlugin` works this way. There loaders are used to mark assets to extract.
- Plugins have access to webpack's **compiler** and **compilation** processes. Both provide hooks for different stages of webpack's execution flow and allow you to manipulate it. This is how webpack itself works.
- Plugins can emit new assets and shape existing assets.
- Plugins can implement plugin systems of their own. `HtmlWebpackPlugin` is an example of a such plugin.
- Plugins can run compilers of their own. The isolation gives more control and allows plugins like *offline-plugin* to be written.

Conclusion

As this book has demonstrated, webpack is a versatile tool. To make it easier to recap the content and techniques, go through the checklists below.

General Checklist

- **Source maps** allow you to debug your code in the browser during development. They can also give better quality stack traces during production usage if you capture the output. The *Source Maps* chapter delves into the topic.
- To keep your builds fast, consider optimizing. The *Performance* chapter discusses a variety of strategies you can use to achieve this.
- to keep your configuration maintainable, consider composing it. As webpack configuration is JavaScript code, it can be arranged in many ways. Find a way you are comfortable with and apply it. The *Composing Configuration* chapter discusses the topic.
- The way webpack consumes packages can be customized. The *Package Consuming Techniques* chapter covers specific techniques related to this.
- Sometimes you have to extend webpack. The *Extending with Loaders* and *Extending with Plugins* chapters show how to achieve this. You can also work on top of webpack's configuration definition and implement an abstraction of your own for it to suit your purposes.

Development Checklist

- To get most out of webpack during development, use webpack-dev-server[13] (WDS). You can also find middlewares which you can attach to your Node server during development. The *Automatic Browser Refresh* chapter covers WDS in greater detail.
- Webpack implements **Hot Module Replacement** (HMR). It allows you to replace modules without forcing a browser refresh while your application is running. The *Hot Module Replacement* appendix covers the topic in detail. If you are using React, read the *Hot Module Replacement with React* appendix.
- **Linting** is a technique that allows you to detect code related issue through static analysis. You can disallow certain kind of usage while enforcing coding style using linting tools. Particularly ESLint[14] is a popular option for JavaScript code. Stylelint[15] can be used with CSS. The *Linting JavaScript* and *Linting CSS* chapters cover the topic in detail. See also the *Customizing ESLint* appendix to learn how to expand ESLint.

Production Checklist

Styling

- Webpack inlines style definitions to JavaScript by default. To avoid this, separate CSS to a file of its own using `ExtractTextPlugin` or an equivalent solution. The *Separating CSS* chapter covers how to achieve this.
- To decrease the number of CSS rules to write, consider **autoprefixing** your rules. The *Autoprefixing* chapter shows how to do this.
- Unused CSS rules can be eliminated based on static analysis. The *Eliminating Unused CSS* chapter explains the basic idea of this technique.

---

[13]https://www.npmjs.com/package/webpack-dev-server

[14]http://eslint.org/

[15]https://www.npmjs.com/package/stylelint

Assets

- When loading images through webpack, optimize them, so the users have less to download. The *Loading Images* chapter shows how to do this.
- Load only the fonts you need based on the browsers you have to support. The *Loading Fonts* chapter discusses the topic.
- Minify your source files to make sure the browser to decrease the payload the client has to download. The *Minifying* chapter shows how to achieve this.

Caching

- To benefit from client caching, split a vendor bundle out of your application. This way the client has less to download in the ideal case. The *Bundle Splitting* chapter discusses the topic. The *Adding Hashes to Filenames* chapter shows how to achieve cache invalidation on top of that.
- Use webpack's **code splitting** functionality to load code on demand. The technique is handy if you don't need all the code at once and instead can push it behind a logical trigger such as clicking a user interface element. The *Code Splitting* chapter covers the technique in detail. The *Dynamic Loading* chapter shows how to handle more advanced scenarios.
- Add hashes to filenames as covered in the *Adding Hashes to Filenames* chapter to benefit from caching and separate a manifest to improve the solution further as discussed in the *Separating Manifest* chapter.

Optimization

- Use ES6 module definition to leverage **tree shaking**. It allows webpack to eliminate unused code paths through static analysis. See the *Tree Shaking* chapter for the idea.
- Set application specific environment variables to compile it production mode. You can implement feature flags this way. See the *Environment Variables* chapter to recap the technique.
- Analyze build statistics to learn what to improve. The *Analyzing Build Statistics* chapter shows how to do this against multiple available tools.
- Push a part of the computation to web workers. The *Web Workers* chapter covers how to achieve this.

Output

- Clean up and attach information about the build to the result. The *Tidying Up* chapter shows how to do this.
- If you are authoring a package, take care with how you bundle it. The *Authoring Packages* chapter covers the related considerations.

Conclusion

Webpack allows you to use a lot of different techniques to splice up your build. It supports multiple output formats as discussed in the *Output* part of the book. Despite its name, it's not only for the web. That's where most people use it, but the tool does far more than that.

Appendices

As not everything that's worth discussing fits into the main content, you can find related material in brief appendices. These support the primary content and explain certain topics, such as Hot Module Replacement with React, in greater detail. You also learn to troubleshoot webpack.

Comparison of Build Tools

Back in the day, it was enough to concatenate scripts together. Times have changed, though, and now distributing your JavaScript code can be a complicated endeavor. This problem has escalated with the rise of single page applications (SPAs). They tend to rely on many hefty libraries.

For this reason, there are multiple strategies on how to load them. You could load them all at once or consider loading libraries as you need them. Webpack supports many of these sorts of strategies.

The popularity of Node and npm[16], its package manager, provide more context. Before npm became popular, it was hard to consume dependencies. There was a period when people developed frontend specific package managers, but npm won in the end. Now dependency management is easier than before, although there are still challenges to overcome.

Task Runners and Bundlers

Historically speaking, there have been many build tools. *Make* is perhaps the best known, and it's still a viable option. Specialized *task runners*, such as Grunt and Gulp were created particularly with JavaScript developers in mind. Plugins available through npm made both task runners powerful and extendable. It's possible to use even npm `scripts` as a task runner. That's common, particularly with webpack.

Task runners are great tools on a high level. They allow you to perform operations in a cross-platform manner. The problems begin when you need to splice various assets together and produce bundles. *bundlers*, such as Browserify, Brunch, or webpack, exist for this reason.

---

[16]https://www.npmjs.com/

For a while, RequireJS[17] was popular. The idea was to provide an asynchronous module definition and build on top of that. The format, AMD, is covered in greater detail later in this chapter. Fortunately, the standards have caught up, and RequireJS seems more like a curiosity now.

Make

Make[18] goes way back, as it was initially released in 1977. Even though it's an old tool, it has remained relevant. Make allows you to write separate tasks for various purposes. For instance, you could have different tasks for creating a production build, minifying your JavaScript or running tests. You can find the same idea in many other tools.

Even though Make is mostly used with C projects, it's not tied to C in any way. James Coglan discusses in detail how to use Make with JavaScript[19]. Consider the abbreviated code based on James' post below:

Makefile

```
PATH  := node_modules/.bin:$(PATH)
SHELL := /bin/bash

source_files := $(wildcard lib/*.coffee)
build_files  := $(source_files:%.coffee=build/%.js)
app_bundle   := build/app.js
spec_coffee  := $(wildcard spec/*.coffee)
spec_js      := $(spec_coffee:%.coffee=build/%.js)

libraries    := vendor/jquery.js

.PHONY: all clean test
```

---

[17] http://requirejs.org/

[18] https://en.wikipedia.org/wiki/Make_%28software%29

[19] https://blog.jcoglan.com/2014/02/05/building-javascript-projects-with-make/

```
all: $(app_bundle)

build/%.js: %.coffee
    coffee -co $(dir $@) $<

$(app_bundle): $(libraries) $(build_files)
    uglifyjs -cmo $@ $^

test: $(app_bundle) $(spec_js)
    phantomjs phantom.js

clean:
    rm -rf build
```

With Make, you model your tasks using Make-specific syntax and terminal commands making it possible to integrate with webpack.

RequireJS

RequireJS[20] was perhaps the first script loader that became genuinely popular. It gave the first proper look at what modular JavaScript on the web could be. Its greatest attraction was AMD. It introduced a define wrapper:

```
define(['./MyModule.js'], function (MyModule) {
  return function() {}; // Export at module root
});

// or
define(['./MyModule.js'], function (MyModule) {
  return {
    hello: function() {...}, // Export as a module function
  };
});
```

---

[20]http://requirejs.org/

Incidentally, it's possible to use `require` within the wrapper:

```
define(['require'], function (require) {
  var MyModule = require('./MyModule.js');

  return function() {...};
});
```

This latter approach eliminates a part of the clutter. You still end up with code that feels redundant. ES6 and other standards solve this.

 Jamund Ferguson has written an excellent blog series on how to port from RequireJS to webpack[21].

npm scripts as a Task Runner

Even though npm CLI wasn't primarily designed to be used as a task runner, it works as such thanks to *package.json* `scripts` field. Consider the example below:

package.json

```
"scripts": {
  "stats": "webpack --env production --json > stats.json",
  "start": "webpack-dev-server --env development",
  "deploy": "gh-pages -d build",
  "build": "webpack --env production"
},
```

These scripts can be listed using `npm run` and then executed using `npm run <script>`. You can also namespace your scripts using a convention like `test:watch`. The problem with this approach is that it takes care to keep it cross-platform.

Instead of `rm -rf`, you likely want to use utilities such as rimraf[22] and so on. It's possible to invoke other tasks runners here to hide the fact that you are using one. This way you can refactor your tooling while keeping the interface as the same.

---

[21]https://gist.github.com/xjamundx/b1c800e9282e16a6a18e

[22]https://www.npmjs.com/package/rimraf

Grunt

Grunt

Grunt[23] was the first popular task runner for frontend developers. Its plugin architecture contributed towards its popularity. Plugins are often complex by themselves. As a result, when configuration grows, it can become difficult to understand what's going on.

Here's an example from Grunt documentation[24]. In this configuration, you define a linting and a watcher tasks. When the *watch* task gets run, it triggers the *lint* task as well. This way, as you run Grunt, you get warnings in real-time in the terminal as you edit the source code.

---

[23]http://gruntjs.com/

[24]http://gruntjs.com/sample-gruntfile

Gruntfile.js

```javascript
module.exports = (grunt) => {
  grunt.initConfig({
    lint: {
      files: ['Gruntfile.js', 'src/**/*.js', 'test/**/*.js'],
      options: {
        globals: {
          jQuery: true,
        },
      },
    },
    watch: {
      files: ['<%= lint.files %>'],
      tasks: ['lint'],
    },
  });

  grunt.loadNpmTasks('grunt-contrib-jshint');
  grunt.loadNpmTasks('grunt-contrib-watch');

  grunt.registerTask('default', ['lint']);
};
```

In practice, you would have many small tasks for specific purposes, such as building the project. An important part of the power of Grunt is that it hides a lot of the wiring from you.

Taken too far, this can get problematic. It can become hard to understand what's going on under the hood. That's the architectural lesson to take from Grunt.

 grunt-webpack[25] plugin allows you to use webpack in a Grunt environment while you leave the heavy lifting to webpack.

---

[25] https://www.npmjs.com/package/grunt-webpack

Gulp

Gulp

Gulp[26] takes a different approach. Instead of relying on configuration per plugin, you deal with actual code. Gulp builds on top of the concept of piping. If you are familiar with Unix, it's the same idea here. You have the following concepts:

- *Sources* to match to files.
- *Filters* to perform operations on sources (e.g., convert to JavaScript)
- *Sinks* (e.g., your build directory) where to pipe your build results.

---

[26]http://gulpjs.com/

Here's a sample *Gulpfile* to give you a better idea of the approach, taken from the project's README. It has been abbreviated a notch:

Gulpfile.js

```
const gulp = require('gulp');
const coffee = require('gulp-coffee');
const concat = require('gulp-concat');
const uglify = require('gulp-uglify');
const sourcemaps = require('gulp-sourcemaps');
const del = require('del');

const paths = {
  scripts: ['client/js/**/*.coffee', '!client/external/**/*.coffee']
};

// Not all tasks need to use streams.
// A gulpfile is another node program
// and you can use all packages available on npm.
gulp.task(
  'clean',
  del.bind(null, ['build'])
);

gulp.task(
  'scripts',
  ['clean'],
  () => (
    // Minify and copy all JavaScript (except vendor scripts)
    // with sourcemaps all the way down.
    gulp.src(paths.scripts)
      // Pipeline within pipeline
      .pipe(sourcemaps.init())
        .pipe(coffee())
        .pipe(uglify())
        .pipe(concat('all.min.js'))
```

```
      .pipe(sourcemaps.write())
      .pipe(gulp.dest('build/js'))
  )
);

// Rerun the task when a file changes.
gulp.task(
  'watch',
  gulp.watch.bind(null, paths.scripts, ['scripts'])
);

// The default task (called when you run `gulp` from CLI).
gulp.task(
  'default',
  ['watch', 'scripts']
);
```

Given the configuration is code, you can always hack it if you run into troubles. You can wrap existing Node packages as Gulp plugins, and so on. Compared to Grunt, you have a clearer idea of what's going on. You still end up writing a lot of boilerplate for casual tasks, though. That is where newer approaches come in.

 webpack-stream[27] allows you to use webpack in a Gulp environment.

 Fly[28] is a similar tool as Gulp. It relies on ES6 generators instead.

---

[27] https://www.npmjs.com/package/webpack-stream
[28] https://www.npmjs.com/package/fly

Browserify

Browserify

Dealing with JavaScript modules has always been a bit of a problem. The language itself didn't have the concept of modules till ES6. Ergo, the language was stuck in the '90s when it comes to browser environments. Various solutions, including AMD[29], have been proposed.

Browserify[30] is one solution to the module problem. It allows CommonJS modules to be bundled together. You can hook it up with Gulp, and you can find smaller transformation tools that allow you to move beyond the basic usage. For example, watchify[31] provides a file watcher that creates bundles for you during development saving effort.

---

[29] http://requirejs.org/docs/whyamd.html

[30] http://browserify.org/

[31] https://www.npmjs.com/package/watchify

The Browserify ecosystem is composed of a lot of small modules. In this way, Browserify adheres to the Unix philosophy. Browserify is easier to adopt than webpack, and is, in fact, a good alternative to it.

 Splittable[32] is a Browserify wrapper that allows code splitting, supports ES6 out of the box, tree shaking, and more.

JSPM

Frictionless browser package management

JSPM

Using JSPM[33] is quite different than previous tools. It comes with a command line tool of its own that is used to install new packages to the project, create a production bundle, and so on. It supports SystemJS plugins[34] that allow you to load various formats to your project.

---

[32] https://www.npmjs.com/package/splittable
[33] http://jspm.io/
[34] https://github.com/systemjs/systemjs#plugins

Brunch

Seeing your build tool in nightmares?
Try Brunch!

Brunch lets you focus on what matters most — solving real
problems instead of messing around with the glue.

Brunch

Compared to Gulp, Brunch[35] operates on a higher level of abstraction. It uses a declarative approach similar to webpack's. To give you an example, consider the following configuration adapted from the Brunch site:

```
module.exports = {
  files: {
    javascripts: {
      joinTo: {
        'vendor.js': /^(?!app)/,
        'app.js': /^app/,
      },
    },
    stylesheets: {
      joinTo: 'app.css',
    },
  },
  plugins: {
    babel: {
      presets: ['es2015', 'react'],
    },
    postcss: {
      processors: [require('autoprefixer')],
```

---

[35] http://brunch.io/

```
    },
  },
};
```

Brunch comes with commands like brunch new, brunch watch --server, and brunch build --production. It contains a lot out of the box and can be extended using plugins.

 There is an experimental Hot Module Reloading runtime[36] for Brunch.

Webpack

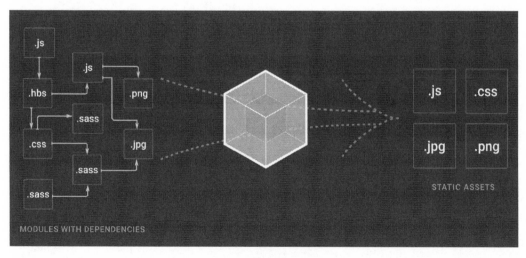

webpack

You could say webpack[37] takes a more monolithic approach than Browserify. Whereas Browserify consists of multiple small tools, webpack comes with a core that provides a lot of functionality out of the box.

---

[36] https://www.npmjs.com/package/hmr-brunch

[37] https://webpack.js.org/

Webpack core can be extended using specific *loaders* and *plugins*. It gives control over how it *resolves* the modules, making it possible to adapt your build to match specific situations and workaround packages that don't work correctly out of the box.

Compared to the other tools, webpack comes with initial complexity, but it makes up for this through its broad feature set. It's an advanced tool that requires patience. But once you understand the basic ideas behind it, webpack becomes powerful.

Other Options

You can find more alternatives as listed below:

- pundle[38] advertises itself as a next generation bundler and notes particularly its performance.
- Rollup[39] focuses particularly on bundling ES6 code. *Tree shaking* is one of its selling points. You can use Rollup with webpack through rollup-loader[40].
- AssetGraph[41] takes an entirely different approach and builds on top of HTML semantics making it ideal for hyperlink analysis[42] or structural analysis[43]. webpack-assetgraph-plugin[44] bridges webpack and AssetGraph together.
- FuseBox[45] is a bundler focusing on speed. It uses a zero-configuration approach and aims to be usable out of the box.
- StealJS[46] is a dependency loader and a build tool which has focused on performance and ease of use.
- Flipbox[47] wraps multiple bundlers behind a uniform interface.

---

[38] https://www.npmjs.com/package/pundle

[39] https://www.npmjs.com/package/rollup

[40] https://www.npmjs.com/package/rollup-loader

[41] https://www.npmjs.com/package/assetgraph

[42] https://www.npmjs.com/package/hyperlink

[43] https://www.npmjs.com/package/assetviz

[44] https://www.npmjs.com/package/webpack-assetgraph-plugin

[45] https://www.npmjs.com/package/fuse-box

[46] https://stealjs.com/

[47] https://www.npmjs.com/package/flipbox

Conclusion

Historically there have been a lot of build tools for JavaScript. Each has tried to solve a specific problem in its own way. The standards have begun to catch up and less effort is required around basic semantics. Instead, tools can compete on a higher level and push towards better user experience. Often you can use a couple of separate solutions together.

To recap:

- **Task runners** and **bundlers** solve different problems. You can achieve similar results with both but often it's best to use them together to complement each other.
- Older tools, such as Make or RequireJS, still have influence even if they aren't as popular in web development as they once were.
- Bundlers like Browserify or webpack solve an important problem and help you to manage complex web applications.
- A number of emerging technologies approach the problem from different angles. Sometimes they build on top of other tools and at times they can be used together.

Hot Module Replacement

Hot Module Replacement (HMR) builds on top of the WDS. It enables an interface that makes it possible to swap modules live. For example, *style-loader* can update your CSS without forcing a refresh. As CSS is stateless by design, implementing HMR for it's ideal.

HMR is possible with JavaScript too, but due to application state, it's harder. The *Hot Module Replacement with React* appendix shows how to set it up with React. You can use the same idea elsewhere as well. Vue and vue-hot-reload-api[48] is a good example.

Enabling HMR

To enable HMR, the following things have to happen:

1. WDS has to run in hot mode to expose the hot module replacement interface to the client.
2. Webpack has to provide hot updates to the server. This is achieved using `webpack.HotModuleReplacementPlugin`.
3. The client has to run specific scripts provided by the WDS. They are injected automatically but can be enabled explicitly through entry configuration.
4. The client has to implement the HMR interface through `module.hot.accept`.

Using `webpack-dev-server --hot` solves the first two problems. In this case you have to handle only the last one yourself if you want to patch JavaScript application code. Skipping the `--hot` flag and going through webpack configuration gives more flexibility.

---

[48] https://www.npmjs.com/package/vue-hot-reload-api

The following listing contains the most important parts related to this approach. You will have to adapt from here to match your configuration style:

```
{
  devServer: {
    // Don't refresh if hot loading fails. Good while
    // implementing the client interface.
    hotOnly: true,

    // If you want to refresh on errors too, set
    // hot: true,
  },
  plugins: [
    // Enable the plugin to let webpack communicate changes
    // to WDS. --hot sets this automatically!
    new webpack.HotModuleReplacementPlugin(),
  ],
}
```

If you implement configuration like above without implementing the client interface, you will most likely end up with an error:

No refresh

The numbers are cryptic but the problem can be fixed with the `NamedModulesPlugin`.

 webpack-dev-server can be picky about paths. Webpack issue #675[49] discusses the problem in more detail.

 You should **not** enable HMR for your production configuration. It likely works, but it makes your bundles bigger than they should be.

Making the Module Ids More Debuggable

When webpack generates a bundle, it needs to tell different modules apart. By default, it uses numbers for this purpose. The problem is that this makes it difficult to debug the code if you must inspect the resulting code.

To overcome this problem, it's a good idea to use an alternative module ID scheme. Webpack provides a plugin that's ideal for debugging. This plugin, `NamedModulesPlugin`, emits module paths over numeric IDs to make the output easier to understand.

You can enable this better behavior as follows:

```
{
  plugins: [
    new webpack.NamedModulesPlugin(),
  ],
}
```

[49] https://github.com/webpack/webpack/issues/675

If you restart the development server (terminate it and run `npm start`), you should see something more familiar:

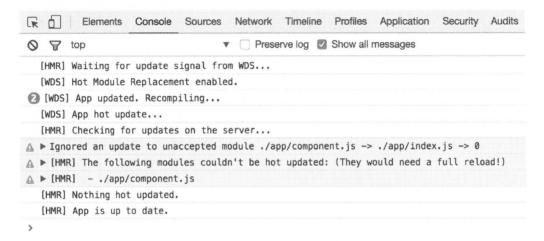

No refresh, but better output

The message tells that even though the HMR interface notified the client portion of the code of a hot update, nothing was done about it. This is something to fix next.

 The same idea works for production usage as you see in the *Adding Hashes to Filenames* chapter.

 A similar effect can be achieved by setting `output.pathInfo = true`. It still uses number based indices while emitting the path to the module within a comment. This should be used for development purposes only.

Implementing the HMR Interface

Webpack exposes the HMR interface through a global variable: `module.hot`. It provides updates through `module.hot.accept(<path to watch>, <handler>)` function and you need to patch the application there.

The following implementation illustrates the idea against the tutorial application:

app/index.js

```
import component from './component';

let demoComponent = component();

document.body.appendChild(demoComponent);

// HMR interface
if(module.hot) {
  // Capture hot update
  module.hot.accept('./component', () => {
    const nextComponent = component();

    // Replace old content with the hot loaded one
    document.body.replaceChild(nextComponent, demoComponent);

    demoComponent = nextComponent;
  });
}
```

If you refresh the browser, try to modify *app/component.js* after this change, and alter the text to something else, you should notice that the browser does not refresh at all. Instead, it should replace the DOM node while retaining the rest of the application as is.

The image below shows possible output:

| <svg></svg> | Elements | Console | Sources | Network | Timeline | Profiles | Application | Security |

Ø ▽ top   ▼ ☐ Preserve log

```
[HMR] Checking for updates on the server...
[HMR] Updated modules:
[HMR]  - ./app/component.js
[HMR] App is up to date.
[WDS] App updated. Recompiling...
[WDS] App hot update...
[HMR] Checking for updates on the server...
[HMR] Updated modules:
[HMR]  - ./app/component.js
[HMR] App is up to date.
>
```

Patched a module successfully through HMR

The idea is the same with styling, React, Redux, and other technologies. Sometimes you don't have to implement the interface yourself even as available tooling takes care of that for you.

To prove that HMR retains application state, set up a checkbox[50] based component next to the original. The module.hot.accept code has to evolve to capture changes to it as well.

The if(module.hot) block is eliminated entirely from the production build as minifier picks it up. The *Minifying* chapter delves deeper into this topic.

Setting WDS Entry Points Manually

In the setup above, the WDS-related entries were injected automatically. Assuming you are using WDS through Node, you would have to set them yourself as the Node API doesn't support injecting. The example below illustrates how to achieve this:

```
entry: {
  hmr: [
    // Include the client code. Note host/post.
    'webpack-dev-server/client?http://localhost:8080',

    // Hot reload only when compiled successfully
    'webpack/hot/only-dev-server',

    // Alternative with refresh on failure
    // 'webpack/hot/dev-server',
  ],
  ...
},
```

Conclusion

HMR is one of those aspects of webpack that makes it attractive for developers and webpack has taken its implementation far.

To recap:

- To work, HMR requires both client and server side support. For this purpose, webpack-dev-server provides both. Often you have to implement the client side interface although loaders like *style-loader* implement it for you.
- It's a good idea to use the NamedModulesPlugin during development as that gives you better debug information.

Hot Module Replacement with React

Hot module replacement was one of the initial selling points of webpack and React. It relies on the react-hot-loader[51] package. At the time of writing, version 3 of *react-hot-loader* is in beta. It requires changes to three places: Babel configuration, webpack configuration, and application.

Before proceeding, make sure you have HMR set up as discussed in the *Hot Module Replacement* appendix.

To get started, install the upcoming version of *react-hot-loader* as a normal dependency as it comes with a small application dependency:

```
npm install react-hot-loader@next --save
```

Setting Up Babel

To connect Babel with *react-hot-loader*, it needs to become aware of its plugin portion:

.babelrc

```
{
  "plugins": ["syntax-dynamic-import"],
  "plugins": ["syntax-dynamic-import", "react-hot-loader/babel"],
  ...
}
```

---

[51]https://www.npmjs.com/package/react-hot-loader

Setting Up Webpack

On the webpack side, *react-hot-loader* requires an additional entry it uses to patch the running application. It's important the new entry runs first as otherwise the setup fails to work reliably:

webpack.config.js

```
module.exports = (env) => {
  const pages = [
    ...
    parts.page({
      title: 'React demo',
      path: 'react',
      entry: {
        react: reactDemo,
        react: env === 'production' ?
          PATHS.reactDemo :
          ['react-hot-loader/patch', PATHS.reactDemo],
      },
      chunks: ['react', 'manifest', 'vendor'],
    }),
  ];
  ...
};
```

Patching is needed still as you have to make the application side aware of hot loading.

 This tweak is not required in the future as *react-hot-loader* evolves. It's possible to inject an empty module for 'react-hot-loader/patch' if it detects that production environment is used. For now, it's needed, though.

Setting Up the Application

On React side, *react-hot-loader* relies on an `AppContainer` that deals with patching. You still have to implement the Hot Module Replacement interface as earlier. Set up an entry point for the demo as follows:

app/react.js

```javascript
import React from 'react';
import ReactDOM from 'react-dom';
import Counter from './counter';
import { AppContainer } from 'react-hot-loader';

const app = document.createElement('div');
document.body.appendChild(app);

const render = App => {
  ReactDOM.render(
    <AppContainer><App /></AppContainer>,
    app
  );
};

render(Counter);

if (module.hot) {
  module.hot.accept('./counter', () => render(Counter));
}
```

To test the setup, a component is needed as well. In this case, it's going to be a counter so you can see how the hot replacement mechanism maintains the state:

app/counter.js

```
import React from 'react';

class Counter extends React.Component {
  constructor(props) {
    super(props);

    this.state = { amount: 0 };
  }
  render() {
    return (
      <div>
        <span className="fa fa-hand-spock-o fa-1g">
          Amount: {this.state.amount}
        </span>
        <button onClick={() => this.setState(addOne)}>
          Add one
        </button>
      </div>
    );
  }
}

const addOne = ({ amount }) => ({ amount: amount + 1 });

export default Counter;
```

If you run the application after these changes and modify the file above, it should pick up changes without a hard refresh while retaining the amount.

Removing *react-hot-loader* Related Code from the Production Output

If you build the application (npm run build) and examine the output, you spot references to __REACT_HOT_LOADER__ there due to the Babel setup. It uses react-hot-loader/babel plugin regardless of the build target. To overcome this slight annoyance, you should configure Babel to apply the plugin only when you are developing.

Babel provides an env option[52] for this purpose. It respects both NODE_ENV and BABEL_ENV environment variables. If BABEL_ENV is set, it receives precedence. To fix the issue, you can push the problematic Babel plugin behind a development specific env while controlling its behavior within webpack configuration by setting BABEL_ENV.

The webpack portion should be adjusted:

webpack.config.js

```
module.exports = (env) => {
  process.env.BABEL_ENV = env;


  ...
};
```

Now Babel will receive the same env as webpack allowing you to fix the behavior.

---

[52]https://babeljs.io/docs/usage/babelrc/#env-option

Tweak Babel setup, so it matches the fields below. The key part is in pushing react-hot-loader/patch below env:

.babelrc

```
{
  "plugins": [
    "syntax-dynamic-import",
    "react-hot-loader/babel"
  ],
  "plugins": ["syntax-dynamic-import"],
  ...
  "env": {
    "development": {
      "plugins": [
        "react-hot-loader/babel"
      ]
    }
  }
}
```

 This tweak may not be required in the future as *react-hot-loader* evolves further. See the *Loading JavaScript* chapter to learn more about Babel env.

The development setup should work after this change still. If you examine the build output, you should notice it's missing references to __REACT_HOT_LOADER__.

Even after this change, the source can contain references still due to a bug in react-hot-loader[53] as it has been built so that it loses information. The issue can be worked around by implementing a module chooser pattern as in the *Environment Variables* chapter. AppContainer provided by *react-hot-loader* should be mocked with a dummy.

---

[53]https://github.com/gaearon/react-hot-loader/issues/471

Configuring HMR with Redux

Redux[54] is a popular state management library designed HMR in mind. To configure Redux reducers to support HMR, you have to implement the protocol as above:

```
const configureStore = (initialState) => {
  const store = createStoreWithMiddleware(
    rootReducer,
    initialState
  );

  if(module.hot) {
    // Enable webpack hot module replacement for reducers
    module.hot.accept(
      '../reducers',
      () => store.replaceReducer(reducers)
    );
  }

  return store;
}

export default configureStore;
```

 You can find a full implementation of the idea online[55].

---

[54] http://redux.js.org/

[55] https://github.com/survivejs-demos/redux-demo

Configuring Webpack to Work with JSX

Sometimes people prefer to name their React components containing JSX using the .jsx suffix. Webpack can be configured to work with this convention. The benefit of doing this is that then your editor is able to pick up the right syntax based on the file name alone. Another option is to configure the editor to use JSX syntax for .js files as it's a superset of JavaScript.

Webpack provides resolve.extensions[56] field that can be used for configuring its extension lookup. If you want to allow imports like import Button from './Button'; while naming the file as *Button.jsx*, set it up as follows:

```
{
  resolve: {
    extensions: ['.js', '.jsx'],
  },
},
```

To resolve the problem at loader configuration, instead of matching against /\.js$/, you can expand it to include .jsx extension through /\.(js|jsx)$/. Another option would be to write /\.jsx?$/, but the explicit alternative is more readable.

 In webpack 1 you had to use extensions: ['', '.js', '.jsx'] to match files without an extension too. This isn't needed in webpack 2.

Get Started Fast with *create-react-app*

create-react-app[57] allows you to get started fast with webpack and React. It's a zero configuration approach that encapsulates a lot of best practices allowing you to get started fast with minimal setup.

---

[56]https://webpack.js.org/guides/migrating/#resolve-extensions
[57]https://www.npmjs.com/package/create-react-app

create-react-app allows you to extract a full-blown webpack setup by **ejecting**. There's a problem, though. After you eject, you cannot go back to the dependency-based model, and you have to maintain the resulting setup yourself.

Conclusion

react-hot-loader allows you to set up HMR with webpack. It was one of the initial selling points of both and is still a good technique. The setup takes care, but after you have it running, it's nice.

To recap:

- Setting up *react-hot-loader* requires changes to Babel, webpack, and application.
- On Babel level you must enable *react-hot-loader/babel* plugin.
- Webpack configuration has to inject `'react-hot-loader/patch'` entry before the application.
- Application has to be wrapped into `AppContainer` provided by *react-hot-loader*.
- The setup may get easier to manage as *react-hot-loader* develops further.
- HMR can be configured to work with Redux by implementing `module.hot.accept` against reducers.
- Webpack makes it convenient to work with `.jsx` files.
- *create-react-app* allows you to get started fast with webpack and React.

Customizing ESLint

Even though you can get far with vanilla ESLint, there are certain techniques you should know. For instance, sometimes you want to skip specific rules per file. You can even implement rules of your own.

Skipping ESLint Rules

ESLint allows you to skip rules on several levels. Consider the following examples:

```
// everything
/* eslint-disable */
...
/* eslint-enable */


// specific rule
/* eslint-disable no-unused-vars */
...
/* eslint-enable no-unused-vars */


// tweaking a rule
/* eslint no-comma-dangle:1 */


// disable rule per line
alert('foo'); // eslint-disable-line no-alert
```

The rule specific examples assume you have the rules in your configuration in the first place! You cannot specify new rules here. Instead, you can modify the behavior of existing rules.

Setting Environment

Sometimes, you want to run ESLint in a specific environment, such as Node or Mocha. These environments have certain conventions of their own. For instance, Mocha relies on custom keywords (e.g., describe, it) and it's good if the linter doesn't choke on those.

ESLint provides two ways to deal with this: local and global. If you want to set it per file, you can use a declaration at the beginning of a file:

```
/*eslint-env node, mocha */
```

Global configuration is possible as well. In this case, you can use env key:

.eslintrc.js

```
module.exports = {
  env: {
    browser: true,
    commonjs: true,
    es6: true,
    node: true,
  },
  ...
};
```

Writing ESLint Plugins

ESLint plugins rely on Abstract Syntax Tree (AST) definition of JavaScript. It's a data structure that describes JavaScript code after it has been lexically analyzed. There are tools, such as recast[58], that allow you to perform transformations on JavaScript code by using AST transformations. The idea is that you match a structure, then transform it somehow and convert AST back to JavaScript.

---

[58]https://github.com/benjamn/recast

Understanding AST

To get a better idea of how AST works and what it looks like, you can check Esprima online JavaScript AST visualization[59] or AST Explorer by Felix Kling[60]. Alternately, you can install recast and examine the output it gives. That is the structure you work with for ESLint rules.

 Codemod[61] allows you to perform large-scale changes to your codebase through AST based transformations.

Writing a Plugin

In ESLint's case, the AST structure can be checked. If something is wrong, it should let you know. Follow the steps below to set up a plugin:

1. Set up a new project named eslint-plugin-custom. You can replace custom with whatever you want. ESLint follows this naming convention.
2. Execute npm init -y to create a dummy *package.json*
3. Set up index.js in the project root with content.

---

[59] http://esprima.org/demo/parse.html

[60] http://astexplorer.net/

[61] https://github.com/facebook/codemod

You can get started with a skeleton as below:

eslint-plugin-custom/index.js

```javascript
module.exports = {
  rules: {
    demo: {
      docs: {
        description: 'Demo rule',
        category: 'Best Practices',
        recommended: true,
      },
      schema: [{
        type: 'object',
        // JSON Schema to describe properties
        properties: {},
        additionalProperties: false,
      }],
      create(context) {
        return {
          Identifier(node) {
            context.report(node, 'This is unexpected!');
          },
        };
      },
    },
  },
};
```

In this case, you report for every identifier found. In practice, you likely want to do something more complex than this, but this is a good starting point.

Next, you need to execute `npm link` within `eslint-plugin-custom` to make your plugin visible to your system. `npm link` allows you to consume a development version of a library you are developing. To reverse the link, you can execute `npm unlink` when you feel like it.

If you want to do something serious, you should point to your plugin through *package.json.*

You need to alter the project configuration to make it find the plugin and the rule within.

.eslintrc.js

```
module.exports = {
  ...
  plugins: [
    ...
    'custom'
  ],
  rules: {
    ...
    'custom/demo': 1,
  }
};
```

If you invoke ESLint now, you should see a bunch of warnings. Of course, the rule doesn't do anything impressive yet. To move forward, check out the official plugin documentation[62] and rules[63].

You can also check out the existing rules and plugins for inspiration to see how they achieve certain things. ESLint allows you to extend these rulesets[64] through extends property. It accepts either a path to it ("extends": "./node_modules/coding-standard/.eslintrc") or an array of paths. The entries are applied in the given order, and later ones override the former.

---

[62] http://eslint.org/docs/developer-guide/working-with-plugins.html

[63] http://eslint.org/docs/developer-guide/working-with-rules.html

[64] http://eslint.org/docs/user-guide/configuring.html#extending-configuration-files

ESLint Resources

Besides the official documentation available at eslint.org[65], you should check out the following blog posts:

- Detect Problems in JavaScript Automatically with ESLint[66] - A good tutorial on the topic.
- Understanding the Real Advantages of Using ESLint[67] - Evan Schultz's post digs into details.
- eslint-plugin-smells[68] - This plugin by Elijah Manor allows you to lint against JavaScript smells. Recommended.

If you want a starting point, you can pick one of eslint-config- packages[69] or go with the standard[70] style.

Conclusion

Especially the fact that you can customize ESLint to various purposes makes it a powerful tool. Thanks to its vibrant ecosystem, it's likely you find rules that are close to your purposes. Those make excellent starting points for your own development.

To recap:

- ESLint allows rules to be skipped locally. Use this feature sparingly.
- You can override ESLint environment per file. It's good to consider other solutions if you notice a lot of overrides in your source, though.
- ESLint can be extended through plugins. They allow you to adjust its behavior to your liking. Given the ecosystem is strong, check it first before going this way.

---

[65] http://eslint.org/

[66] http://davidwalsh.name/eslint

[67] http://rangle.io/blog/understanding-the-real-advantages-of-using-eslint/

[68] https://www.npmjs.com/package/eslint-plugin-smells

[69] https://www.npmjs.com/search?q=eslint-config

[70] https://www.npmjs.com/package/standard

Searching with React

Let's say you want to implement a rough little search for an application without a proper backend. You could do it through lunr[71] and generate a static search index to serve.

The problem is that the index can be sizable depending on the amount of the content. The good thing is that you don't need the search index straight from the start. You can do something smarter instead. You can start loading the index when the user selects a search field.

Doing this defers the loading and moves it to a place where it's more acceptable for performance. Given the initial search is slower than the subsequent ones, you should display a loading indicator. But that's fine from the user point of view. Webpack's *Code Splitting* feature allows to do this.

Implementing Search with Code Splitting

To implement code splitting, you need to decide where to put the split point, put it there, and then handle the `Promise`:

```
import('./asset').then(asset => ...).catch(err => ...)
```

The nice thing is that this gives error handling in case something goes wrong (network is down etc.) and gives a chance to recover. You can also use `Promise` based utilities like `Promise.all` for composing more complicated queries.

---

[71]http://lunrjs.com/

In this case, you need to detect when the user selects the search element, load the data unless it has been loaded already, and then execute search logic against it. Consider the React implementation below:

App.js

```
import React from 'react';

export default class App extends React.Component {
  constructor(props) {
    super(props);

    this.state = {
      index: null,
      value: '',
      lines: [],
      results: [],
    };
  }
  render() {
    const { results, value } = this.state;

    return (
      <div className="app-container">
        <div className="search-container">
          <label>Search against README:</label>
          <input
            type="text"
            value={value}
            onChange={e => this.onChange(e)} />
        </div>
        <div className="results-container">
          <Results results={results} />
        </div>
      </div>
    );
```

```
  }
  onChange({ target: { value } }) {
    const { index, lines } = this.state;

    // Set captured value to input
    this.setState(() => ({ value }));

    // Search against lines and index if they exist
    if(lines && index) {
      return this.setState(() => ({
        results: this.search(lines, index, value),
      }));
    }

    // If the index doesn't exist, it has to be set it up.
    // You could show loading indicator here as loading might
    // take a while depending on the size of the index.
    loadIndex().then(({ index, lines }) => {
      // Search against the index now.
      this.setState(() => ({
        index,
        lines,
        results: this.search(lines, index, value),
      }));
    }).catch(err => console.error(err));
  }
  search(lines, index, query) {
    // Search against index and match README lines.
    return index.search(query.trim()).map(
      match => lines[match.ref],
    );
  }
};

const Results = ({results}) => {
```

```
  if(results.length) {
    return (<ul>{
      results.map((result, i) => <li key={i}>{result}</li>)
    }</ul>);
  }

  return <span>No results</span>;
};


function loadIndex() {
  // Here's the magic. Set up `import` to tell Webpack
  // to split here and load our search index dynamically.
  //
  // Note that you will need to shim Promise.all for
  // older browsers and Internet Explorer!
  return Promise.all([
    import('lunr'),
    import('../search_index.json')
  ]).then(([{ Index }, { index, lines }]) => {
    return {
      index: Index.load(index),
      lines,
    };
  });
}
```

In the example, webpack detects the import statically. It can generate a separate bundle based on this split point. Given it relies on static analysis, you cannot generalize loadIndex in this case and pass the search index path as a parameter.

Conclusion

Beyond search, the approach can be used with routers too. As the user enters a route, you can load the dependencies the resulting view needs. Alternately, you can start loading dependencies as the user scrolls a page and gets adjacent parts with actual functionality. import provides a lot of power and allows you to keep your application lean.

You can find a full example[72] showing how it all goes together with lunr, React, and webpack. The basic idea is the same, but there's more setup in place.

To recap:

- If your dataset is small and static, client-side search is a good option.
- You can index your content using a solution like lunr[73] and then perform a search against it.
- Webpack's *code splitting* feature is ideal for loading a search index on demand.
- Code splitting can be combined with a UI solution like React to implement the whole user interface.

---

[72] https://github.com/survivejs-demos/lunr-demo
[73] http://lunrjs.com/

Troubleshooting

Using webpack can lead to a variety of runtime warnings or errors. Often a particular part of the build fails for a reason or another. A basic process can be used to figure out these problems:

1. Pass `--display-error-details` flag to webpack to get a more accurate error to study. Example: `npm run build -- --display-error-details`.

2. Study the origin of the error carefully. Sometimes you can infer what's wrong by context. If webpack fails to parse a module, it's likely not passing it through a loader you expect for example.

3. Try to understand where the error stems from. Does it come from your code, a dependency, or webpack?

4. Remove code until the error goes away and add code back till it appears again. Simplify as much as possible to isolate the problem as this helps in the later steps.

5. If the code worked in another project, figure out what's different. It's possible the dependencies between the projects vary, or the setup differs somehow. It takes only one subtle difference. At the worst case, a package you rely upon has gained a regression. In that case, you have to fix the package version carefully. Using a Yarn *lockfile* is a good idea for this reason.

6. Study the related packages carefully. Sometimes looking into the package *package.json* can yield insight. It's possible the package you are using does not resolve the way you expect.

7. Search for the error online. Perhaps someone else has run into it. Ideally doing this leads to a quick solution. Stack Overflow[74] and the official issue tracker[75] are good starting points.

8. Enable `stats: 'verbose'` to get more information out of webpack. The official documentation covers more flags[76].

---

[74] https://stackoverflow.com/questions/tagged/webpack

[75] https://github.com/webpack/webpack/issues

[76] https://webpack.js.org/configuration/stats/

9. Add a temporary `console.log` near the error to get more insight into the problem. A heavier option is to debug webpack through Chrome Dev Tools[77].
10. Ask a question at Stack Overflow[78] or use the official Gitter channel[79] to get more ideas.
11. If everything fails and you are convinced you have found a bug, report an issue at the official issue tracker[80] or at other appropriate places if it's an issue in a dependency. Follow the issue template carefully, and provide a minimal runnable example as it helps to resolve the problem.

Sometimes it's fastest to drop the error to a search engine and gain an answer that way. Other than that this is a good debugging order. If your setup worked in the past, you could also consider using commands like git bisect[81] to figure out what has changed between the known working state and the current broken one.

You'll learn about the most common errors next and how to deal with them.

ERROR in Entry module not found

You can end up with this error if you make an entry path point at a place that does not exist. The error message is clear in this case and tells you what path webpack fails to find.

ERROR ... Module not found

You can get the error in two ways. Either by breaking a loader definition so that it points to a loader that does not exist, or by breaking an import path within your code so that it points to a module that doesn't exist. Reading the error message points out what to fix.

---

[77] https://medium.com/webpack/webpack-bits-learn-and-debug-webpack-with-chrome-dev-tools-da1c5b19554

[78] https://stackoverflow.com/questions/tagged/webpack

[79] https://gitter.im/webpack/webpack

[80] https://github.com/webpack/webpack/issues

[81] https://git-scm.com/docs/git-bisect

Loader Not Found

There's another subtle loader related error. If a package matching to a loader name that does not implement the loader interface exists, webpack matches to that and gives a runtime error that says the package is not a loader.

This mistake can be made by writing `loader: 'eslint'` instead of `loader: 'eslint-loader'`. If the loader doesn't exist at all the previous 'Module not found' error will be raised.

 A loader definition missing `-loader` was valid in webpack 1. It has been disallowed in webpack 2. The behavior can be enabled again through `resolveLoader.moduleExtensions` array.

Module parse failed

Even though webpack could resolve to your modules fine, it can still fail to build them. This case can happen if you are using syntax that your loaders don't understand. You could be missing something in your processing pass.

Module build failed: Unknown word

This error fits the same category. Parsing the file succeeded, but there was the unknown syntax. Most likely the problem is a typo, but this error can also occur when Webpack has followed an import and encountered syntax it doesn't understand. Most likely this means that a loader is missing for that particular file type.

SyntaxError: Unexpected token

`SyntaxError` is another error for the same category. This error is possible if you use ES6 syntax that hasn't been transpiled alongside UglifyJS. As it encounters a syntax construct it does not recognize, it raises an error.

Conclusion

These are only examples of errors. Certain errors happen on the webpack side, but the rest come from the packages it uses through loaders and plugins. Simplifying your project is a good step as that makes it easier to understand where the error happens.

In most cases, the errors are fast to solve if you know where to look, but in the worst case, you have come upon a bug to fix in the tooling. In that case, you should provide a high-quality report to the project and help to resolve it.

Glossary

Given webpack comes with specific nomenclature, the main terms and their explanations have been gathered below based on the book part where they are discussed.

Introduction

- **Static analysis** - When a tool performs static analysis, it examines the code without running it. This is how tools like ESLint or webpack operate. Statically analyzable standards, like ES6 module definition, enable features like **tree shaking**.
- **Resolving** is the process that happens when webpack encounters a module or a loader. When that happens, it tries to resolve it based on the given resolution rules.

Developing

- **Entry** refers to a file used by webpack as a starting point for bundling. An application can have multiple entries and depending on configuration, each entry can result in multiple bundles. Entries are defined in webpack's `entry` configuration. Entries are **modules** at the beginning of the dependency graph.
- **Module** is a general term to describe a piece of the application. In webpack, it can refer to JavaScript, a style sheet, an image or something else. **Loaders** allows webpack to support different file types and therefore different types of module. If you point to the same module from multiple places of a code base, webpack will generate a single module in the output. This enables the singleton pattern on module level.
- **Plugins** connect to webpack's event system and can inject functionality into it. They allow webpack to be extended and can be combined with loaders for maximum control. Whereas a loader works on a single file, a plugin has much broader access and is capable of more global control.

- **Hot Module Replacement (HMR)** refers to a technique where code running in the browser is patched on the fly without requiring a full page refresh. When an application contains complex state, restoring it can be difficult without HMR or a similar solution.
- **Linting** relates to the process in which code is statically analyzed for a series of user-defined issues. These issues can range from discovering syntax errors to enforcing code-style. Whilst linting is by definition limited in its capabilities, a linter is invaluable for helping with early error discovery and enforcing code consistency.

Loading

- **Loader** performs a transformation that accepts a source and returns transformed source. It can also skip processing and perform a check against the input instead. Through configuration, a loader targets a subset of modules, often based on the module type or location. A loader only acts on a single module at a time whereas a plugin can act on mulitple files.
- **Asset** is a general term for the media and source files of a project that are the raw material used by webpack in building a bundle.

Building

- **Source maps** describe the mapping between the original source code and the generated code, allowing browsers to provide a better debugging experience. For example, running ES6 code through Babel generates completely new ES5 code. Without a source map, a developer would lose the link from where something happens in the generated code and where it happens in the source code. The same is true for style sheets when they run through a pre or post-processor.
- **Bundle** is the result of bundling. Bundling involves processing the source material of the application into a final bundle that is ready to use. A bundler can generate more than one bundle.

- **Bundle splitting** offers one way of optimising a build, allowing webpack to generate multiple bundles for a single application. As a result, each bundle can be isolated from changes effecting others, reducing the amount of code that needs to be republished and therefore re-downloaded by the client and taking advantage of browser caching.
- **Code splitting** produces more granular bundles than bundle splitting. To use it, the developer has to enable it through specific calls in the source code. Using a dynamic `import()` is one way.
- **Chunk** is a webpack-specific term that is used internally to manage the bundling process. Webpack composes bundles out of chunks, and there are several types of those.

Optimizing

- **Minifying**, or minification, is an optimization technique in which code is written in a more compact form without losing meaning. Certain destructive transformations break code if you are not careful.
- **Tree shaking** is the process of dropping unused code based on static analysis. A good ES6 module definition allows this process as it's possible to analyze in this particular manner.
- **Hashing** refers to the process of generating a hash that is attached to the asset/bundle path to invalidate it on the client. Example of a hashed bundle name: *app.f6f78b2fd2c38e8200d.js*.

Output

- **Output** refers to files emitted by webpack. More specifically, webpack emits **bundles** and **assets** based on the output settings.
- **Target** options of webpack allow you to override the default web target. You can use webpack to develop code for specific JavaScript platforms.

Made in the USA
Middletown, DE
17 April 2018